THE JEWS OF IRAQ

THE JEWS OF IRAQ

3000 Years of History and Culture

by Nissim Rejwan

FONS VITAE

First published in Great Britain in 1985 by
George Weidenfeld & Nicholson Limited
91 Clapham High Street, London SW4 7TA

New edition in the United States in 2009 by
Fons Vitae
49 Mockingbird Valley Drive
Louisville, KY 40207
http://www.fonsvitae.com
Email: fonsvitaeky@aol.com

Library of Congress Control Number: 2009933713
ISBN 9781891785399

Printed in Canada

Cover Image:

The Great Synagogue in Baghdad, with its dean Hakham Ezra Dangoor, who later became Chief Rabbi. On this site stood the great synagogue of the Head of Captivity, where new Exilarchs were installed from the ninth to the thirteenth centuries AD.

Spiritual Affinities
Judaism and Islam

A Fons Vitae Project

Fons Vitae would like to draw attention to the profound spiritual affinities of Judaism and Islam by establishing new ground where these two faiths can stand together. We invite scholars from the world over to contribute to these efforts. We have opened a home at Fons Vitae where the two traditions can work together in the enduring world of the Spirit.

Fons Vitae is now dedicated to making available scholarly work on the common spiritual and doctrinal themes in Judaism and Islam, with the express purpose of publishing works in this field of study. Such shared elements have been called, and coined, 'elective affinities' by Jewish studies scholar Paul Fenton, a term that many of our scholars have adopted. In the stated aims of one book for the project, author Rabbi Aubrey Glazer writes that "through this approach, a non-syncretistic exploration of a given mystical path is possible. This comparative analysis allows for the mystic in each tradition to encounter the tradition of the other, and through this encounter catalyze a deeper immersion in [his] own tradition." This non-syncretistic approach is in keeping with Fons Vitae's mission, which began, precisely, with a series of books exploring Thomas Merton's study of and inspiration by other faiths. This deepening of his own faith was truly the fruit of his immersion in the study of other spiritual taditions, as well as his friendships with people of those faiths.

Much is being done on the relationship between Christians and Muslims, as well as Christians and Jews, concerning the affinities between these traditions, at the level of both scholarship and action. We felt that the particular relationship between Judaism and Islam has been hitherto mostly neglected, and are responding to this need.

Foreword

Joseph V. Montville

In 1998, Nissim Rejwan won a National Jewish Book Award for *Israel's Place in the Middle East: A Pluralist Perspective.*[1] The Jewish Book Council, born in Boston in 1924, and based in New York, annually recognizes fiction and non-fiction works of Jewish content in several categories. Among many noteworthy prize-winners have been Saul Bellow, Cynthia Ozick, Bernard Malamud, Aharon Applefeld, Philip Roth, Allen Ginsberg, Leon Wieseltier, Peter Cole and Benny Morris. This is a serious award conferred by a prestigious organization governed almost entirely by American Jews who trace their family ties to Europe. It is thus remarkable that the Book Council's citation for *Israel's Place in the Middle East,* said, "In a very engaging manner, Rejwan points out the error of those who think that Jews and Arabs stand in opposition, representing two clashing cultures, mentalities, and temperaments. From the standpoint of history, religion, and ethnicity, Israel is an integral part of the Middle East." This is exactly the point Rejwan intended to make. But it is not at all one that is accepted by the dominant political culture in Israel today.

Thus the reprinting of Nissim Rejwan's *The Jews of Iraq: 3000 Years of History and Culture,* first published in London by Weidenfeld and Nicholson and Westview Press in Boulder, Colorado in 1985, is an event to be celebrated. The new edition is a product of the Spiritual Affinities: Judaism and Islam project that Fons Vitae launched in 2009, which aims to document cultural, religious and spiritual connectedness between Jews and Muslims. *The Jews of Iraq* sets out to achieve such a goal. The narrative is divided in the three sections: the Babylonian period from the beginning of captivity from 731 BCE to 641 CE; the encounter with Islam from 641-1850; and the modern period through 1951 including the migration of almost the entire Iraqi Jewish population of some 125,000 souls to Israel.

When it was first published, Professor David Semah of Haifa University called the third part of *The Jews of Iraq:*

> "...the most personal and therefore, the most absorbing...shaped by the author's own experience and convictions, and on specific points, it is not in full agreement with the attitudes commonly held in Israel in recent years. Underlying Rejwan's account...is the notion that in modern times Iraqi Jews no longer sat by the rivers of Babylonia, weeping as they remembered Zion. They did not arrive in Israel in the 1950's as destitute Babylonian exiles returning to their ancient home. Iraq had long been their home. Their lives were two seemingly contradictory impulses: in adhering to their Jewish heritage, they lived as though they had themselves been driven out of Jerusalem, but in playing a

very active role in all aspects of Iraqi society, they lived as though Iraq had always been and would always be their only homeland."[2]

In other words, the Jews of Iraq had a history, a memory, and a positive sense of their value or collective self-worth. And Nissim Rejwan set out to record this history which Iraqi Jews and most Jews who immigrated to Israel from Muslim majority countries came to feel was not recognized, and certainly not respected by the receiving culture of the new Jewish state. There is irony in the fact that among some of the earliest East European Zionists to immigrate to Palestine in the first *aliyah* or ascent to the Land of Israel that began in 1882, there were some who idealized the Oriental or Levantine culture of the native Palestinian Arabs. A few even discussed conversion to Islam as a way to cleanse themselves of a Jewish identity degraded by their lives in Christian Europe. (Alas, such Ashkenazi idealization of Arab Muslim peasants was not to be extended to Arab Jews.)

A Hebrew writer named Mordechai Zeev Feierberg created a Russian Jew who tells his people, "Europe is sick; everybody senses that its foundations are rotten and its society crumbling. Our destiny lies in the East...And you, my brethren, when you go now eastward, you must always remember that you are Oriental by birth....The worst enemy of the Jews is the West and what, therefore, is unnatural is that we, the Hebrew, Oriental people, should put our lot with the nations of the West.... If it is true that the people of Israel have a mission, let them bear it and carry it to the Orient..."[3] The Israeli politician. lawyer, journalist and former Member of Knesset, Amnon Rubenstein has written that, "Many authors" in the early days of Zionist settlement in Palestine, "filled their writings with empathy and admiration for the native-born, free-spirited, local Arabs. If the Jews sought a release from *galut* [exilic] images and searched for their new, authentic identity, the distant relative rediscovered, the uninhibited Arab was a figure worthy of emulation." [4]

But the romantic vision of the noble Arab before World War I was not to last. As European Jewish immigration to Palestine increased, the predictable social and political stresses grew also. Tensions throughout the 1920's climaxed in a terrible massacre of Jews in Hebron on August 23 and 24. Reportedly spurred by rumors that Jews were killing Arabs in Jerusalem and planning an attack the Al-Aqsa Mosque there, a mob killed 67 Jews. Some analysts marked the Hebron massacre as the decisive end to any romanticizing of the noble Oriental culture in which Eastern European Jews could return to their Semitic roots in the Land of Israel.

Previously, in January, 1919, as an adjunct to the Paris Peace Conference ending World War I, Emir Feisal, son the Sherif Hussein, leader of the Hijaz, the western province of Arabia, signed an agreement with Chaim Weizmann, soon to become head of the World Zionist Organization. The Feisal-Weizmann agreement was short-lived, but it did lay the framework for considerably increased European Jewish immigration to Palestine and in accordance with the 1917 Balfour Declaration, the establishment of a Jewish home in Palestine under British protection and in full respect of the rights of the native Arab Palestinian population. The greater Arab reward for rebelling against the Ottoman Empire during the Great War would be the establishment of a large, yet to be defined, Arab state created from the Ottoman provinces. Feisal famously referred to "our Jewish cousins," and elsewhere wrote, "The two main branches of the Semitic family understood one another."[5] And on March 3, 1919, Feisal wrote to Felix Frankfurter, then President of the Zionist Organization of America saying, "The Arabs, especially the educated among us, look with the deepest sympathy on the Zionist movement."[6] Such a statement may seem strange in the current context of the Israeli-Palestinian conflict, but is not inconsistent with a tradition of symbiosis between Jewish minorities under Muslim majorities during long stretches of history. Of course Feisal's remarks were no doubt also part of a political strategy designed to help the Hashemites establish their position in the Arab successor provinces taken from the defeated Ottoman Turks.

However, as Nissim Rejwan reports in *Israel's Place in the Middle East*, citing a strongly Zionist thinker, "A product of Europe and its civilization, Zionism was caught up in the notion of the superiority of Western, i.e., European civilization. This notion caused the Zionists—and the Jews as a whole—to look down upon the Arabs and their ancient culture....The [Ashkenazi] Jews came to Palestine with the determination to make the country an outpost of Western civilization and to 'civilize the Arab nations'. The unequivocal cultural identification of the Yishuv [Zionist settlement in Palestine] with the West...disabused the Arabs of the hope, expressed by Feisal, that the Jewish 'cousins" were *cousins* by Arab definition."[7]

There is pathos in this situation that was to become an indescribable tragedy once the Nazi movement came to power in Germany in the 1930's. What might have been a potentially negotiable social and political—even Abrahamic religious—contract between Zionism and Arab nationalism based on the flickers of mutual recognition and respect noted above, disappeared in the vortex of European political collapse that produced World War II and the tragedy of the Holocaust. There have been and continue to be Palestinian and other Arab and Israeli voices calling for genuine negotiation of a new social and political—even religious—contract based on a shared history of cultural and religious heritage and symbiosis. But they face an uphill battle against the fear and loathing that dominate domestic Israeli and Palestinian politics and the regional setting now exacerbated by Iran's major new role as a player especially in the new century.

Yet there have been accomplished the Israeli peace treaties with Egypt and Jordan and the Arab League/Muslim world proposal first advanced by King Abdullah of Saudi Arabia, in 2002, promising full diplomatic recognition of

Israel in exchange for withdrawal from the occupied territories with minor adjustments, recognition of East Jerusalem as the capital of the new Palestinian state and proper arrangements for the Palestinian refugees of 1948. No serious observer of the Israeli-Palestinian conflict believes that an agreement that meets the basic needs of both sides can be achieved without the intense political and moral engagement of the United States. President Barack Obama appears determined to make such a commitment. What he, the Israelis, the Palestinians and the other Arab and Muslim states will need for a genuine peace among Jews, Muslims and Christians in the Holy Land, will be a concerted effort, necessarily undertaken at first by non-official actors, to begin a process of healing the wounds of history in our unhappy Abrahamic family. On close examination, Christians—but especially Jews and Muslims share an intertwined legacy of moral and spiritual values that can inform and inspire a deeply rooted process of reconciliation. The Fons Vitae Spiritual Affinities: Judaism and Islam project is committed to doing its part in this effort.

Nissim Rejwan in first undertaking to write *The Jews of Iraq: 3000 Years of History and Culture* has helped us to understand why Abrahamic peace is plausible and possible. Fons Vitae is honored to have the opportunity to reintroduce this work to a world more than ready for it.

Joseph V. Montville is a retired American diplomat who chairs the Center for World Religions, Diplomacy, and Conflict Resolution at George Mason University and is Distinguished Diplomat in Residence at American University. He is also a member of the Fons Vitae Spiritual Affinities: Judaism and Islam advisory board.

Endnotes

1. University Press of Florida, 1998.

2. New Outlook, September-October, 1986, p. 46.

3. Quoted in Zion Zohar, ed., *Sephardic and Mizrahi Jewry: From the Golden Age of Spain to Modern Times,* New York University Press, 2005, p. 302.

4. In *The Zionist Dream Revisited,* (Schocken, 1984), p. 50.

5. Quoted in *The Times* of London, December 12, 1918, p. 7.

6. Text in *amislam.com.*

7. Rejwan, op. cit., p. 117, citing Trude Weiss-Rosmarin, *Toward Jewish-Muslim Dialogue* (New York, 1967), 6-7. The bitter irony was that this Eastern European disdain for Arabs came to be extended to the Jews "ingathered" to the Land of Israel from Muslim countries. David Ben Gurion said in *Look* magazine of October 5, 1965, "[Jews] from Morocco have no education. Their customs are those of Arabs. They love their wives, but they beat them…Maybe in the third generation something will appear in Oriental Jews that is a little different." And Golda Meir, then prime minister, told a meeting of the Zionist Federation of Great Britain on March 8, 1964, "We in Israel need immigrants from countries with a high standard, because the question of our future social structure is worrying us. We have immigrants from Morocco, Libya, Persia, Egypt, and other countries with a 16th century level. Shall we be able to elevate these immigrants up to a suitable level of civilization? If the

present state of affairs continues, there will be a dangerous clash between the Ashkenazim, who will constitute the elite, and the Oriental communities of Israel. This is the most tragic thing that can befall us. We need ...immigrants from countries of a high level." Reported in the Tel Aviv daily *Yediot Aharonot,* March 9, 1964.

Contents

PREFACE ix

Part One: From the Assyrian Captivity to the Arab Conquest (731 BC–AD 641) 1

1 Roots 3
2 The Lure of Exile 11
3 The Scribes and the Birth of the Synagogue 17
4 The Way They Lived 24
5 Greeks, Romans, Seleucids, Sassanians 30
6 Family, Home and Education 36
7 A Neat Division of Labour: Exilarch and *Gaon* 47
8 From Mishnah to Talmud 53
9 The Talmud in Action 61
10 Babylonia Assumes Leadership 70

Part Two: The Encounter with Islam (641–1850) 77

11 A Deep Sigh of Relief 79
12 Islam and the Jews: Theory and Practice 85
13 Baghdad's Jewish Population 94
14 Messianism and Karaism: Rabbinic Judaism Challenged 104
15 Saadia's Legacy 117
16 The Last of the *Geonim* 130
17 The Dark Ages of Iraqi Jewry 136
18 Lasting Imprint 144
19 100 Years of Turmoil 155
20 Recovery and Reassertion 161

Part Three: A Century of Radical Change (1850–1951) 169

21 The Road to Equality 171
22 Exilarch to *Nasi* to *Hakham Bashi* 177
23 The Impact of Modern Education 185
24 World War I 192
25 Rumours of a Brave New World 200
26 Mandate and Independence 210
27 The *Farhud* and its Consequences 217
28 Youth in Revolt 225
29 The Politics of Extortion 233
30 The Exodus 243

APPENDIX: THE ORGANIZATION OF THE COMMUNITY 249
CHRONOLOGY 254
SELECT BIBLIOGRAPHY 258
SOURCE NOTES 260
INDEX 267

MAPS: Jewish settlements in Babylonia in the Talmudic period 49
The city of Baghdad in the seventeenth century 165

Preface

Apart from the last few chapters, where I made use of my own limited first-hand knowledge and observation, this book makes no claims to original research, its chief merit being the way the information is collated, summarized and organized. For some time now, the need has been felt for a straight, comprehensive and brief account of the Jews of Iraq, their history, culture and society, and in putting this account together I have tried to do something by way of filling that need.

The nearly three millennia of Iraqi Jewish history surveyed here are covered in three parts, dealing respectively with the period extending from the first Assyrian captivity in the early eighth century BC to the Arab conquest in the middle of the seventh century AD; the encounter with Islam (641–1850); and the last hundred years (1850–1951), a period of political upheaval and radical change culminating in the mass exodus of the Jews to Israel. Learning from my experience as a reader, I have also attempted to depict the story of the Jews of Iraq in its wider context of general Jewish and of Iraqi and regional history. My hope has been to spare the reader the difficulty of trying to fit the account into events and developments in the surrounding world.

I am indebted to the many authors and scholars whose own labours have provided the groundwork for this book. My thanks also go to Dr Davide and Mrs Irene Sala (Salman), whose active interest and whose encouragement made the production of this book possible. I have also benefited greatly from the comments and suggestions offered by friends who read the work in manuscript. My thanks to all of them – and to my editor at Weidenfeld and Nicolson, Ms Linda Osband, for her diligence, patience and forbearance.

Nissim Rejwan
Jerusalem, May 1985

PART ONE

From the Assyrian Captivity to the Arab Conquest (731 BC–AD 641)

From the Maccabean era to the middle of the eleventh century, when the Babylonian academies fell into oblivion, the development of the Talmud and its elevation to a position of classical authority constitute the most significant achievement of the Jewish people. And this, too, may be added: the intellectual *qui vive* so characteristic of Jews throughout the Middle Ages despite contumely and persecution was the result of the Talmud.

Judah Goldin[1]

CHAPTER I

Roots

For close on four millennia the fortunes of the Jewish people, the growth of their religious beliefs and the shaping of their culture were in one way or other inextricably linked with 'the land of the twin rivers', now known as Iraq. At first glance Egypt, the ancient Hebrews' other close neighbour, would seem to have exercised a more decisive influence, if only because of its geographical proximity to the Land of Israel. However, in the cultural sphere Israel's contacts with Mesopotamia were far closer than they were with Egypt. Indeed, most of the important outside influences – as reflected in the Bible – came from the direction of Mesopotamia, and much of the contents of the early chapters of Genesis points unmistakably to that land.

> The founding Patriarch came from Mesopotamia; he had been bidden to leave that land for the very purpose that is to become the leading theme of the Bible, namely, the quest of an enduring and universally valid way of life. The story of the ages anterior to the period of Abraham should, therefore, bear the distinctive imprint of his original homeland. That it does so in fact is but further proof that the account as a whole is based on genuine traditions instead of being the invention of some imaginative writer, or school of writers.[1]

It was thanks to this affinity with Mesopotamia, which goes back far into the past, that the people of Israel was able to go on to its unique and enduring achievement by filling the vast spiritual vacuum that had caused Abraham to leave Mesopotamia and proceed to the Promised Land. 'That the original promise was fulfilled remains to this day one of the great wonders of history. The credit, however, for giving Israel its all-important start, physically and culturally, belongs to ancient Mesopotamia.'[2]

The ancestors of the present-day Jews were members of a clan of no clear ethnicity or peoplehood led by Terah, father of the Patriarch Abraham. The clan left Ur of the Chaldees in Sumer, spent some time in Harran in upper Mesopotamia, and finally left for Hebron in the land of Canaan. This emigration, which took place in the year 1850 BC or thereabouts, is invested in the Bible with the character of a religious movement. The Terahites, in leaving Ur, left behind them the kindred Arameans; they also left behind the gods they and their fathers had worshipped. According to the biblical account, Abraham was 'called'. It was by the grace of prophetic inspiration, in obedience to the divine voice, that he set foot upon a land (Canaan as it was known then, the Land of Israel as it came to be called by the Jews, and Palestine to the Romans) which he received as a promise to be his and his seed's 'for ever'.

Early historians of this period, writing before the great archaeological discoveries were made in Mesopotamia, tended to depict Abraham and his fellow migrants from Ur as simple nomads, originating in the desert. Later findings tended to tell a rather different story. Ur, it transpired, was a trading and manufacturing centre whose business extended far afield. Raw materials were imported, some from overseas, to be worked up in the factories of Ur. A bill of lading belonging to a merchant ship which came up the canal from the Persian Gulf to discharge its cargo in Ur details gold, copper ore, hardwoods, ivory, pearls and precious stones. According to Sir Leonard Woolley, who was in charge of a joint Anglo-American archaeological expedition which began its work on the site in 1923, Ur of the Chaldees at the beginning of the second millennium BC was a powerful, prosperous, colourful and busy capital city. 'We must', Woolley writes, 'radically alter our view of the Hebrew Patriarch when we see that his earlier years were passed in such sophisticated surroundings. He was the citizen of a great city and inherited the traditions of an old and highly organized civilization. The houses themselves reveal comfort and even luxury.'[3]

Yehezkel Kaufmann, a biblical scholar of the first rank and a prominent historian of ancient Israel, indirectly confirms Woolley's verdict. 'The Biblical story', he writes, 'which has the family of Abraham wander north, then southwest – from Ur of the Chaldees to Harran, then to Canaan – is . . . important because it confutes the notion that the Israelite tribes were desert barbarians with a low culture and religion at the time of the Exodus and Conquest.'[4] Enumerating some of the contributions made by Babylonian civilization to the culture of early Israel, Kaufmann continues:

> Israeli traditions regarding the Creation, the Antediluvians, the Flood, and the Tower of Babel have striking parallels in Babylonian

literature which show that the [Hebrew] tribes were influenced by Mesopotamian culture during their stay in that area. The social and legal backgrounds of the patriarchal narratives likewise reveal cultural contacts with Mesopotamian legal traditions. Elements of Israel's hymnal and wisdom literature, along with certain cultic practices, also stem from the period of the tribes' stay in the land between Ur and Harran.[5]

Our story starts with a cataclysm. A Sumerian lamentation over the fall of Ur, situated half-way between Baghdad and the head of the Persian Gulf, was discovered at Nippur in the year 1900. With a population of between 250,000 and 500,000 engaged in agriculture, handicraft and commerce, Ur's glory was not to last. Sweeping down from their mountain fastness across the Persian Gulf, Elamite hordes attacked Sumeria, and in the year 1960 BC Ur went down in disaster and shame. The Sumerian lamentation describes 'the all-annihilating destruction' wrought by the invaders. The city's walls were razed to the ground, its buildings reduced to ashes, and its gates filled with bodies of the slain. Both weak and strong perished by famine or were overtaken in their houses by fire, while those who managed to survive were scattered far and wide. Families were broken up. Parents abandoned their children, and husbands their wives.

It is generally assumed that among those who escaped the cataclysm was Terah, the head of an Aramean nomadic family whose original home had been at Harran, in north-west Mesopotamia, but who for some time had taken up residence in the capital city of Ur. Terah, together with his sons and kinsmen, made their way back to Harran, which he intended to be a temporary halting-place, on the way to the far safer land of Canaan. Terah, however, died in Harran and the succession fell to his eldest son, Abram. Abram had a different approach to things, and different ideas from his father's. Unlike his father, a polytheist worshipping a congeries of idols, Abram was a monotheist; upon succession to the family headship, he promptly broke with idolatory and turned to the service of the one and only God whom he recognized as the creator of heaven and earth. Abram's one God, moreover, differed from the deities recognized and worshipped in other contemporary religions – such as the Sumerian high-god Anu and the Babylonian universal-god Shamash – in that He was not a nature god, nor was He a territorial god restricted to a particular locality or country. Abram's god, as the creator of heaven and earth, was independent of nature and of any geographical limitations.

Furthermore, unlike the other known deities, Abram's God was essentially an ethical god to whom justice and righteousness was of supreme concern.

There is reason to believe that round about this time Abram became convinced that he was to become the founder of a new nation – a nation which was to bring the knowledge of God to the world. Detaching himself and his wife and household from the heathen environment of Harran, Abram thus resumed the family trek to Canaan, which he thought would be eminently suitable for the fulfilment of the destiny to which he believed himself to have been appointed. Proceeding south along the eastern bank of the Jordan, he crossed the river into Canaan and reached Shechem, some twenty-seven miles north of Jerusalem, and there he learned in a revelation that the land he had entered and chosen as his new home was the very land which had been predetermined in the counsels of God to be given to him and his descendants. Coming as they did from the other side of the river Euphrates, Abram and his family became known in their new surroundings as 'Hebrews', a term derived from a root, *'eber*, meaning 'the other side'.

The process of the Hebrews' settlement in the land of Canaan was a slow one. Fresh kindred groups followed from the Aramean borderland of the desert. Abram (whose name now appears in the Bible as Abraham) pitched his tents around Hebron; his son Isaac dwelt in Gerar and the Negev; Isaac's son Jacob, also named Israel, dwelt in Shechem. The Israelites, the Children of Israel, now counted twelve tribes. Two chief divisions marked themselves off according to descent from Leah or Rachel, the two wives of the ancestor Israel: Reuben, Simeon, Levi, Judah, Issachar and Zebulun claimed descendency from Leah, while Joseph and Benjamin were the sons of Rachel. Two other groups were considered of somewhat inferior lineage as the children of concubines – Gad and Asher, and Dan and Naphtali. However, they all knew themselves to be united in blood, the children of one father.

It was in the Hyksos period (1700–1580 BC) that Joseph, Israel's favourite son, was reportedly sold by his jealous brothers to an Ishmaelite caravan as it passed through on the way to Egypt. For at least four centuries following this forced migration, the Israelites lived, multiplied and prospered in the Nile delta – until they were driven out by a Pharaoh 'whose heart the Lord had hardened' (thought by historians to be Rameses II, 1290–1224 BC). It was at this juncture that the first great religious reformer in the history of mankind, a man of supreme intelligence and powerful personality, made his appearance.

Moses was born at a time when the tyrannical Pharaoh had ordered all new-born male children of the Hebrews to be cast into the river, but Moses was said to have been saved by the ruler's own daughter. It was Moses who managed to unite the Israelites around the cult of a unique and universal God, and led their long march across the Sinai peninsula; he died just as they were on the threshold of the Promised Land.

After the death of Moses, leadership of the Israelites passed on to Joshua, who led them to victory in the conquest of Canaan. In reality, however, victory was achieved by each of the twelve tribes fighting for its own territory under elected chiefs, or 'Judges', and may have taken up to a hundred years to complete. The establishment of an Israelite kingdom under Saul, and the victories of David (1010–955 BC) over the Philistines, Canaanites and the states lying to the east of the Jordan (Amon, Edom and Moab), finally consecrated the supremacy in Palestine of Abraham's progeny. David, and Solomon after him, succeeded in building a veritable empire, and according to biblical sources the reign of the latter was a period of considerable glory for the new nation. Indeed, for the first time in history Palestine came to obey one ruler whose authority extended from Dan in the north to Beersheba in the south. Jerusalem, formerly a small and unimportant town, became a capital city, and it is said that scores of thousands of workmen took part in the building of its Temple. The Israelite army was armed with weapons of iron and was well provided with horses and chariots. From Etzion-Geber near Akaba (now known as Eilat) Solomon's ships sailed down the Red Sea and returned from Arabia and Ethiopia loaded with gold. The King himself, who was credited with proverbial wisdom, lived in a sumptuous palace among 'seven hundred wives and three hundred concubines'. It appears, however, that such pomp and extravagance was more than this small and austere nation could stand, both financially and morally. Solomon's glorious reign ended in revolution, and after his death in 935 BC the kingdom was divided by plebiscite into two parts: the Kingdom of Israel in the north, with Samaria as its capital, and the Kingdom of Judah in the south, its capital continuing to be Jerusalem; the period of united monarchy had lasted somewhat less than a hundred years.

After over a century of unrest and tribulation, and recurrent wars with neighbours from north, east and south, the first half of the eighth century BC witnessed a return of prosperity and peace in Israel, and both Hebrew kingdoms were free of outside molestation. The Aramean kingdom of Damascus was too weak, after her defeats at the hands of the Assyrians, to renew her aggression; the Egyptians were too busy to interfere or just not sufficiently interested; and the frequent palace revolts which had shaken the kingdoms ceased. In the year 745 BC, however, Tiglath-pileser III became King of Assyria and inaugurated a campaign of imperial conquest which in less than a quarter of a century brought an end to the existence of the Kingdom of Israel and to the independence of the Kingdom of Judah. What happened at first was that King Menahem of Israel (*c.* 745–737 BC) paid tribute to Tiglath-pileser, but his successor Pekah pursued an anti-Assyrian policy, allying himself for this purpose with Damascus. Whereupon the Assyrian conqueror took Damascus, abolished the monarchy and proclaimed the territory an Assyrian province. The northern and Transjordanian regions of the Kingdom of Israel were also detached and made into Assyrian provinces. The upper strata of the population of these areas were deported and replaced by immigrants from other parts of the Assyrian Empire.

About ten years after this first deportation of Jews at the hands of the Assyrians, Hoshea, the last king of what remained of the Kingdom of Israel, withheld payment of tribute from Assyria at the instigation of Egypt. Whereupon he was imprisoned and Samaria, his capital, was stormed after a three years' siege and was made the seat of government of the Assyrian province of Samaria. A second deportation took place, involving – according to Assyrian records – 27,290 people, and again foreign settlers were sent to take their place. This took place in the year 721 BC and the exiles were despatched to places in Syria, Assyria and Babylonia.

The fate of Judah, the smaller of the two Hebrew kingdoms, proved to be no better than that of Israel, although the end came 133 years later. Trouble seems to have started in the year 605 BC, with the defeat of the Egyptian forces at Carchemish by the powerful Babylonian king, Nebuchadnezzar. Judah had for some time been under Egyptian rule, and with the Egyptians' defeat this rule was superseded by that of Babylon. However, King Jehoiakim of Judah, who had been chosen by the Egyptians to replace his brother Jehoahaz, staged a rebellion at the instigation of Egypt not long after Nebuchadnezzar established Babylonian supremacy in the kingdom. Retribution came rather swiftly: Nebuchadnezzar laid siege on Jerusalem, and the city fell on 16 March 597 BC, Jehoiakim's young son and successor Jehoiachin (who, in the meantime, had assumed authority) was taken in captivity together with the flower of Judah's inhabitants. Zedekiah, an uncle of Jehoiachin's, was then appointed king of the enfeebled state under an oath of allegiance to Nebuchadnezzar. But he too, deluded by Egyptian promises and encouraged by the false prophets, rebelled – and after a desperate siege lasting two years, Nebuchadnezzar stormed Jerusalem again, this time razing it to the ground in August 586 BC. Judah ceased to exist as a sovereign state and became a colony, and the majority of its inhabitants were deported, with only a remnant of 'vinedressers and husbandmen' being left behind.

It was the third major deportation of Jews to the land of the twin rivers – and the most crucial and surprising in its ultimate consequences. Commenting on the end of Judah, Rabbi Isidore Epstein writes:

> Thus did Judah share the fate of the Ten Tribes – captivity. But whilst the other tribes vanished and merged with their conquerors, Judah alone survived. But that is not all. Out of the crucible of exile and affliction, Judah emerged, purged and purified, into a new people – the Jews. Spreading quickly throughout the earth, the Jews carried wherever they settled a new message – Judaism. Shaped and nurtured by a faith which was impervious to change of circumstance and environment, Judaism in captivity not only survived but also developed a dynamic which in turn was destined to captivate the world.[6]

A fascinating but tricky problem faces the historian here – a problem which will probably remain unsolved. Babylonia had for thousands of years been a highly developed, relatively prosperous and densely populated country. Why then should Nebuchadnezzar have chosen for settlement by the Jews what Josephus describes as 'the most proper places of Babylonia', which the region around Nippur, one of the largest cities in the Empire, certainly was? According to Salo W. Baron, this might have something to do with the fate and places of settlement of the earlier waves of Jewish arrivals in Mesopotamia; it is possible, he writes, that some Jewish – or rather Israelitic – settlements had been established in these regions prior to the deportations of 597 and 586 BC.

Under Assyria, he explains, the cities of Babylon and Nippur were less focal centres, and foreign mass settlements there might have been welcomed by the government of the day.

> The most important group of aliens in Northern Israel after Samaria's fall came from Kuta. If those scholars who identify this place as a district one day's journey from Babylon be correct, it is entirely possible that the Assyrian monarchs, pursuing their ancient policy, settled there, in exchange, some of the Israelites deported in

> 721 and after. With the rise of Chaldaea, this district, because of its proximity to the new capital [Babylon], became one of the central regions of the empire. Many of the Israelitic exiles as well as some voluntary immigrants who perhaps had joined them during the seventh century, may have spread through all Babylonia while it was still under Assyrian domination. Thus later deportees could settle in established Israelitic centres. This concatenation of circumstances would also explain in part the equally astonishing fact that as early as the first third of the sixth century, when Ezekiel prophesied, the Jews had achieved an advantageous economic position. Although in general the policy of Assyrian and Babylonian monarchs toward deported nations was favourable, such a prodigious development in the course of a few decades would otherwise be an almost insoluble riddle.[7]

Conceivably, too, this state of affairs contributed considerably to the other phenomenon which tends to present a problem to the student of this period – namely the speed with which the exiles were integrated in their new surroundings, especially with regard to work. For there was hardly any important vocation, including public office, in which Jews were not represented; the economic activities in which the exiles engaged were even more varied than they were back home. A people of farmers and petty artisans, these Jews entered with alacrity the highest echelons of Babylonia's trade and commerce. But although well integrated in the imperial fabric, these exiles nevertheless retained their cultural and religious identity almost intact.

CHAPTER 2

The Lure of Exile

Sometime during the third century AD, in one of the two great Jewish academies of Babylonia, four rabbis discussed the question as to why the Holy One, blessed be He, chose Babylonia as the place of exile for the people of Israel. Rabbi Hiyya, himself a native of Babylonia, thought it was because they would not have been able to survive the severe decrees of Rome. Another native of Babylonia, Rabbi Eleazar ben Pedath, sought the explanation topographically – namely that Babylonia was a low-lying land, resembling the nether world, and from such a land the Jews would soon be redeemed. A third sage, Rabbi Hanina bar Hamma, suggested the reason that the language of Babylonia was akin to that of the Torah. The fourth and last of the group, Rabbi Yohanan bar Nappaha, was brief and much more direct: God, he said, sent the children of Israel back to their mother's home.

It will be noted that the deliberations of these four worthy sages took place almost exactly eight centuries after the Babylonian monarch, Nebuchadnezzar, drove the population of Judah into exile in Babylonia – and some 750 years after the Persian King, Cyrus, issued his famous edict allowing the Jews of Babylonia to return to Jerusalem and rebuild their Temple there. During these long centuries many shifts occurred in the fortunes of the exiles. The exiled King of Judah, Jehoiachin, was favourably treated by Nebuchadnezzar's successor Amel-Marduk (562–560 BC), but he was assassinated by Nebuchadnezzar's son-in-law Neri-glissar; after some twenty years of internal rifts and foreign wars the country became weak and divided and fell easily to the rising power of the Achaemenids. Cyrus, who had by that time taken over Media, Persia and Elam, entered Babylon on 16 October 539 BC following its capture by his general, Gobryas.

While these and other momentous events were taking place, the exiles were busy establishing themselves in their new homes. When the last group of Jews arrived in Babylonia in 586 BC, they found two other groups of Hebrews already there. One group, there for only eleven years, consisted of their friends and relatives, recent newcomers still groping their way in their new surroundings and into a new life. The other group, in so far as its members were still identifiable, consisted of the great-grandchildren of those Israelites who comprised the second Assyrian deportation, which took place in 721 BC. These Israelite Hebrews – as distinct from Judean Hebrews – were descendants of the Ten Tribes. What differentiated the newcomers from the Israelites was that the latter had probably been fairly completely absorbed into the foreign environment by the time the former arrived, though some of them, later to be merged with the Jewish people, must have maintained their identity in the Median highlands and beyond. Nevertheless, this second group of deportees are considered virtually lost to the Jewish people, hence the reference to 'the lost ten tribes'.

An interesting phenomenon confronts the student here – namely the fact that, unlike their brethren from Israel who assimilated into the Assyrian world, the exiles from Judah did not assimilate into the Babylonian world. The phenomenon is especially striking because, in the final analysis, the downfall of the southern Kingdom of Judah followed the same pattern as that of the northern Kingdom of Israel, whose fall resulted in an equally massive deportation. How did it come to pass that – in the words of Bernard J. Bamberger – 'the power that brought Judaism to full maturity – the fire that fused its component materials into a unified whole – was national destruction and exile'? On this perplexing problem, on the fact that 'it was in the ashes of the Jewish state that the Jewish religion ripened', Bamberger submits the following explanation:

> It was not because [the exiles from Judah] were more numerous; the reverse was the case. It was not because the Babylonians were unfriendly or exclusive; on the contrary, the exiles soon became adjusted economically and even socially, and established themselves comfortably in their new homes. It was simply because the Judean exiles regarded themselves in a special light, and took a distinctive view of their destiny and experience. It was because the outlook of the prophets had made a deep impression upon them. In sober fact, the Jews survived because of their religion.[1]

Of these prophets, two exercised a most decisive influence at this difficult phase of Jewish history – Jeremiah and Ezekiel. All his life Jeremiah had predicted tragedy, and he consistently urged submission to the Chaldean masters and firm adherence to the pledges of loyalty the Judeans had given them. When these pledges were broken, he insisted that Jerusalem was doomed. However, as disaster approached and as his prophecies were proving to be valid, he began to reach out towards a more distant future. He wrote to the earlier exiles in Babylonia counselling them to be patient and of good cheer, and at a time of despair he preached that there was still hope for Israel. But although this hope included the restoration of the Jewish state, its most significant feature was the prophecy that God would make a new covenant with His chastened and purified people.

Ezekiel, who was among those who had been exiled to Babylonia in 597 BC, likewise changed from a prophet of doom to a prophet of hope. The first thing he tried to do was to persuade the Jews that the God of Israel had not been defeated and had not abandoned them. The reason why national disaster had come upon the Jews, he preached, was that they were disloyal to Him, and that He was using Babylonia to punish wicked peoples. Combining the old nationalism with the new growing universalism, Ezekiel taught that though God was the God of the whole world, He was recognized only by Israel – adding, however, that His name could attain recognition in the world only if the people that worshipped him was preserved and ultimately restored to greatness.

> To a deeply depressed Israel, whom he describes symbolically as a heap of dry bones, the prophet brings the hope and assurance of rebirth. God will put a new spirit into the people; He 'will remove the stony heart from them and give them a heart of flesh'. Made worthy of His favour through this act of grace, they will be restored to land and to Temple. There they will follow the double rule of ethical rectitude and ceremonial precision; and Ezekiel gave detailed plans for rebuilding the sanctuary and conducting its rituals.[2]

Ezekiel was an early product of the Babylonian exile, although he was born and bred in Palestine. As such, his teachings are highly important as a case study of the way in which the new community managed the feat of preserving and strengthening its faith while at the same time adjusting to the new environment and to a vastly different life. Ezekiel's greatest single contribution to Judaism probably lay in his treatment of the problem of reward and punishment, which he presented in a new and remarkable light. In earlier days, it had been generally supposed that the nation was responsible as a unit to the Deity, and that adversity or prosperity came upon men in accordance with their deserts; the sin even of a few might be visited upon the entire community. The prophets modified this doctrine by representing God as judging the nation by the law of righteousness, and not on the basis of ritual conformity. But they too thought in terms of national retribution.

However, once the ethical note was introduced, once righteousness became the true measure of salvation, the question arose as to the lot of the individual Jew: why should the righteous suffer because of the sins of the wicked, and why is it that the fortunes of men are so much at variance with their deserts?

The question was not quite new; it appears already in the confessions of Jeremiah. But in Ezekiel's day the problem became acute in another form. The exiles argued that, while Israel deserved punishment, the actual suffering had been inflicted on innocent parties. 'The fathers have eaten sour grapes and the teeth of the children are set on edge.' Ezekiel's answer was clear and uncompromising, and it contained an aspect quite new to Judaism. Every individual, he insisted, receives reward or punishment according to his or her own conduct. No one suffers for the sins of another, and each individual must expiate his or her own wrongdoings. Before Jerusalem was sacked, Ezekiel declared, a heavenly agent marked the brow of every righteous person, and none of these was killed. The wicked, however, met their death, each and every one of them.

This remarkable viewpoint had a bearing on another, no less crucial, aspect of the Jewish religion, namely the subject of salvation. With the earlier prophets, salvation that came from deliverance from evil was a political and social force, and what was contemplated was the salvation not only of Israel but of humanity as a whole. The salvation of the individual would be a necessary consequence – a salvation to be achieved through the universal triumph of justice. In this universalization, however, the individual does not really count. For Ezekiel, on the other hand, the freeing of the individual from sin is all-important. His chief concern was the reconciliation with God, not of the whole people or of humanity but of the individual human being – making him into a just man. This, in turn, demanded a recognition of individual guilt. However, as Rabbi Epstein points out:

> Ezekiel was not a prophet of doom: he was essentially the prophet of hope. Merely to arouse the people to a deeper sense of sin, without at the same time holding out to them the prospect of release from its burden, would have only served to drive them to despair. His task therefore was to proclaim to them a divine promise of individual deliverance from sin, and to bring to all sin-conscious individual souls a message of divine reconciliation through an inward renewal wrought by the power of God. 'From all guilt there may be a release and new life', is the burden of his message. The initiative, however,

he insisted must come from the individual himself. 'Cast away from you all your transgressions wherein you have transgressed; and make you a new heart and a new spirit.' The individual must will to be delivered from sin and make for himself, through penitence and confession, a new spirit. Having done his share, he is reconciled with God who through His loving-kindness recreates him in spirit and life. . . .[3]

This new perception of the reality of a personal relationship with God, Rabbi Epstein concludes, 'was of tremendous significance for the exiled people. It meant that city, Temple and sacrifices were no longer indispensable, and that the people in exile could individually as well as corporately be both loyal to their new home and worshippers of God who would be with them wherever they might be.'[4]

Meanwhile, events of great moment were taking place. Less than one year after seating himself upon the throne of Babylon, in the spring of 538 BC, Cyrus from his summer residence at Ecbatana issued a royal decree granting permission to the Jews to return to Jerusalem and rebuild the Temple. He decreed that the sacred vessels of the Temple, originally carried by the Babylonians back with the deportees, should be returned to the Jews. It is to be noted, however, that this unusual act was not a gesture confined to the Jews. The truth of the matter was that Cyrus had new ideas about how to govern the vast empire which he had won from the Babylonians. Instead of trying to mingle together all the conquered peoples in the hope that they would become one nation, he decided to send each nation back to its original home, and in this way to give each satisfaction. Indeed, it was the policy of the Achaemenian rulers, from Cyrus down, to tolerate the cults of the subjugated nationalities throughout the empire.

The Jews, of course, were overjoyed. Their hopes revived with the restoration of their land and the proposed rebuilding of the Temple. However, while everybody wanted Judea to be rebuilt, the question was who should leave Babylonia to go there to do the building? For the fact was that many of the Babylonian Jews had in the meantime become prosperous and well established in business and farming; the journey to Judea was long and hazardous, and life there would obviously be rugged and full of hardships. Moreover, the Jews in Judea were poor and it was necessary to take considerable amounts of money for the rebuilding of Jerusalem. It was remarkable, therefore, that the caravan which eventually left Babylonia consisted of 42,360 persons, not counting 7,337 slaves of both sexes. The returnees took with them all their worldly goods as well as the contributions of gold and silver made not only by the Jews who chose to remain in Babylonia but by the King out of his treasury. Most started out on foot, some rode on camels' backs, others on donkeys. It took them several months to travel the long, dusty miles of desert, but when they arrived they greeted the land of their fathers with song and rejoicing. This is how one song commemorates the occasion, preserved in Chapter 126 of the Book of Psalms:

> When the Lord brought back those that returned to Zion,
> We were like unto them that dream.
> Then was our mouth filled with laughter,
> And our tongue with singing;
> Then said they among the nations:
> 'The Lord hath done great things with these.'
> The Lord hath done great things with us;
> we are rejoiced.

The joy of the arrival, however, was soon to be dashed. Looking about to see what was to be done, the newcomers were overwhelmed by what they saw. To start with, the territory assigned to them was rather small, comprising Jerusalem and the land about it. But even this land was not entirely theirs to distribute among themselves, since the descendants of the poorer folk who had never left Judea laid claim to it now that they had cultivated it for years. Moreover, disagreements erupted among the returned exiles themselves, principally over the question of what to build first – the walls around the city or the Temple in the city. In addition there was trouble from the neighbouring nations, who, since the deportation of the bulk of the population, had been having it very much their own way. Feeling threatened by the prospect of a wall around Jerusalem, they wrote a letter to the Persian King falsely reporting that the Jews were again planning rebellion.

As time went on and the quarrels and hardships continued, some of the returned exiles openly regretted that they had left their comfortable homes in Babylonia. Nevertheless, in the year 516 BC the modest Temple was completed – exactly seventy years after the first Temple was razed and nearly twenty-one years after the first group of Jews returned from Babylonia. It is to be noted here, however, that the Jews have continued to think of the Babylonian exile as having lasted seventy years, since they considered the rebuilding of the Temple, not the Cyrus declaration, as marking the end of the exile.

CHAPTER 3

The Scribes and the Birth of the Synagogue

The task which the Prophet Ezekiel took upon himself was difficult and rather ambitious. He sought to persuade the Jews that the God of Israel had not been defeated and had not abandoned them. Moreover, he deplored the division among the Hebrews and sought to unite both Judeans and Israelites into a common group, and to look forward to being one people when the time came for restoration to their old country. Finally he sought to keep alive in the Jews their national hopes, and encouraged them with assurances of spiritual blessings and promises of restoration. In these hopes of restoration he never wavered. When the elders came to him and suggested the erection of a Temple on Babylonian soil, he vigorously and relentlessly set himself against such a plan, which he considered tantamount to a renunciation of future restoration at home. Subsequently, and with painstaking detail, he laid out the plan of a new Temple, as well as the lines of the future policy of the nation based on the Torah even though he ventured some modifications.

Ezekiel was not alone in seeking to impress upon the exiles the importance of the Torah for their individual and national well-being. He was probably assisted, and was certainly followed, by a long line of teachers known as *soferim* (scribes), under whom the Torah came to occupy a central place in the religious life of the people. The scribes were men whose main interest lay in the preservation of the old literature of the Hebrews. They collected the writings of famous men and the utterances of notable prophets spoken in Israel and Judah and made them available for the Babylonian exiles to read and ponder. In this way, and because Ezekiel's ideas were similar to those of the great prophets, the scribes helped to spread the message of the Babylonian prophet.

With the appearance of the scribes and their assumption of the role of teachers, the school took the place of the Temple and the teacher that of the sacrificing priest; the religious observances, especially the Sabbath, prayer and fasting, took the place of the sacrificial rites. It was at this time that the foundations of the synagogue were laid. The synagogue met the needs of the exiles in more than one sense. The Jews, of course, lived in groups, and it was thus natural for those living near one another to meet on the days that they did no work. On Sabbaths, feast days and fast days they would gather together and reminisce and talk about the glories of the past. For obvious reasons, they could not perform the sacrifices which the priests used to offer up on such occasions; but they could sing the songs that accompanied the sacrifices, and which the scribes had preserved. It is likely that such gatherings were precisely the occasions on which the prophets used to address the people and give them words of encouragement and hope. A prophet, teacher or scribe present would most probably read to the assembly portions of the Torah or the written work of a prophet of Israel who had lived long before and whose words provided the encouragement and the hope which the exiles needed to preserve themselves and their Jewishness. These were the origins of the institution we now know as the synagogue.

Prior to the rise of the synagogue, however, and constituting one of the main factors leading to that development, the Babylonian exiles introduced certain changes and modifications in their religion which proved to be essential in their new environment, cut off as they were from the seat of their religion and peoplehood. As Solomon Grayzel puts it, the Jews in Babylonia developed their religion in such a way as to make their future more secure:

> They had become accustomed to rest from work on the Sabbath and on such holidays as Passover, Sukkot, and Shabu'ot. In Judea they had refrained from working on these days because their religion forbade them. In Babylonia, as we now know, many of them supposed that they no longer needed to observe their religion. Nevertheless, most of them continued to rest on such occasions. They probably argued that they were doing this in memory of the old days when their nation was free and independent. Besides the feasts and the days of rest, they also began to observe days of fasting. All of them mourned on the anniversary of the day when the wall of Jerusalem began to crumble under the attacks of the Babylonians, and on the day when the city fell. For these reasons the 10th of Tebet, the 17th of Tammuz and the 9th of Ab were observed as fast days. Such days of rejoicing and of mourning were almost enough to keep the Jews separate from the Babylonians, and to unite them in common memories.[1]

Whether these changes and readjustments in themselves would have proved sufficient to preserve both the faith and identity of the Babylonian Jew without the fall of the Babylonian Empire and the partial return to Jerusalem is a moot question. Some historians, including Grayzel, tend to believe that the Babylonian Jews would most probably have succumbed to the lure of their environment had not the Babylonian Empire come to a sudden and unexpected end. Other historians are silent on this issue. However, the fact remains that although the overwhelming majority of the Babylonian Jews chose not to take advantage of Cyrus's offer of return, it was in Babylonia rather than in Jerusalem that the Jewish religion was preserved and codified. Moreover, the work of restoration 'back home' was itself effected only thanks to the continued efforts and assistance provided from the Babylonian exile.

In Chapter 2 we saw how difficult the act of return and restoration proved to be, beset as it was by many stumbling-blocks. In fact, the returned exiles became disappointed and exhausted after years of hard labour. The land had grown wild during their fifty years of absence, quarrels amongst themselves and disputes with their neighbours weakened their will to work, and their hopes for full restoration began to wane. Finally, in the year 516 BC the modest Temple was completed and, alongside their brethren in Jerusalem, the Jews of Babylonia rejoiced in the belief that all was finally well in the old country. They also imagined that, unlike themselves who were finding it hard to lead a full Jewish existence in a foreign land, the Jews of Judea were finding it a simple matter to live a Jewish life. Proceeding on this assumption a man named Ezra, one of the most pious of the Babylonian Jews, decided about one generation after the rebuilding of the Temple to emigrate to the Holy Land, to live, study and pray as a Jew in the land of the Jews.

Ezra, who was by descent a priest and by profession a scribe, was joined on his long trip by some 2,000 men, women and children – and with great joy and high hopes the group set out on the long and arduous journey. Ezra, who was loved and respected and enjoyed a good reputation as a pious and learned Jew, carried letters from the Persian king ordering all his officials along the way to protect the travellers. The king also issued a decreee conferring upon Ezra authority to appoint upon his arrival judges and magistrates, with plenary powers of jurisdiction in accordance with the rules of the Torah. Moreover, he carried large gifts from the king and his council for the Temple in Jerusalem, and was also permitted to secure funds from the Jews of

Babylonia and to lead back to Jerusalem all those who expressed the wish to go there.

The men who accompanied Ezra – and whose number some historians put at 1,800 not counting women and children – came from priestly, Davidic and other families, including a number of Levites and other subordinate Temple survivors. They arrived in Jerusalem in the month of Ab, 458 BC. After spending four months acquainting himself with the situation, Ezra was shocked and horrified by what he saw; it was far worse than he or any of his fellow Babylonian Jews had expected. To start with, while the Temple service went on under a descendant of Joshua, the Jews were respectful neither towards the priests nor towards the Temple, and even failed to support it properly; it transpired, too, that the neighbouring peoples had as much to say about the Temple and the running of its affairs as did the Jews. Secondly, Ezra was horrified at the extent to which intermarriage had gone: the Jews appeared to have freely intermarried with the pagan peoples in the neighbourhood of Judea, and the daughters of these pagans usually brought into the Jewish community their family gods, their specific religious notions and their own forms of sacrifice; even the language spoken by their children was not Hebrew.

Observing this state of affairs, Ezra decided that unless this foreign influence was removed the Jews could not maintain their belief in one God. He went on a fast, mourning his cherished dreams – and at the end of three days called the leaders of the people and told them how he felt, how hopeless the outlook for the survival of the Jews seemed to him. He expressed his belief that the Jews would be finished as Jews unless they returned whole-heartedly to their belief in one God and to the good life which that implied. Asked by the elders if he could lead them towards the life and the beliefs he wanted them to accept, Ezra said he could, provided they met one condition. They agreed, and on the twentieth of the month of Kislew he and the representatives of the community approved by an overwhelming majority a resolution decreeing that all unlawful marriages be dissolved. This meant that all foreign wives and the children born of them must be sent away. A commission was then appointed to draw up a list of the transgressors. This took the whole winter, and on the first of the month of Nisan, 457 BC, the measure was officially put into effect – but in practice it failed.

The plain truth was that Ezra's plan could not be carried through. It demanded that hundreds of men break up their families and send those whom they loved and cherished out of their homes. This was too much to ask of human beings. But Ezra was adamant, being something of a doctrinaire. He demanded this supreme sacrifice because he believed that the nation and its ideals were more important than the feelings of individual men and women. As Grayzel puts it: 'He was serving as general in a war for the preservation of the Jews, and like every general he considered his objective of greater importance than the lives of his soldiers.'[2]

Ezra's difficulties came from outside the community as well as from inside. The Samaritans and the other neighbouring nationalities were angered by the affront to their womenfolk; they were unwilling to permit their sons, daughters and grandchildren to be expelled from the country where they had settled, and they threatened revenge. Ezra realized that in order to defend Jerusalem from a sudden attack by these pagan nations the city should be suitably fortified, and he duly started to make preparations to rebuild the walls. That undertaking, however, was seen as being in excess of the royal authority granted to him on his departure from Babylonia. His enemies were quick to seize the opportunity. Rehum, the governor of Samaria, signed a petition addressed to the king, and the king gave orders for the immediate cessation of the work and for razing the part already constructed. Despite the first expressions of willingness on the part of the city's elders to obey him, Ezra could not fail to notice that matters were returning to what they had been before his arrival. It is assumed by a number of historians that Ezra, disappointed and virtually defeated, at this juncture decided to return to Babylonia, and that he revisited Judea only many years later. Other chroniclers take the view that Ezra merely chose to leave public life and disappeared from the public eye, but that he remained in Judea. According to this version Ezra, who was primarily a scribe and a teacher rather than a man of action, gathered about himself a small group of close disciples and acquainted them with the great literary and religious treasures of the Jewish people. He is thought to have achieved more, in this way, than he could possibly have accomplished by his interest in practical government.

Ezra's next appearance in public life came some twenty years later, when another great name in the annals of Babylonian Jewry appeared in troubled Judea. Nehemiah, son of Hacaliah, was a Jew who stood high in the favour of the Persian king. Though his official title was 'King's Cupbearer', he was one of the king's advisers and shared in the government of the empire. When news of what was going on in Judah reached him through Hanani, one of his brethren, he 'sat down and wept, and mourned for days, and . . . continued fasting and praying before the God of heaven'. As further told in the Book of Nehemiah, he approached the king and asked for permission to go to Jerusalem and rebuild the walls of the city. The king, after obtaining Nehemiah's promise that he would not stay away permanently, granted him leave and appointed him military governor of Judah. Nehemiah arrived in Jerusalem in the summer of 445 BC, and three days after his arrival, in the dead of night, he rode out to survey the walls. In the morning he called the leaders of the Jewish people together, showed them the king's commission appointing him governor, and announced that he expected them to help in rebuilding the wall around the city. Disregarding their objections and protests, and dismissing the argument that the neighbouring Samaritans and Ammonites would be sure to resent such an act, Nehemiah succeeded in arousing the workmen and artisans of Jerusalem to volunteer, and in a very short time the work was completed.

It was at this point that Ezra made another appearance. Together with Nehemiah, who seems to have had similar thoughts of reformation and rejuvenation for his people, he decided what the Jewish community needed in order to be brought closer to the ideal which it was destined to represent. Using his unchallenged authority as governor, Nehemiah now ordered the gates of the new wall to be closed at sundown on Friday and not to be opened till sundown on Saturday. He did this to stop pagan merchants from making the Sabbath their market day by bringing their wares into the city. He paid little attention to the protests from these merchants, and similar protests later from the city's Jewish merchants; eventually both classes of merchants got used to doing their business deals on weekdays. Nehemiah's next step was to forbid all outside interference in internal Jewish affairs, and followed this by measures aimed at reforming and improving the administration of the Temple, including the levying of a regular tax for its support.

Apart from a number of social and economic reforms which he then introduced, Nehemiah finally joined with Ezra in establishing the Torah as the constitution of the new community. On the first of Tishri (the Jewish New Year) in the year 444 BC, a large number of people gathered in the court of the Temple, watching with deep interest the priests and Levites at the service and the offering of the sacrifices. After the service and the offerings, Ezra read sections of the Torah to the assembled people, the Levites making the rounds and elucidating the text. On the twenty-fourth day a fast was observed, and the people solemnly bound themselves to order their lives in accordance with the Torah. A document of ratification was drafted, subscribed by

Nehemiah, the governor, then by representatives of the priests, the Levites and the laity. Specific mention was made of those prescriptions of the Torah which were particularly relevant to the situation: no marriages should be contracted with the surrounding nations; the land should lie fallow and all debts be remitted every seventh year; the prescribed dues for the upkeep of the Temple worship and the maintenance of priests and Levites should be regularly paid; and the Sabbath and holy days must be so honoured as to exclude any manner of business transaction even with non-Jewish traders.

By now Ezra was an old man, and he died not long after this ceremony was held. Nehemiah, too, had to depart, having been recalled back to his post in Persia. It did not take long for the opposition elements to raise their head, and the wealthy classes among the Jews duly fell back to their old ways.

CHAPTER 4

The Way They Lived

> Build houses and live in them; plant gardens and eat their produce. Take wives and have sons and daughters . . . multiply there, and do not decrease. But seek the welfare of the city where I have sent you into exile, and pray to the Lord on its behalf, for in its welfare you will find your welfare.

This rare piece of advice, sent forth by the prophet Jeremiah (29: 5–7) in Jerusalem to the elders, priests, prophets and people who had been carried off to Babylonia after the destruction of the Temple, could not have been more apt or better considered. The exiled Jews of Babylonia took it with alacrity and energy; they sought and worked for 'the welfare of the city' and they duly found their own welfare therein. Although we read of the Jews of Babylonia sitting by 'the rivers of Babylon' and weeping, they appeared to have done this only in a manner of speaking – or that those who did sit there and weep in memory of Jerusalem were a group of zealots. The majority of the Jews quickly set out to rebuild their homes and their lives; they worked hard, prospered and multiplied.

But they did not start from scratch. Babylon in those days was a great centre of commerce, industry, trade and finance. Babylonian trade routes took the Jews to every corner of the known world, making them men of commerce and international trade. This, however, applied only to a few. The most important and commonest occupation of the Babylonian Jews was agriculture. Having been farmers from their days in Palestine, the Jews naturally turned to farming in Babylonia as well. A few of them had large tracts of agricultural land which they parcelled out among others either leasing or renting, paying an agreed share of the produce to the landowner. A large number possessed small farms of their own; but a considerable proportion were farmhands who worked for a daily wage. The pages of the Babylonian Talmud are dotted with references to the farmer and his daily life and affairs; and in keeping with its main aim as a compendium of laws and precepts, it also expounds laws regulating the wages, work conditions, leases, rents and other matters pertaining to farming.

The men who tilled the soil, especially those amongst them who had to pay exorbitant rates to landowners, underwent great hardships, as they toiled to convey the waters from the canals to the irrigation ditches or strove to keep them from overflowing. Taxes, too, were high, and the tax-gatherers were generally strict and ruthless. Yet the farmers, however small their plots of land, seem to have been of good cheer; in the words of a popular saying of the time, 'A yoke of arable land is worth more than a storeful of merchandise.'

While the farmer and the farmhand were content with their lot, the craftsman generally considered himself a happier man. As another popular saying had it: 'Seven years of famine, but never did it cross the threshold of the craftsman.' Jews in Babylonia worked as bakers and brewers; weavers, dyers and tailors; shipbuilders and woodcutters; and we have records of Jewish blacksmiths, tanners, fishermen, sailors and porters. The farmer took his produce to town once a week; in the markets there was a stall for each trade, and a market inspector watched over the measures and weights and settled disputes according to law and custom. On the one hand, there were street vendors and retail traffickers eking out a modest living, and on the other there were the princes of commerce who exported grain, wine, wool and flax, and imported silk, iron and precious stones. Differences between rich and poor were great; men of business suffered less at the hands of the authorities and lived far better. The rich merchants, who travelled by water or by caravan routes to distant marts, led a life of luxury amid a retinue of slaves and menials.[1]

These rich Jews did not have a reputation for generosity or undue hospitality. In one of the tractates of the Mishnah (*Betza'* 32b) we find the following passage:

> Rabbi Nathan ben Abba said in the name of Rab: The rich Jews of Babylonia will go to hell. Sabbatai ben Marinos went to Babylon and asked for work. They refused to give it him. He asked for sustenance; they refused to give it him. Then he said: These people must be descended from the mixed multitude who went out of Egypt with the Israelites [Exodus 12:38], for he who has no pity upon his fellow-creatures is assuredly not of the seed of Abraham our father.

Together with farming, the Jews of Babylonia took to growing products from which wine and other alcoholic drinks could be made. These included not only grapes but also, and perhaps mainly, dates, from which a strongly intoxicating drink is extracted. One Arab chronicler of the seventh century of the Common Era quotes lines of poetry in which wines produced by the Jews of Sura are highly praised. Another side occupation of the Jews was the raising of cattle, but for some reason this was not considered as respectable an occupation as farming, shepherds in those days being generally held in low esteem in Babylonia.

In urban centres, apart from trade, commerce and finance, a significant class of Jews engaged in manual labour, hiring themselves out by the day or the week. These included masons, carpenters, potters, tailors, weavers and others. They thronged the towns, and from the Talmud one learns of groups of Jews, with no permanent employment or shops or stalls of their own, gathering in the market-places waiting for an employer to come and hire them. Here again the detailed rules and laws expounded in the Talmud testify to the great interest which the rabbis of the day took in regulating the relations between employer and employee. By implication, they also furnish proof that the employers of these Jews were as often as not Jewish themselves.

These better-off Jews, who could afford to employ others, were generally men who engaged in commerce and industry. As time went on, the number of these Jews increased. For the most part the commerce they engaged in was local, restricted to the cities, towns and villages of Mesopotamia. This country-wide movement of goods and produce in turn gave rise to a shipping industry, and a number of Jews became boatmen. This of course was something new for those who came from Judah, where rivers and canals, in so far as they existed, were not of the size or width to allow boats to pass. In Babylonia, however, the same canals and rivers which were used for irrigation served for the transportation of goods to various parts of the country, as these canals connected the two great rivers which ran parallel and covered the length and breadth of the land. Wine, fruit, vegetables, grain and goods of all kinds moved up and down the rivers and were then taken either for local consumption or for export to foreign lands. Despite the repeated wars with Rome, there was an unceasing exchange of goods between the Roman and the Persian Empires. Babylonian Jews were no doubt active in this import–export trade – an activity, incidentally, which was to continue to be one of their most important occupations throughout the centuries. The export–import trade from Babylonia did not stop with the Roman Empire, however; there were Jews who dealt with lands farther to the east. Silk was imported from China, while several other luxury goods were imported from India. In this sense Babylonian Jewry could be said to have served as a bridge between Europe and the Far East, between West and East.

Commercial activity on such a scale naturally required a banking system of some kind – and even some form of insurance arrangement. Here the story of one Jewish family is worth telling, especially since it is fully documented and verified. 'Murashu and Sons' – International Bank – Insurance, Conveyancing, Loans – Personal and Real Estate – is one firm which has left to posterity its business documents almost intact; these were excavated not long ago and are written on clay. The head office of the firm is given as Nippur, and the claim is made that it has 'branches everywhere'. Keller outlines the story as told in the documents and deeds discovered by scholars from the University of Pennsylvania in its former business premises in Nippur.

The Murashus, exiles from Jerusalem, apparently did very well for themselves after their arrival in Nippur in the year 587 BC. They were an old, well-established firm which continued to stand for something in Mesopotamia throughout the Persian era. The books of Murashu and Sons contain, apart from the firm's deeds and transactions, some invaluable information about the life of the Jewish exiles, their names, their occupations and their property. The offices of Murashu and Sons are described as having been 'a hive of activity'. For some 150 years or more the firm enjoyed the full confidence of its clients, whether it was a matter of conveyance of large estates and sections of the canals or slaves. The nature of the business deals which the firms engaged in can be fathomed from some of those recorded in the documents and the deeds that have been deciphered so far.

One of these documents relates the story of three jewellers who one day called on Murashu and Sons and addressed one of the sons: 'In the case of this emerald ring we give a twenty-year guarantee that the stone will not fall out of the gold. If the emerald falls out of the ring before the expiry of twenty years, [we] undertake to pay Murashu and Sons damages amounting to ten Minas of silver.' The document is signed by seven people. Before the lawyer's name the clay bears the imprint of three finger-nails. These were the signatures of the three jewellers who could not write.

A Babylonian exile named Mannudannijama one day came to Murashu and Sons, because he wanted to arrange a deed of conveyance with a Babylonian concerning an important herd of cattle – 'thirteen old rams, twenty-seven two-year-old rams, 152 lambing ewes, forty year-old rams, an old he-goat, a two-year-old he-goat . . . a total of 276 white and black, large and small sheep and goats . . . cash on delivery

. . . Mannudannijama to be responsible for pasture, feeding and safe custody.' It was dated Nippur, the twenty-fifth of Ulul, and signed with Mannudannijama's finger-nail.

The firm engaged in other business and banking activities. Securities for those imprisoned for debts were deposited with the bank, which had special departments to meet and provide for all eventualities of life. The rate of interest was 20 per cent annually. This was the normal rate in those days and not peculiar to Murashu and Sons.

It was in Babylonia, then, that the occupations of merchant, trader, financier and banker were introduced to Jewry – professions which continue to be favourites with Jews up to our own day. In Palestine, the Jews had only been peasants, settlers, cattle-breeders and tradesmen; the Torah had made no provisions for commerce. It was an alien occupation; the words 'shopkeeper' and 'merchants' were synonymous with 'Canaanites', people whom the prophets had vigorously castigated for their sins. 'A trader, in whose hands are false balances, he loves to oppress' (Hosea 12:7). 'When will the new moon be over, that we may sell grain? And the sabbath, that we may offer wheat for sale . . . and deal deceitfully with false balances – that we may buy the poor for silver and the needy for a pair of sandals, and sell the refuse of the wheat?' (Amos 8:5–6) As Keller sums it up:

> The switch over to this hitherto forbidden profession was extremely clever – a fact that is seldom properly understood. For it proved to be in the last resort, when added to a tenacious attachment to their old faith, the best guarantee of the continuance of Israel as a people. As farmers and settlers scattered throughout a foreign land they would have intermarried and interbred with people of other races and in a few generations would have been absorbed and disappeared. The new profession demanded that their houses should be in more or less large societies, within which they could build themselves into a community and devote themselves to their religious practices. It gave them cohesion and continuity.[2]

How did their life in Babylonia, the economic prosperity, the social cohesion and the communal solidarity affect the numbers of the exiles? There are of course no statistics of the kind to which we in the modern world are accustomed. However, estimates based on the Jews' manner of life and on figures scattered here and there throughout the Babylonian Talmud would show that about the year 70 AD the Jews of Babylonia numbered about a million. They continued to increase, both by birth and by immigration from Palestine; in Roman times, indeed,

Jews beyond the Euphrates are said to have been counted by millions. The most important and populous communities were those of Nehardea, at the junction of the Euphrates and the Royal Canal; Nisbis and Mahoza on the same canal; and Sura, to the south of Mahasia. But Jews of course lived also outside the large cities, in villages and hamlets. It is estimated, therefore, that between AD 200 and 500 the number of Jews in Babylonia approached the two-million mark.

CHAPTER 5

Greeks, Romans, Seleucids, Sassanians

In the year 539 BC, when the armies of Cyrus entered Babylon, its ancient capital, Babylonia lost its independence for ever and the Achaemenian era of Mesopotamian history started, itself to end a little over two centuries later, in 331 BC. The Achaemenians lost control of Babylonia when their armies were defeated by troops led by Alexander the Great in the battle of Gaugamela (near Arbil) on the first day of October, 331 BC. It was a victory which opened the road to Babylonia and Persia for Alexander – just as the battle of Issus two years previously had opened the road to Syria and Egypt for him. The Persian troops stationed in the capital Babylon surrendered without fighting, and the Macedonian conqueror made a triumphal entry into the old Semitic metropolis. Relaxed, leisurely, slow-moving and rather inefficient, the Persian Empire fell an easy prey to the youthful and ambitious Alexander and his well-trained army.

A new and more trying period was opened for the Jews as a whole, and for the Jews of Babylonia in particular. Neither Babylonian nor Persian culture had managed fully to integrate, assimilate and finally destroy Judaism, thanks partly to the work of the scribes and the decisive role which the Babylonian academies played in the maintenance and preservation of the faith. In the Greeks, however, the Jews were confronted with a more persistent, subtle and alluring opponent. Like Cyrus before him, Alexander realized that he could never rule over 'a hundred different nations' unless he won their hearts, so he acted accordingly. Unlike the Persians, however, he did not dream of uniting all his conquests into one great empire, but instead wanted to merge all the conquered peoples into one great cultural unity:

> He admired the philosophy and the literature of Greece, but he also liked the grandeur and the wealth and the ease of life which he found in Persia. He thought it possible to combine the two and create a nation which would have the best features of Greek and Oriental

> civilizations. He built new cities and he enlarged old ones; and he encouraged Greeks, especially the veterans of his army, to settle in these cities and teach the native population how to live like Greeks. Within a generation the entire ancient East throbbed with new life. New ideas, new names for old gods, new methods of administration, a new language, new military tactics and, not the least, new markets for trade awakened the East from the lethargy into which it had sunk during the centuries of easygoing Persian rule.[1]

The Jews soon realized that they were surrounded by a new world, and the impression made upon them by Alexander and his exploits and ambitions was great. However, although the conflict generated by his appearance and his later attempts at Hellenization was long and profound, its effects were far more evident in Palestine and among the Jews of Egypt than they were among the Jews of Babylonia. Nor were these effects felt more by the deeds of his successors. After the death of Alexander in 323 BC, the disruption of the empire and the wars among his generals led to a renewal of the age-old struggle for the possession of Palestine between the north and the south. Ptolemy, the general who ruled Egypt, successfully and swiftly invaded the country in 320; Seleucus, another of Alexander's generals, made himself master of Babylonia *c.*312. Eventually Seleucus won for himself all the lands which Alexander had conquered in Asia. The Seleucids ruled Babylonia for just over two centuries (331–126 BC), giving way to the Parthians. Their empire finally crumbled when its last vestige, a small state in northern Syria torn apart by dynastic crises, fell an easy prey to the Romans in 63 BC.

As far as Babylonian Jewry was concerned, the main impact of Greek rule appears to have been a negative one. For a number of centuries following this period the Greeks maintained closer and broader contacts with the lands to the west than with Babylonia to the east. The great debate over Hellenization, which raged in the Holy Land and threatened to tear its Jewish society asunder, does not seem to have deeply affected the Babylonian Jews. Despite the many vicissitudes which characterized the government of the Parthians (126 BC–AD 227) who succeeded the Seleucids, the Jews of Babylonia managed to weather the storms which swept Palestine and other lands where substantial Jewish communities lived. Indeed, while Palestine was struggling, first to stave off the dangers of Hellenization, and then to liberate itself from the yoke of Rome, Diaspora communities – of which the Babylonian was by far the largest and most important – became increasingly important for the maintenance of Judaism and the Jewish way of life.

To achieve this whilst living as a minority among a non-Jewish majority, the Jews of Babylonia and other Diaspora communities fought a threefold struggle: they strove to preserve themselves, to gain the goodwill of their neighbours, and to live in accordance with Jewish tradition. Babylonian Jewry, at this time the only major Jewish community not under Roman rule, appeared dormant for almost two centuries, lying low and waiting for the storm to pass. But with the steady deterioration of conditions in Palestine, and after the last vestige of Jewish independence was crushed there with the fall of Masada in the spring of AD 73, Babylonian Jewry assumed a much greater role in Jewish life than it had had at any time in the past. It seems certain, however, that for the first two centuries AD the Jewish communities that lived under the rule of Rome held a more central role in Jewish life than the Jewish community of Babylonia.

Losing the war in Palestine, the Jews were deprived of a central authority – a loss that was felt by the Jews of the Diaspora even more acutely than by the Palestinians themselves. The Jews of the world had always looked to Palestine for guidance in religion and mores. Now, with the loss of Jerusalem and the destruction of the Temple, there was nowhere for these communities to look for guidance. However, at this very critical moment in Jewish history there were some who did not believe that losing the war to Rome was necessarily fatal to Jewish life. Study and religious observance, they maintained, would guarantee the continuance of the people.

This rather optimistic point of view – optimistic because conditions were such that few people could take it seriously – was maintained and gained strength mainly in the Diaspora communities, where the Jews for the most part had given very little aid to their Palestinian co-religionists during the first rebellion against Rome. When the Romans eventually failed to be impressed by this display of loyalty to themselves, and when the surrounding Gentile world refused to make any distinction between 'good' Diaspora Jews and 'bad' Palestinian Jews, the Diaspora to the west of Palestine started to show signs of discontent and at least one minor attempt at a revolt was made, although swiftly crushed, in Egypt.

One generation after the defeat in Palestine, around the year AD 110, Emperor Trajan began planning another campaign in the East. Parthia, Rome's rival in Asia, was weak at the time and the Roman emperor thought he would repeat the performance of Alexander the

Great by conquering Persia and India. However, in order to conduct a successful campaign of conquest in that part of the world it was considered advisable to gain the goodwill of the Jews, both because Judah was a border province and because so many Jews lived in the western parts of Parthia. To appease the Jews of Palestine Trajan seems to have even given them a promise to permit the rebuilding of the Temple.

Whether or not he succeeded in this part of his strategy, however, Trajan failed as far as the Jews of Babylonia were concerned. Quickly overrunning the district of Parthia which lay on the other side of the Euphrates where the Jews were settled in large numbers, Trajan crossed the Tigris and annexed Adiabene, whose royal house had embraced Judaism during the reign of Claudius and had fought on the side of the Jews during the great war against Rome two generations before. He then continued eastwards, following Alexander's footsteps. At this point, however, he had to turn back, for at the rear of his army the provinces he had just conquered rebelled. Among the fighters, threatening to cut off Trajan's return and thus capture and annihilate his army, were the Jews of Parthia, who were not enthusiastic about coming under the rule of their traditional enemies and the destroyers of Jerusalem. Although in the end this rebellion was put down with barbaric cruelty and order eventually restored, Trajan was forced however to abandon all thought of further conquest, his attention having now been turned to the uprising of the Jews in various other parts of the empire.

In the meantime, Palestine continued to suffer badly and to decline as the centre of Jewish life. The devastation wrought by the Romans in the course of suppressing the two great Jewish revolts of AD 66–70 and AD 132–5 left a permanent mark from which the country was never to recover. Economic conditions deteriorated; taxation became cripplingly heavy as misgovernment worsened; and every civil or military disturbance tended to affect the Jews more than any other section of the population. Those Jews who survived the disaster of the Bar Kochba revolt began to ask themselves if this was the end. And no wonder. Five hundred and eighty thousand men are said to have been killed in battle alone, while tens of thousands more must have perished before the systematic destruction had been started by the Romans.

But the Jews of Palestine somehow survived, their hopes for salvation not completely crushed. They alternately waited and hoped for divine intervention to save Jerusalem from pagan hands or for the Parthians to grow strong and come to their rescue. As time passed, however, a growing number of Jews became convinced that a way other than continued revolts and bloodshed existed for ensuring their survival as a people. Rabbi Yohanan ben Zakkai, seeing that Jerusalem was doomed, asked Vespasian in the year AD 70 for permission to open a school in a little town by the seacoast called Yavneh. This simple request, which Vespasian granted, was meant to show the Jews an alternative way:

> They laid down the sword of the soldier and raised high the more lasting pen of the scholar .... Rome might destroy the Jewish nation, the city of Jerusalem, the Temple and the Sanhedrin. It might kill hundreds of thousands of men and women and lay waste the land of Israel. But there were some portions of Jewish life which Rome could not touch, namely those which did not exist in any physical form, but were nevertheless part of the people's being.[2]

This was the state of affairs which prevailed in Palestine between the year 70 and 200 AD. Meantime, in Babylonia the decline of the culture and the civilization as a whole was being hastened by a series of almost uninterrupted wars between the Romans (or the Byzantines) and the Persians. According to Greek and Latin sources of the period, four centuries of such warfare resulted in the complete destruction of the northern part of the country. Very little is known, however, of the economic, social and administrative shifts in Mesopotamia after the country came under the rule of the Sassanians, who somewhat uncharacteristically maintained their hold for over four centuries (227–636). We know, for example, that the northern city of Assur was destroyed by Shapur I in 256, while the remains of a magnificent palace at Ctesiphon has been identified as the residence of Chosroes I. The residence of another Sassanian king, far more modest than this, has been excavated at Kish, and shards of Sassanian pottery testify to the occupation or reoccupation of other ancient sites.

> But at the beginning of the seventh century, shortly before the Islamic conquest, the usual combination of military set-backs, internal strife and economic difficulties brought about the decline of the Sassanian kingdom and the ruin of Mesopotamia. Many canals left unattended dried up; the rivers, unchecked, could meander freely; scattering to outlying villages, people abandoned the towns deprived of water, and the ancient cities of Mesopotamia were rapidly buried beneath the sand of the desert and the silt of the valley.[3]

It is one of the oddities of Jewish history that the 400 years during which the Persian sovereigns of the Sassanid line ruled Mesopotamia witnessed an intellectual and literary activity whose intensity was matched only by the poor and steadily deteriorating material conditions in which the Jews lived. Under the Sassanians, the Jews lost the right of inflicting capital punishment and were excluded from certain government appointments previously open to them. About the year 261, the city of Nehardea, which until then was the centre of Jewish life in Babylonia, was captured and destroyed by Odenath, Prince of Palmyra. Conditions for the Jews were not greatly affected by this blow since Sura soon took Nehardea's place as a centre of learning. It was indeed, in the 200 years or so that followed that the Babylonian Jewish community was to attain its greatest importance and made its lasting contribution to Jewish thought and literature.

Although the shifts and vicissitudes which characterized the fortunes of Babylonian Jewry from the middle of the fifth century onwards came while this work was not quite finished, they did not affect the literary and religious activities of the rabbis, which for some time now had been concentrated on the organization and redaction of the Talmud. The fact that they were able to continue the work amidst all these shifts and set-backs serves only to illustrate the background of

the thriving, well-organized life of the Jews in Babylonia in the first few centuries of the Christian era. The total number of Jews there was to be reckoned in hundreds of thousands. By the time of the Patriarchate (in Palestine), it had numerically equalled, or perhaps even outstripped, that of Palestine. Above all, it had become the seat of a unique intellectual life which was to have a permanent influence upon the being and the mentality of the Jewish people at large.[4]

CHAPTER 6

Family, Home and Education

Judaism regards marriage and the establishment of family life as a duty obligatory upon mankind. The Tannaite Rabbi Eliezer pronounces the man who through bachelorhood shirks the duty of rearing children to be guilty of murder against the human race; another rabbi calls him a despoiler of the divine image; and a third says that such a man renounces his privilege of true humanity, in so far as only in the married state can happiness, blessing and peace be attained. It is indicative of the attitude of Judaism on this subject that, while other religions regard the celibacy of the priests and saints as signs of higher sanctity, Jewish law expressly commands that the high priest shall not be allowed to observe the solemn rites of the Day of Atonement if unmarried.

In Babylonia, this and other Jewish religious ideals seem to have been cherished and observed somewhat more than they were in Israel or Judah. Reasons for this are not difficult to find. One was in the differences between the respective social conditions of the Jews in Palestine and those of the Jews of Babylonia. The Jews of Babylon and of the other large urban centres in Babylonia lived in large homogeneous groups and – as we will see in another chapter – enjoyed a great measure of autonomy. Consequently, the rule of the rabbis possessed greater authority in Babylonia than it did in Palestine, and their decisions were more easily enforced. To give only one example, many of the wealthier Babylonian Jewish homes had slaves. To be sure, Jewish slaves among Jews were comparatively rare, and where any existed they had to be treated in accordance with biblical law and released after the sixth year. In cases where non-Jewish slaves lived in Jewish homes, however, the slave frequently was either absorbed or freed. Occasionally, a freedman married a Jewess, or a Jew took to wife a former slave. Such alliances were not only frowned upon but a public record was kept of them in order that no Jewish person might marry into the disgraced family. It is obvious that such close scrutiny could not be imposed in small and far-off villages and hamlets where the majority of Palestinian Jewry lived.

As a rule, Jews in Babylonia married early in life – the young men anywhere between sixteen and twenty, the young women even younger. Marriage being such a serious undertaking and surrounded by such a halo of sanctity, eligible young men were allowed to bide their time between betrothal and formal matrimony – a period which could take up to twelve months or more. After the marriage ceremony, the bride was led to the home of her husband amid great festivity with music and lighted tapers. Frequently, the father of the bridegroom bestowed a house on the newly married couple, since it was not considered good form to dwell in the home of one's father-in-law. The women were given to personal adornment, and the use of cosmetics was quite common. In Jewish homes womenfolk had their own chambers, and while man was as a rule the provider, the tasks of the household absorbed the woman's whole attention. Mothers also looked after the education of their children.

The wife was held in high esteem. And no wonder, considering the care and the thought invested in selecting her. In *Pessahim* 49a, we find the following elaborate piece of advice:

> A man should sell all he possesses in order to marry the daughter of a learned man, for if he were to die or be exiled he may be confident that his children will be learned. And let him not marry the daughter of an ignoramus, for if he were to die or be exiled his children will be ignorant. A man should sell all that he has in order to marry the daughter of a scholar or give his daughter to a scholar in marriage. That is like uniting grapes of the vine to grapes of the vine, which is good and acceptable. But let him not marry the daughter of an ignoramus, because that is like uniting grapes of the vine to berries of the bush, which is something unattractive and unacceptable.

Considering what a wife could do for him, the Jew was enjoined to love his wife like his own self and to honour her even more. Few things were considered as important as peace within the home and the family. This is one reason why polygamy seems to have been rare amongst Babylonian Jewry; they practised monogamy despite the fact that the Bible permits a man to have more than one wife. Certainly, there were cases of Jews practising polygamy, but they were rare. Also, because of the insistence upon a quiet, peaceful and dignified family life, great care was exercised in the selection of a husband or a wife for one's daughter or son. Disparity in age between husband and wife was discouraged, and marriages based primarily on financial or material considerations were greatly condemned. Hereditary hazards were stressed, and the probability of children who would be freak or extreme was avoided as much as it was possible. Thus the rabbis urged that a tall man should not marry a tall woman lest their children be lanky; while a short man should not marry a short woman lest the children be dwarfish. Even a fair man should avoid marriage with a fair woman, lest their children be 'extremely fair'; while a dark man should not marry a dark woman lest their children be exceedingly dark (*Bekoroth* 45b).

While parents usually did the choosing and took care of the matchmaking, it was considered proper among the Jews of Babylonia for the young man or woman to have the final word. Again, one of the chief requirements in the choice of husband or wife was that the family standing of the proposed in-laws should not be either much lower or much higher than one's own. A man who insisted on marrying too far beneath his social standing could be cut off from his family. However, in this respect the woman was considered to find it easier to adjust herself socially – hence the dictum: 'Descend a step in choosing a wife' (*Yebamoth* 63a). A woman of higher social status, on the other hand, may put the man in an embarrassing position and create in him feelings of inferiority. Children were considered a necessity as well as a blessing – hence a childless marriage could be dissolved. The community held the parents responsible not only for educating their children but also for preparing them for life outside the home.

On the whole, the religious life of the Jews in Babylonia was ordered on the Palestinian pattern. Following the traditions of the Pharisees, Babylonian Jews adopted the principle that Judaism must be present and must influence every aspect of life. Back in Palestine, regular daily services were not held in the villages because of the lack of the required number of men, while in the towns ten men of leisure, mostly of the student class, were paid to attend the synagogue. In Babylonia, the synagogue was the tallest and handsomest building in any Jewish community of suitable size. Prayers and benedictions accompanied every act. The Bible, as interpreted by the rabbis, and the Mishnah were the standard works for the guidance of men and their lives, or were supposed to be – for this had not always been the case. It is told that when Rab (Abba Areka) first returned from his studies in Palestine (*c.* AD 220) and undertook a journey through the Jewish settlements in Babylonia, he was shocked by the ignorance of the Jews about matters of Jewish observance. He decided there and then to establish himself in the midst of this ignorant population, open a school and instruct the people in proper Jewish living. He succeeded so well that within a generation that part of Jewish Babylonia become the model for the rest of the country.[1]

The story of Rab and his journey to Palestine to complete his studies is of some interest here. The Babylonian Jews, like their co-religionists everywhere, were always intensely interested in study and always established schools. However, though they found themselves in far more congenial conditions economically and communally, their intellectual activity was not as intensive or as deep as it had been in Palestine – at least for the first few centuries of their exile. So when a student showed an unusual desire to pursue his studies further he would go to Palestine. A number of these are known to have chosen to stay there, as happened to the famous Hillel – known as Hillel the Babylonian (Ha-Babli). He was born in Babylonia around the year 75 BC, but went to Palestine to pursue his studies and stayed there to become the head of the Sanhedrin. His example was followed by a good many others, but an overwhelming majority of these eventually returned to their birthplace, there to become prominent in the study of the Torah and to raise the intellectual level of Babylonian Jewry as a whole. The most outstanding among these was Abba Areka, later to be known by the unusually prestigious name Rab, meaning Rabbi or *the* Rabbi.

Foundations for an extensive educational system were in fact laid by the Pharisees long before the talmudic era, and were built on antecedents going back to the schools of wisdom and the priestly training of ancient Israel. After the destruction of the Temple, however, the rabbis intensified their efforts to develop a comprehensive and efficient school system. Declaring that the acquisition of a good education was one of the primary duties of each individual, they went into great detail concerning facilities for the instruction of children and outlined a general educational programme for the entire Jewish world. They ruled that provision for education was a major responsibility of the community, elaborating this at great length. They ruled, for example, that wherever there were twenty-five children of school age a teacher must be supplied by the community, and that when the number increased to forty an assistant teacher was to be appointed. Scholars were advised never to choose a residence where there was no elementary teacher.

Insistence on adult education was equally pronounced:

> As long as he lives, every Jew must set aside for daily study as much time as he can possibly afford. . . . In Palestine and in Babylonia

great teachers often delivered public discourses for businessmen and farmers, and, after arriving in Babylonia, Palestinian scholars addressed the large crowds usually assembled before the exilarch's palace. The Babylonian rabbis set aside early morning hours for the instruction of those engaged during the day in earning a living, while farmers and artisans residing at a great distance had an opportunity to hear a distinguished leader during the Sabbaths preceding the holidays. The semi-annual *kallah* gathering enabled men of various walks of life, residing in distant parts of the country, to devote the month, or a part of the month preceding the High Holidays or Passover, to concentrated study and exchange of thought with one another, under the experienced guidance of the greatest rabbis of the generation.[2]

A statement like the one cited in *M. Horayoth* III, 8, to the effect that 'a bastard, if he be learned, takes precedence over an uneducated high priest', may sound grossly exaggerated. There is, however, no doubt that learning opened the road to the highest prestige in public and private life. As Baron has found, 'a glance into the relatively well-transmitted biographies shows that many leading rabbis of the age rose from the lowest strata to win uncontested leadership in social as well as intellectual life'.[3] As a matter of fact, a deep-rooted suspicion is easily discernible at this juncture that the rich were not really interested in learning. A favourite saying of Yohanan ben Zakkai's was: 'Separate the children from the wealthy [literally the 'landlords'], because they keep people away from the words of the Torah.'

After the return of Rab from his studies in Palestine, education made rapid strides among the Jews of Babylonia. In the years between the middle of the third century and the late fourth century the level of education among adults and children alike was raised to a hitherto unknown height. The biblical injunction, 'Thou shalt teach them to your children', put elementary education into the hands of the parents. The result of this was that where the parents were illiterate or poorly educated, the child would be brought up virtually ignorant. Accordingly Rab concentrated his efforts on raising the standard of knowledge among the adults. He strengthened among the Babylonian Jews the idea, long current in Palestine, that an ignoramus was to be despised. As this idea took root, and as a man's standing in the community began to depend not so much upon family and wealth as upon intellectual endeavour and achievement, young and old became interested in acquiring knowledge. Before long, there was hardly a

Jewish community in Babylonia which did not consider the education of its children a matter of the highest importance:

> No idea became more characteristic of Jewish life than that study is a religious duty. What is still more remarkable is that in the matter of study there were no distinctions between rich and poor; all studied the same material with the same zeal. In fact one of the famous Talmudic sayings has it: 'Watch over the children of the poor, for out of them will knowledge come forth.' The Jewish people became a cultural democracy.[4]

The ultimate aim of education was not to accumulate knowledge, although that in itself was important. The real aim was to establish good habits of life. Jews studied the laws that regulated man's relations to God; but these laws also regulated man's relations to his fellow men. Business, philanthropy, wages, morality and ethics, the rules of common politeness – these were as much part of their religious studies as were synagogue regulations, prayer, and the rules of penitence for sins committed. Indeed, a Jew's attitude to his fellow human beings was as much a subject for discussion as was, say, the observance of the Sabbath. One striking aspect of this attitude to education and to learning was that any learned man in a community was competent to decide civil suits (criminal cases were heard before a tribunal of three judges). Moreover, such a man, if confirmed by the exilarch or directly appointed by him, had the advantage that he could not be sued for damages for an error of judgement. These judges, unsalaried and barred from accepting fees, had the power to inflict corporal punishment, to imprison or to pronounce the ban; they could also, if properly authorized, impose fines. Finally, it was within the province of a judge, should he find it fit to do so, to remove the communal council, appoint physicians and collectors of charity, and proclaim fast days.[5]

What with this rather peculiar attitude to learning and study, Jewish society in Babylonia was becoming dominated by a new sort of theocracy rather than by an aristocracy of birth or money, 'a theocracy, however, not of a professional or charismatic priesthood, but of rabbis recruited from all social classes, whose claim to leadership consisted exclusively in learning and personal piety'.[6]

Another feature of Jewish life in Babylonia which was to flourish and be fully developed there was the synagogue. It was something entirely new in Jewish life. All earlier shrines, Jewish and non-Jewish, had been built around an altar for sacrifice. They were regarded as in some special sense the dwelling place of deity, their basic ritual usually performed by priests. The synagogue (a Greek word meaning assembly) was a gathering of the people to advance their communal and spiritual interests. Its novelty was that such an assembly might be held in any convenient place. It had no sacrificial procedures. Any person, regardless of birth or title, who was qualified to instruct the group or to lead them in prayer, might do so. In his *Book of Jewish Thoughts* Rabbi Hertz quotes this passage from K. Kohler:

> A unique creation of Judaism was the Synagogue, which made Torah the common property of the entire people. Devised in the Exile as a substitute for the Temple, it soon eclipsed it as a religious force and a rallying point for the whole people, appealing through the prayer and Spiritual lesson to the congregation as a whole. The Synagogue was limited to no one locality, as was the Temple, but raised its banner wherever Jews settled throughout the globe. It was thus able to spread the truths of Judaism to the remotest parts of the earth, and to invest the Sabbath and Festivals with deeper meaning by utilizing them for the instruction and elevation of the people. What did it matter, if the Temple fell a prey to the flames for a second time, or if the whole sacrificial cult of the priesthood with all its pomp were to cease? The soul of Judaism lived indestructibly in its House of Prayer, Assembly and Learning.[7]

If the school in Babylonia served to make the Jewish people what Grayzel has called a 'cultural democracy', the synagogue, by eliminating the need for priestly intermediaries, became the embodiment of religious democracy. Indeed, its democratic character was enormously enhanced by the element of popular education, which from the start was a basic function of the synagogue. Every precaution was taken, moreover, to make the Torah available to all classes of the people. A passage of the Torah was read and explained to the people assembled in synagogues on Sabbaths and festivals; but since farmers who lived at some distance from villages could not travel on the Sabbath, portions of the Torah were also read on the market days, Mondays and Thursdays, when the country people could be present. This custom has persisted up to our own day.

It is in the Babylonian exile that the synagogue is thought to have originated; it was there that biblical monotheism first had to fashion a centre for itself on foreign soil.

> How strong its [the synagogue's] influence was is illustrated by the active missionary campaign that Babylonian Jews conducted among

the Gentile population. One of the most curious events in the first century was the conversion of the queen and prince of the petty kingdom of Adiabene to Judaism. By the middle of the second century Babylonian Jewry was probably the most secure and flourishing of all Jewish communities, and it is no wonder that many Palestinians sought permanent refuge there from the heavy hand of Rome. Parthian toleration had been such as to allow the Jews virtually to fashion their own state within the Babylonian Empire.[8]

The extent and nature of the differences between Babylonian and Palestinian Judaism are of interest to us here only in so far as they derived from the different environments and the varying cultural and economic conditions of the two Jewish groups living there. Officially, religious life in Babylonia lay within the purview of the exilarch's powers. However, the ever-growing number of rabbinic scholars and the establishment of academies in the second century created a polarity of powers within the Babylonian community.

The arrival of the Mishnah and of Palestinian-trained scholars gained for the masters of learning increasing recognition among the masses and power commensurate with that of the exilarch's office. To be sure, we hear of tension and even open conflict between rabbis and exilarchs, but in the last analysis each side had to recognize the authority of the other. Judges were appointed from the academies' rolls, while the *yeshivot* [Talmudic academies] requested exilarchal approval of their leadership.[9]

In this respect, however, differences between the two communities may seem slight. Even the subject matter of the *yeshivah* curriculum in the two countries were more or less identical, namely the elucidation of Jewish law and, later, the Mishnah. Like its Palestinian counterpart, the Babylonian academy was primarily concerned with the application of Jewish law. However, those aspects of the law that were relevant only to the Holy Land were largely omitted from the Babylonian curriculum, while greater attention was given to the adjustment of Jewish civil and religious law to the Gentile environment in which the Jews lived. *Dina di malkhutah din* ('The law of the state is the law' – that is, binding on the Jew) was a principle first enunciated in the Babylonian academies. To quote Gerson D. Cohen :

Certainly the historical circumstances which permitted the Babylonian academies to flourish for centuries after those of Palestine had closed or dwindled to inconsequentiality provided a transitional centre for the young Jewish communities of Western Europe. Above all, however, it made the Babylonian Talmud, and its recension of the tradition, the normative canon for the whole Jewish world. Thus a Jewish community of the Diaspora mediated the tradition to scores of generations and countries beyond its own.[10]

The synagogue, which in Palestine assumed a central position in Jewish life only after the elimination of the Temple and its sacrificial worship, had always played a crucial role in the life of Babylonian Jewry. But synagogues were more than just houses of worship; they were also places for teaching and instruction, both for children and adults. However, as popular participation in the worship and the instruction alike increased, an inevitable lowering of standards followed, and the taste in learned discourse became less sophisticated. The Babylonian Rabbi Isaac Nappaha put it thus : 'At first, when the penny was more readily available, man wished to hear something about the Mishnah or Talmud; now that the penny is scarce and government makes us ill, he prefers to listen to a discussion of Bible or Aggadah.' Living in a period of military anarchy, this same rabbi once pathetically described how starving people ate unripe grain in the fields – and was in a good position clearly to perceive the impact of political and economic pressures on what he considered a serious deterioration in the public taste.

Some of Nappaha's more fastidious colleagues are now even said to have lost all interest in attending synagogue services.

> One generation earlier Rabbi Simon ben Laqish had called a man failing to attend the synagogue of his locality 'a bad neighbour'. Rabbi Yohanan ben Zakkai, too, had placed synagogue attendance in the dispersion on a par with living in Palestine, and thus explained the fact why so many Jews in Babylonia were enabled to reach ripe old age. But their immediate successors, Rabbi Ammi and Rabbi Assi, refused to attend any of the thirteen Tiberian synagogues and preferred to pray in their own studies (*Berakhoth* 8a). This example was followed by several Babylonian scholars, until Rab became so convinced of the superiority of study over prayer that, when he once saw Rabbi Hamnuna unduly prolonging his prayers, he exclaimed: 'They leave matters of eternity and busy themselves with the life of the moment' – a remarkably lopsided evaluation in the eyes of most modern theologians. To which stricture Rabbi Hamnuna could but lamely reply: 'There is a special time for prayer and another for study.' (*Sabbath* 10a)[11]

Within the walls of the schoolhouse or synagogue, the Jewish people weathered all storms:

> This sense of security was enhanced by the essentially intangible character of the synagogue. The word refers primarily to the congregation, and only secondarily to the 'house' of worship. Unlike the Temple, a synagogue could not be destroyed by an enemy. With the burning of the Temple, its entire sacrificial system was obliterated. The destruction of any number of synagogue buildings, such as at times occurred even in Persia (*Yoma* 10a), entailed no change in the established liturgy or mode of worship. Ten Jews assembled anywhere in public or in private . . . could conduct a regular service like that held in the largest and most elaborate structure. . . . The loss of synagogue buildings or sacred objects having become a matter of financial rather than intrinsically religious concern, the community became more immune to strictly religious intolerance than it was to political and economic antagonisms.[12]

Moreover, the relatively secondary position of the *house* of worship bred a certain indifference to synagogue architecture. In fact, some rabbis resented the diversion of substantial building funds from educational budgets.

Unlike synagogues, which were a communal responsibility, cemeteries and burial of the dead were considered a family responsibility. The family could use its discretion in burying the deceased on its own land or in any one of the numerous Palestinian caves that had been set aside as family graveyards. Since rabbinic law insisted on a speedy burial, any nearby plot seemed preferable to long-distance transportation. Babylonia's geological composition, on the other hand, led to the early formation of large communal graveyards.

The community also tried to reduce differences between rich and poor in regard to shrouds, although it could not prevent the wealthy from building imposing mausolea. The Babylonian Talmud quotes in succession a number of tannaitic sources attesting to this protracted struggle:

> At first they carried to the mortuaries the corpses of the rich in vase-shaped baskets of silver or gold, while the poor were brought in wicker baskets of peeled willow twigs. Since poor families were thus put to shame, the leaders ordained that everybody be carried in wicker

> baskets in honour of the poor. . . . At first the rich mourners in the mortuary were served drinks in white glasses, while the poor drank from coloured glasses. Since this custom put the poor to shame, the leaders ordained that everybody be served in coloured glasses in honour of the poor. . . . At first they carried the corpses of the rich with their faces uncovered, while the poor men's faces, blackened by prolonged starvation, were covered. Since the poor were thus put to shame, the leaders ordained that everybody be carried with his face covered in honour of the poor. . . . At first the burial of a deceased person was more burdensome for his relatives than his last illness, until some relatives left the corpse behind and ran away. Then Rabban Gamliel, disregarding his own dignity, willed that he be buried in a simple linen shroud, whereupon the whole people began using linen shrouds.

To which the fourth-century Babylonian Rabbi Papa added: 'Today people use even a rough cloth worth one *zuz*.'[13]

CHAPTER 7

A Neat Division of Labour: Exilarch and *Gaon*

During the third century AD two misfortunes befell the Jews of Babylonia. In 226, a few years after Rab's return to his native land, a brief civil war broke out as a result of which a Persian dynasty, the Sassanians, seized power from the ruling Parthian one, the Arsacids. Thus the Arsacid Empire, which had endured for close on three and a half centuries, came to an end. The Arsacids were favourably inclined to the Jews, and their last king, Artaban IV, was personally acquainted with Rab and held him in high regard. It is even said that when the Arsacids made way for the Sassanians, Rab exclaimed in grief, 'The bond is broken.' His forebodings were not unfounded. The new king, Ardashir I, had grown up under the influence of the fire-worshipping Magians, who zealously and scrupulously observed the expanded Zoroastrian ritual and were intolerant of all other creeds. In the case of the Jews, these priests objected to a number of their most cherished religious customs. They forbade them from lighting candles in celebration of Sabbaths and holidays; they forbade the slaughtering of animals for food unless certain parts of them were offered on their altars, thus making it practically impossible for the Jews to eat meat; they ordered the dead in Jewish burial-grounds exhumed and cast out to the vultures and dogs because their religion enjoined them not to pollute the earth with corpses; and they set out to destroy synagogues and ritual baths on the ground that immersion was forbidden.

Fortunately, this persecution did not last long enough permanently to affect Jewish life in Babylonia. Samuel, Rab's lifelong colleague and successor, did his utmost to appease the government, at the same time telling the Jews that their new disabilities were a token of their sinfulness and that they were called upon to mend their ways and redouble their zeal for their own faith. His efforts met with success under Ardashir I's heir Shapur I (274–72), who did not have to depend upon the priests to the same extent as his father had and who, moreover, was in need of money for his campaigns against the Roman provinces to the west. He is also said to have had high regard for Samuel, and that in deference to him he spared the lives of Jews in the conquered countries unless they offered resistance.

The second misfortune came hard on the heels of the first. In the year AD 258, four years after Samuel's death, the recurrent warfare between Rome and the Persian Empire was renewed. Shapur I then had the whole of Syria in his hands, and the emperor Valerian, who had marched to meet him on the battlefield, was defeated and taken prisoner in 260. This Persian victory, however, was soon offset by one of Rome's allies in the region, Prince Odenath of Palmyra, who in the years 263–5 twice forced the Persians back to their capital Ctesiphon and overran Babylonia which lay nearest to them. As the Jews fought the Palmyrenes with particular bitterness, many Jewish settlements were destroyed and the invaders spent their fury upon Nehardea, in which the Jewish population predominated and where the oldest and most famous Jewish academy had been located. This flourishing city was razed to the ground. The blow proved fatal to the academy which, founded by Samuel, was now presided over by his pupil and disciple Nahman, son of Jacob. Nehardea was never to return to be the seat of the academy, which after years of effort was found a resting-place at Mahoza.[1]

Throughout all these shifts and turns of fortune which characterized Jewish life in Babylonia the communal life of the Jews was ordered and dominated by a distinctive institution called the Exilarchate. The Greek word *exilarch* means 'head of the exile' (*resh galutha* in Aramaic) and was adopted for the head of Babylonian Jewry. The Exilarchate was a hereditary office traditionally originating with King Jehoiachim and hence looked upon as in some way maintaining the continuity of Davidic rule; those who held it continued to trace their ancestry to the House of David in the male line. The Exilarch was the highest official of Babylonian Jewry, to whom the Jews looked up with awe and to whose authority they submitted willingly. The Persian court, too, considered him as the representative of Jewry, answerable for whatever taxes were levied upon them and serving as their leading spokesman.

Tracing the origin of the Exilarchate makes a fascinating story. The four closing sentences of the Second Book of Kings speak of the last king but one of Judah, who was eventually pardoned by his captor, the King of Babylonia, and given high rank in the Babylonian court. The Jewish king, of course, was Jehoiachim, and it is very likely that his descendants continued to hold this high rank under the subsequent

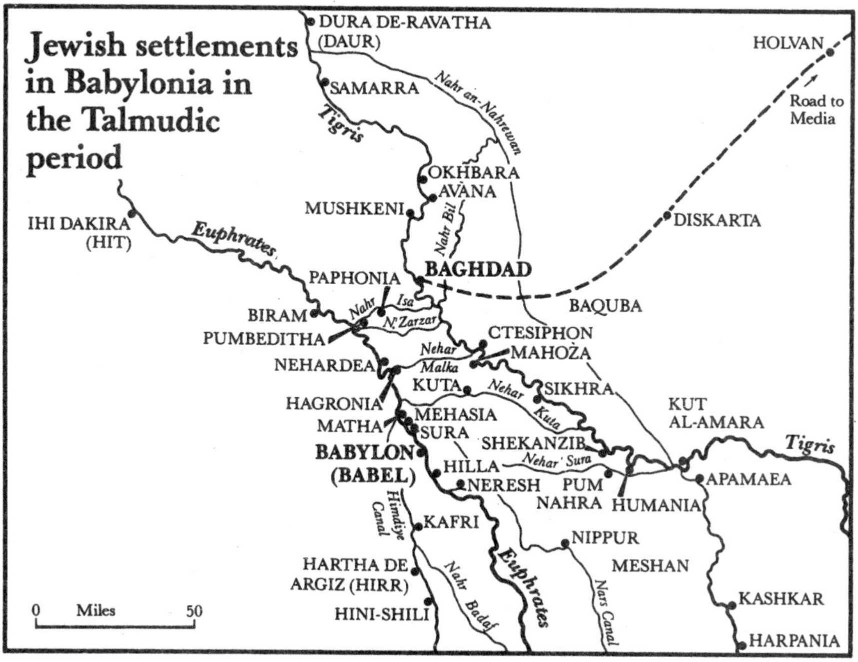

Jewish settlements in Babylonia in the Talmudic period

rulers of Babylonia. According to calculations made on the basis of this version, no ruling house in the whole world continued uninterruptedly to hand authority down from father to son as did the House of David. Considering that the Exilarchate lasted beyond the year AD 1000, this house can be said to have exercised authority for more than 2,000 years.

It is no wonder, therefore, that the Exilarch's investiture was such a solemn act, in which lay as well as spiritual leaders participated, with the laying on of hands and blowing of trumpets. On the Sabbath following the elevation, an elaborate service was held in synagogues throughout the country, where the new prince was proclaimed. The Exilarch, in possession of extensive estates and enriched by gifts from his devoted people, maintained a regal establishment.

> At his table rich and varied dishes were served and wine flowed freely. The company included a host of poor scholars who wore a badge as his dependants; the more punctilious would as often as feasible keep away because they suspected ritual irregularities in the preparation of the food. On the festivals the people thronged about the palace. The prince was always richly clad. When he appeared at court, as for example on the occasion of the Persian new year when he carried with him a gift of money, he wore a wide belt inwoven with

> gold and silver threads. The members of his suite disported themselves in silk garments. The prince's seal bore the heraldic device of a fly. So at least in later times; but at an earlier period the seal was adorned with the design of a lion, the Lion of Judah.[2]

It is interesting, and something of an historical enigma, that although the institution of the Exilarchate is traceable to the very beginning of the Babylonian exile, the first time we hear of the Exilarch is about the year AD 200. When we first meet him, we find him possessed of certain powers and duties, some of which were mentioned above. These powers, however, derived solely from the fact that the Jews of Babylonia, from the start, enjoyed the right to rule themselves in accordance with Jewish law. This is what we now call autonomy. The Exilarch appointed judges and was himself the final court of appeal. In his name punishment was inflicted upon condemned Jews who might be made to suffer imprisonment, stripes, paying fines or excommunication from the Jewish community. He also saw to the collection of taxes from the Jews of the entire country, and turned over a certain portion of the money to the government. However, since certain cities in the Persian Empire were populated by a large percentage of Jews, these cities were to all intents and purposes under the direct and full authority of the Exilarch and his officers, even to the extent of supervising their markets and guarding the walls which surrounded them.

If this sounds like something bordering on monarchy, there were extenuating circumstances which made the system seem far more like a true democracy. For the fact was that, although every official in every Jewish community of Babylonia was in theory appointed by the Exilarch, in actual practice he did no more in many instances than ratify the men chosen by the community itself.

> Each community had its head who, with his seven advisers, formed the Community Council. They, divided into a number of committees, supervised the usual civic activities such as charity collection and distribution, the synagogue and other communal property, and the schools which every community was expected to have. They also appointed the officers of the city to maintain order and check weights and measures. Thus every Jewish community was practically an independent municipality.[3]

These municipalities, or local councils, must have had a lot on their hands. Each community, no matter how small, had by its very nature to possess certain property of its own. For example, there had to be a synagogue building and, in many instances, a separate building for the administration. There also had to be a *mikvah*, or ritual bath. Moreover, land had to be apportioned for a cemetery, and this in turn had to be maintained and closely guarded. Finally, the larger cities which enjoyed the presence of a Talmudic academy (*yeshivah*) must have had a *Bet Midrash* ('House of Study') in addition to the synagogue.

The Exilarch was the temporal leader of Babylonian Jewry, its 'emperor' if we use concepts current in those days. The spiritual leaders, the 'popes', were the heads of the Babylonian academies. Addressed as *Gaon* (eminence), these scholars were held in high esteem by Jews and Gentiles alike, and while the Exilarchs held the administrative and judicial powers the *Geonim* held the legislative power. Many of the Exilarchs were acknowledged as learned men; nevertheless, for the most part they depended upon the counsel of the *Geonim*, who at a later period composed for them their inaugural addresses – until gradually the speech in the end was delivered by the *Gaon* of Sura himself. In spiritual matters, however, the Exilarch was duly advised whenever decisions of great moment were taken by the *Geonim*.

This state of affairs was obviously fraught with dangers of disputes and splits between the temporal and spiritual authorities in the community. Indeed, the ever-increasing number of rabbinic scholars, the arrival in Babylonia of the Mishnah and of a number of Palestinian-trained scholars, gained for the masters of learning increasing recognition among the masses and a measure of power and prestige that became almost commensurate with those of the Exilarch's office. Nevertheless, although we hear of tension and even open conflict between rabbis and Exilarchs, we find that in the last analysis each side had to recognize the authority of the other. Judges were appointed from the academies' rolls, while the *yeshivot* required exilarchal approval of their leadership.

The ways in which the work of the academies was transmitted to the people reveal another interesting aspect of the life of Babylonian Jewry. In the main it seems to have been done through lectures in the synagogues and through the elementary schools. The influence of the scholars upon the people was thus fairly limited, and was almost entirely a moral one, with little support from external authority. However, the fact that these scholars and rabbis were recruited from all classes of society, and that many of the most famous of them hailed from the poorer classes must have made them more acceptable to the populace. Generally speaking, their sermons and speeches, which combined instruction in the law with words of encouragement and hope, were well received.

The rabbis' authority was, however, not entirely confined to the moral sphere. They had one way of lending a somewhat more substantial meaning to this authority, namely the ban or excommunication. A person who disobeyed their decisions could be officially suspended from participation in Jewish life, and in cases in which he or she persisted in their defiance the excommunication was made permanent. It is to be noted, however, that this mode of discipline had no theological implications whatsoever. The excommunicated person was not given over to perdition, as in the case of those excommunicated from the church; he or she was simply the object of complete social ostracism. So severe was the punishment, indeed, that most offenders were completely humbled by the temporary ban. This form of discipline had one minor drawback: it depended for its effectiveness on the co-operation of the entire community. Only in so far as they enjoyed the respect and loyalty of members of their respective communities could the scholars make their will effective.

But the work of the academies and their heads and teachers was mainly educational. Apart from the sermons and speeches delivered in synagogues, the Babylonian academies developed an interesting and rather novel medium of communication with the masses of Jewish laity. Two months a year, at the end of the summer and winter seasons, interested laity and scholars convened at the two largest academies, in Sura and Nehardea, for intensive Talmudic discussion. These semi-annual retreats served to make the academies living intellectual centres and to keep the population in constant touch with the sources of law and moral teaching.[4]

CHAPTER 8

From Mishnah to Talmud

> Said Rab Abba in the name of Samuel: 'For three years the Schools of Hillel and Shammai maintained a controversy, each School asserting that the decision should be given in accordance with its opinion. At last a Voice descended in Yavneh and cried out: "The words both of these and these are the words of the Living God, but the decision should follow the School of Hillel." '
>
> It was asked: 'If the words of both are those of the Living God, why was the decision granted to the School of Hillel?' The reply was: 'Because the members of the School of Hillel are amiable of manner and courteous; they teach the opinions of both, and furthermore they always give the opinion of their opponents first.'
>
> *Erubin* 13b

Hillel Ha-Babli (the Babylonian) left his home in Babylon early in the first century AD and went to Palestine to pursue his studies. He studied with the famous *zug* (pair) Shemaiah and Abtalyon, and after spending some time in Babylonia he returned to Jerusalem, where he became the recognized head and *nasi* (president) of the highest academy there. He and a colleague Shammai, with whom he differed basically on matters of legal interpretation, constituted the last of the *zugot* (pairs). Hillel, who unlike Shammai advocated an attitude of leniency in the interpretation of the law, assumed his office at a time when the whole structure of the religious and national life of the people was in danger as a result of the policies pursued by Herod, the Jewish king who through Roman pressure sought to keep the Jews subjugated and humiliated. Dedicating himself to the task of raising an academy for the study of the law, Hillel warned his contemporaries to shun politics, love peace, and draw their fellow men to the Torah. Neither Herod nor the Roman rulers hindered his efforts, and he exerted a major influence on the development of Judaism. So much so that it was said of him that, like Ezra the scribe before him, he restored the Torah, which had been neglected.

Hillel and Shammai, who became the two most noted exponents of Pharisaism during Herod's reign, were responsible for establishing the study of the Oral Law independently of biblical texts. The process had started as far back as the days of Ezra, but it began in earnest only with the work of this pair of scholars. The goal, of course, was to codify the Scriptures, to interpret them and to make them the norm of daily life. In its first stages this was done through translations, the first of which (the Septuagint) was made in Egypt during this period. We do not know precisely what Palestinian influences, if any, were at play in this Greek version. The Aramaic versions, however, were the work of a later generation, and were called *targumim*, plural of the Hebrew word *targum*, meaning translation. During this early age we encounter a mysterious body called the 'Men of the Great Synagogue', who had a good deal to do with the formulation of the liturgy.

The medium of study both in Palestine and Babylonia during these first centuries was oral, and constant repetition was accordingly necessary. Hence, in Hebrew in those days, 'to repeat' meant 'to study', and vice versa. The Hebrew verb for 'repeat' is *shanah*, and the noun is *mishnah*, thus this latter word was applied to the corpus of traditions accompanying the Scriptures and termed the 'Oral Law'. But the Aramaic equivalent of the verb *shanah* is *tena*, and the noun-agent, meaning teacher, is *tanna*. The *tannaim*, therefore, were the first teachers whose names and work were connected with the codification of the Oral Law and the compilation of the two Talmuds. The pre-Tannaic period is usually reckoned from 200 BC to 10 AD, but the starting-point of this period remains a subject of controversy. The Tannaic period itself begins in the year 10 BC and ends around 220 AD with the final redacton of the Mishnah to writing by Judah the Prince.

The pre-Tannaic period ends with five *zugot* of scholars, who include Antigonus of Soko, Simeon ben Shetah and others. The last 'pair' was that of Hillel and Shammai. It was directly after Hillel that the Tannaic period began, and Hillel's sixth descendant was Judah the Prince. It went as follows: Hillel, Simeon, Rabban Gamliel I, Rabban Simon I ben Gamliel I, Rabban Gamliel II, Rabban Simon II ben Gamliel II, and Rabbi Judah the Prince, also known as 'Rabbi'. There were six generations of *tannaim*, beginning with that of Yohanan ben Zakkai, who founded the Yamina (Yavneh) academy after the destruction of Jerusalem in AD 70, and ending with that of Judah the Prince, in whose days the codification of the Mishnah was completed. It was a work of enormous dimensions. Traditions handed down through some 150 scholars were selected and scrutinized. The material gathered in the pre-Tannaic period was revised, supplemented and, where necessary, rearranged, and traditions of doubtful validity were excluded. The division according to subjects was made more clear cut, and the whole was arranged in six Orders (*Sedarim*), each divided into Tractates (*Massekhoth*), Chapters (*Perakim*) and Paragraphs (*Pesukim*). The actual editing was done by Judah the Prince (also known as Patriarch Judah I), who had a predilection for pure, vigorous Hebrew.

It was about this time that the centre of gravity was beginning to shift from Palestine to Babylonia. Rab returned to Babylonia in the year 219 AD. He settled in Sura, on the Euphrates, and founded an academy there. Another academy, in Nehardea further north, was already in existence, founded by Samuel. Some decades later, yet a third academy was founded at Pumbeditha, north of Nehardea, and it was followed by that at Mahoza on the Tigris (headed by Raba) and others. In these academies the codified Mishnah was studied and interpreted; but the teachers here were not called *tannaim*, since that term was associated with the growth and the codification of the work rather than with its study. They were called *amoraim*, plural for *amora*, an Aramaic word which originally meant 'speaker' and which was used of one who repeated the teacher's words to the people; but the word eventually came to be used to denote the teacher himself and not merely his mouthpiece.[1]

The work of the *amoraim* was to 'complete' the Mishnah. For the fact was that, no sooner had that work of compilation and codification been completed than fresh discussions began to be held round it. It was no more possible for it than for the Pentateuch, which contained all the written Law, to be so comprehensive as to meet all conceivable cases and eventualities. Fresh problems of a religious and legal nature were always arising, and these were brought to the schools for decision. Here they would be examined carefully from all sides, in the light of the Mishnah or of less authoritative independent compilations. These included a variety of sources: the *Tosefta* (supplement) and the Baraita (outside statements), both of which stood in the same relation to the Mishnah as the Apocrypha does to the Bible. In addition there was a vast body of traditional lore – history, legend, ethical teaching – which had not found its way into the severely practical code drawn out by Judah the Prince.

The work done by the *amoraim*, the so-called 'completion' of the Mishnah, was called Gemara, a word derived from the verb in Aramaic meaning 'to complete'. Thus the Gemara added to the Mishnah make up the Talmud. It has been said, with justice, that no book – with the exception only of the Bible – has played so important a role in the history of the Jewish people as the Talmud. As it happened, however, there are two Talmuds: the Gemara exists in two versions – that of the Tiberias schools, called the Jerusalem or Palestinian Talmud, and the one produced by the academies of Babylonia and called the Babylonian Talmud. Neither the date of completion nor the name of the redactor of the Palestinian Talmud is certain, and concerning the Babylonian Talmud we know that its codification was begun by Rab Ashi, head of the Sura academy (*c.*367 AD) and completed probably by the year 500.

The work of the Babylonian *amoraim* reached its climax under Rab Abaye (283–338) and his *halakhic* (religious law) opponent Raba (299–352). Layer upon layer of *halakhic* and *aggadic* material continued to be added during the several generations which followed, each generation interpreting, arguing and debating the opinions and judgements of the preceding generations. The mass of the oral traditions and teachings which had accumulated through the centuries by this time assumed such proportions that the time was deemed ripe for the redaction of the vast material, involving the sifting, summarization and systematic arrangement of the whole. This work was started only towards the end of the fourth century.

Rab Ashi became the head of the Sura academy during the seventh or eighth decade of the fourth century, and there began a systematic review of the work done during the preceding century and a half. One by one he examined the treatises (Tractates) of the Mishnah and sifted the material. With the help of students and associates, he then chose what he considered worthwhile among the discussions, comments and additions accumulated around each Mishnaic statement. This material was not all legal material, but included discussions about ethics, history and legend as well as law. Rab Ashi organized this work in such a way that, when after about fifty years of this sifting process he died, any of his students and disciples could easily find out what he was expected to know and what he might ignore. And so Ashi's successors continued the work, following his method and taking up for discussion those treatises of the Mishnah that he had not had time to review.

Ashi's leading successor in this huge project was Rabina II (d. 500), who redacted the new material accumulated since his predecessor's days. Rabina was the last of the *amoraim*, the last to teach the Torah orally. With his work, the Babylonian Talmud may be regarded as having been completed. The turn of the century also brought some measure of peace and quiet to the life of the community following decades of trouble and shifts of fortune. The Jews set out to restore their life as it had been thirty years previously, but with only partial success.

The Exilarchate was restored; communal institutions resumed their functions, and the academies at Sura and Pumbeditha were reopened. Intellectual activity, however, which had been virtually suspended for more than three decades, could not be restored to its old vigour. Students were few and rather ill-equipped to carry on the work of former generations.

With the completion of work on the Talmud, the scholars who succeeded Rabina – the last *amora* – were no longer called *amoraim* but began to be identified as *saboraim*, a word derived from the Hebrew verb meaning 'to reflect'. The *saboraim* 'reflected' upon the sayings and teachings of the *amoraim* contained in the Talmud, discussed and reasoned about them, interpreted and expounded them; they made certain additions to the Talmudic text, but these were principally of an explanatory character. Their contribution, though by no means a major one, was significant in that it helped make parts of the text more understandable by setting them in better order, by expanding some of them, and by adding a word or phrase here and there to indicate how the discussions and disputations are to be read. It is worth noting here that in the case of the Palestinian Talmud no such explanatory revisions and additions were made, and this is why the work remains rather obscure. In the words of one historian, 'The Babylonian Talmud is also far from easy to read and study, but if not for the work of the *saboraim* it would have been very much more difficult.'[2]

The Babylonian Talmud, now available in the original in twelve fairly unmanageable tomes and in an English translation in almost three times as many volumes, was the result of three centuries of scholarly activity and the collective efforts of more than a thousand rabbis, scholars and students. Because it is primarily a legal commentary upon the Mishnah, the interpretation of difficult words and concepts form an integral part of the commentary. Its main concern, however, remains the interpretation and practical application of the Law. Every statement is scrutinized, every division of opinion traced to its source and principle. The discussion, as it grew in the course of generations, is faithfully reproduced, thus presenting a picture of cumulative layers of argumentation. 'The reader is taken into the atmosphere of the schools; he is made to witness the strenuous mental contests as proponent and opponent engage in thrusts and counter-thrusts. Constantly one is led from one subject to another, the very variety keeping the mind agile.' Max Margolis and Alexander Marx, who offer this short profile of the Babylonian Talmud, continue:

> The curt phraseology, half Hebrew half Aramaic, yields now and then to the easy flow of the Aramaic vernacular; the legal tone is dropped, and the strain is relieved by a succession of sententious sayings and quaint tales [*haggadah*]. Sometimes the lighter matter covers several pages and even complete chapters. As a result of the ease with which transitions are effected, the Talmud becomes a veritable encyclopaedia, in which, over and above jurisprudence, there are found embedded theology and esoteric theosophy, moral and natural science, medicine, mathematics, astronomy, history, legend, folklore.
>
> There are two sides to the Talmud – the one rigidly legalistic and intellectual, the product of critical analysis which penetrates to the bottom of things; and the other ethical, spiritual, appealing to the emotions. Jewish life as it developed came to rest wholly on the Talmud. By it religious practice was regulated, Jewish piety in every act and in every thought moulded, and Jewish mentality kept wide-awake even in the darkest period of general stagnation.[3]

This accurate portrayal is applicable both to the Palestinian and Babylonian Talmuds. But the Talmud which the Babylonian scholars and rabbis spent so many years compiling, organizing and redacting, differs in many crucial ways from its Palestinian counterpart. For although it contains discussions and elaborations on only about half of the treatises of the Mishnah, the authors of the Babylonian Talmud worked primarily over those treatises which contained material of importance to Jewish life in the Diaspora. As a result it is seen as having afforded a better and more solid basis for life in later Diaspora lands where Jews and non-Jews lived side by side. Such treatises as those which dealt with agriculture in Palestine, or with laws of ritual purity which applied only to the Holy Land, were largely left out of the record of Babylonian discussions. To be sure, such matters were not left out of the discussion completely, but both *amoraim* and *saboraim* made it clear that they did not consider them of importance in actual life. On the other hand, the Babylonian scholars concentrated their attention on such activities as prayer, the holidays, business conduct, family life and other matters deemed by them to be more relevant to Jewish life in the Diaspora. Thus, besides the relative ease with which it could be studied and understood, the Babylonian Talmud had the added advantage for Diaspora communities of dealing in more detail with matters directly affecting their daily life.

Next to the Bible, the Talmud is considered the most important product of the Jewish mind. Comprising the collective wisdom of the Jewish people, every aspect of Hebrew thought and every topic of human interest are to be found in it, discussed, analysed and dissected sometimes to the point of casuistry. There were indeed periods in their history when Jews paid more attention to the Talmud than to the Bible, looking upon it as what one modern historian called 'the Bible in action': the principles of the Bible applied to daily life.

> The same insistence upon human equality and personal freedom, the same love of justice and hope for a better society which the prophets had spoken of, shine through every discussion of the Tannaim and Amoraim. Scribes and Pharisees had long before established the principle that it is not enough to believe in ideals, but that these ideals must be given meaning through application to human activities. One may talk grandly about human equality or about love as a basis for religion. Such talk comes pretty close to hypocrisy if a man does not *act* accordingly. The Rabbis therefore assumed that not mere expressions of faith but the development of personal and social habits is the best expression of the godly life. The human will must be shaped, controlled, regulated and directed so that, even if a man forgets the fundamental principles expressed by the prophets, he will live according to them because such is the law.[4]

It was from this point of view, as well as others, that the Talmud proved all the more essential for the very reason that the Jews in Babylonia had no central government. A government is able to apply the principles set down in a constitution which speaks in general terms. But these principles need elucidation, and their application requires a suitable judicial apparatus, since individual men and women cannot possibly interpret the constitution independently in a manner acceptable to the society as a whole. The Talmud, on the other hand, comprises both the principles and the ways in which they are applied; and since the tendency of interpreters is to give themselves the benefit of the doubt and to meet every eventuality, the *tannaim* and *amoraim* who worked on it tried to apply these principles to as many actual situations as they met in their day. This is why the Talmud is considered by the Jews as a link in the Chain of Tradition which leads in a straight path back to Moses and Sinai.

The period in which the Babylonian Talmud finally took shape happened to coincide with the growth of independent centres of Jewish life in far-distant regions, which were cut off politically and linguistically from the former large centres. Indeed, the Jewish people at that time was about to enter an entirely new and different phase of its existence, in countries of which the Jews had never heard, and engaged in callings and encountering difficulties with which they had previously been totally unfamiliar. It was thus a great help to them, and a crucial factor in their struggle for survival as Jews, that they possessed in the Talmud a code not merely of religion or of law but of civilization and of daily conduct.

CHAPTER 9
The Talmud in Action

If the Talmud can be said to have one quality which overshadows all others, this would be the quality of pragmatism. The rabbis of the Talmud were not philosophers, nor were they concerned wth theories. They were practical men concerned mainly with conduct, and as such they were generally little interested in speculations that had no bearing on human behaviour. In this they can be said to have acted in the tradition of their spiritual fathers, the Prophets. Nevertheless, they were fairly preoccupied with questions of religious doctrine in so far as these had a bearing on life and conduct. They thus set themselves the task of interpreting, elaborating upon, elucidating and applying these doctrines and the teachings relevant to them, communicating them by means of homily, parable and wise sayings, not as theoretical principles but as practical guides. This practical approach to matters of religion and religious doctrine is so intrinsic to the Talmud that it extends even to the paramount question of belief in God. The rabbis taught that faith is extolled only in so far as it leads to right action. To profess belief in God and to act as if He did not exist is of little value indeed. To know God and not to act in accordance with His will is worse than to deny His existence altogether.

The teachings of the Talmud may best be grouped under three broad headings: Faith, Ethics and Religious Observance. As a doctrine, belief in God was stressed, but the Talmud rabbis refrained from binding themselves by any particular form in which this doctrine was to be understood. Given the faith, they taught, the means whereby this faith was to find expression was of no practical significance.

It is in the sphere of ethics and morality, the second of the three topics which exercised the minds of the Talmud rabbis most, that their genius for penetrating the text of the Holy Writ and discovering in it new ideas of far-reaching practical importance was most conspicuous. As Epstein puts it: 'Here is evidence of a fineness of perception that enabled the Talmudic teachers to draw out the full consequences of the moral injunctions and admonitions of the Bible for the enrichment of Jewish ethical teaching and the general moral culture of mankind.'[1]

The general contents of the Scriptural moral law, with its basic principles of justice and righteousness and the human rights and duties they entail, are known and have been expounded in numerous studies. In Talmudic teaching, however, these rights and duties are developed in such a way as to bring within their scope rules of conduct which no ordinary interpretation of the biblical text could disclose.[2]

First of the human rights discussed is the right to life. This right, as interpreted in the Talmud, is designed not only to provide security for life and limb but also to offer a safeguard against threatened injury. To lift a hand against a fellow creature, even without actually striking him, is branded as an infamy. 'He who lifts a hand against his fellow although he did not strike him is called a wicked man' (*Sanhedrin* 58b). Then comes the right to possession, forbidding any encroachment upon a fellow man's livelihood. The Talmud rabbis, proceeding on the prohibition in the Bible (Lev. 25: 14–17) of 'wrongdoing one another' in business, preclude all kinds of deceit, tricks of trade, or misrepresentation in commercial transactions; strict honesty is demanded of all sides in a business transaction. The Talmud asserts: 'The Holy One, blessed be He, hates a person who says one thing with his mouth and another in his heart' (*Pessahim* 113b), and this applies to business standards as well as to all other facets of daily life.

There is also the right to work, and the right of the labourer to his earnings; the right of the person to safeguard his honour and reputation, and the related right of 'person' which forbids encroachment upon a fellow man's self-respect.

> In its concern for the right of person, the Talmud has taken the greatest pains to explain what kind of acts offend against this fundamental human right. It is, for example, sinful to give someone an address without being sure that it is the correct one. It is likewise sinful to go into a shop and ask the price of an article when there is no intention of buying it. Offences of this type are designated in the Talmud as 'wrongdoing through words' (*onaath debarim*) and considered graver than wrong caused to fellow men in respect of material values (*onaath mamon*), since they are an affront to human personality. Closely allied to wrongdoing with words is ... misrepresentation of the truth, such as practised by the confidence trickster who seeks to influence his victim to think or to act against his own interest or what would have been his better judgement. ... All such deception, whether practised on a Jew or a non-Jew, comes under the category of 'stealing of the mind' (*genebath daath*) and are forbidden.[3]

The duties expounded in the Talmud are in great measure designed to safeguard human rights. For instance, confirming the right of the individual to life, righteousness bids man not to stand idly by if the blood of his fellow is spilt. The right to life also entails the duty of alms-giving by those who can afford it. As a right or just act towards the poor, it is the duty of the donor to enter with sympathy and understanding into the experiences of those who turn to him for help.

> The claims of the poor upon the consideration of the more fortunate are derived from the idea of divine ownership, involving the recognition that whatever man has he holds from God, and that his right of possession is justified only by the opportunities this provides for service. . . . The landowner, whilst enjoying the reward of his toil and diligence, had to recognize that whatever rights he had in the land and its produce were derived from God and were subject to the overruling consideration that He alone had the ultimate ownership. From this followed the corollary that all God's children were entitled to a share in the land as a common heritage. . . . [This] Biblical attitude in respect of the gifts of Nature inspired the Talmudic teachers in their attitude to other gifts which fall to man by good fortune. Though they recognized private property rights, they sought to circumscribe this by social considerations, and only in so far as they provided a basis for service were the claims of private possessions justified. For a man, therefore, to refuse to others what he possesses simply on the ground that what he held is his own is a conduct for which, in the eyes of these teachers, there is no warrant. Provided it involves no loss or damage to the owner, others are entitled to avail themselves of the benefits and advantages which private property could offer. A typical example to which the Talmud applies this principle is a field which has been cleared of crops at the end of the harvest, when it is considered unethical for the owner to refuse to allow the public to enter the field simply because it was his private possession [*Baba Kamma* 81b).[4]

The attitude of the Talmud rabbis to matters of religious observance is similarly characterized by practicality and likewise free of dogmatism and fundamentalist zealotry. The *mitzvot* (commandments) are not a burden: they were given to purify man. It is much better, therefore, to perform them out of love for God than out of fear. The performance of one *mitzvah* paves the way for the next, while one transgression promotes the next. The ways of the Torah 'are ways of sweetness, and all her paths are peace', we are assured (Prov. 3: 17). The Talmud teaches that the positive duties of man, as an individual and as a member of society, embrace and complete his personality which he must strive to develop with all his powers into a harmonious whole. 'Six hundred and thirteen commandments', it says in *Makkoth*

23b, 'were delivered unto Moses on Mount Sinai: three hundred and sixty-five of which are prohibitive laws, corresponding to the number of days of the solar year, whilst the remaining two hundred and forty-eight are affirmative injunctions, being as numerous as the limbs constituting the human body.' This was the rabbis' way of expressing the Jewish ideal that the restraints and disciplines of life constitute an everyday task. Moreover, since *mitzvot* are to develop character, being a Jew's proper adjustments to the spirit of the Torah, the person's attitude to the act and not its details is of prime importance.

Great emphasis is placed in the Talmud on the importance of the Torah and its study. According to the rabbis, Torah is one of the pillars of the world: 'Upon three things is the world based – upon Torah, upon divine worship, and upon acts of benevolence.' In the same Tractate (*Sayings of the Fathers*) we are told about certain age levels in beginning the formal study of Torah: 'At five the age is reached for the study of Scripture; at ten for the study of the Mishnah; and at fifteen for the Talmud.' But there is no age given when one may stop for Torah demands continuous study, which is a lifelong process. No one acquires knowledge of the Torah without study, and throughout one's life one must do so regularly. 'Qualify yourself for the study of the Torah, since it does not come to you as an inheritance. . . . Wander forth to the home of Torah, and say not that the Torah will come after you.' Finally, the rabbis prescribe self-discipline and hard work for those who want to study Torah seriously: 'This is the way that is becoming for the study of Torah: a morsel of bread with salt you must eat, and water by measure you must drink; you must sleep upon the ground and live a life of deprivation while you toil in the Torah (*Aboth* I, II, IV, V, VI].

Of related interest is the emphasis the Talmud rabbis placed on the subject of equality among men. 'Why was man created a solitary human being, without a companion?' they asked (*Sanhedrin* 37a). The reply was: 'So that it might not be said that some races are better than others.' In *Berakhoth* 17a, the Talmud quotes a favourite saying of the rabbis of Yavneh: 'I am a creature of God, and my neighbour is also His creature; my work is in the city, and his in the field; I rise early to my work, and he rises early to his. As he cannot excel in my work so I cannot excel in his work. But perhaps you say, I do great things, and he does small things. We have learnt that it matters not whether a man does much or little, if only he directs his heart to Heaven.' And in *Sanhedrin* 98b, God is cited as saying: 'Both the Gentiles and the Israelites are my handiwork, therefore how can I let the former perish on account of the latter?'

On the subject of Jew and non-Jew, the Talmud carries on the universal spirit of the Bible. 'Gentiles living outside of Palestine', we are instructed in *Hulin* 13b, 'are not to be considered wilful idolaters, even though they maintain idolatrous worship, but merely as continuing the traditional customs of their ancestors.' Rabbi Judah and Raba, two eminent sages, sent presents to their Gentile friends on their holy days, explaining that they did not consider them idolaters. 'It is incumbent upon the Jew', we are further told (*Gittin* 50b–51b), 'to make no distinction in charitable assistance between Jew and non-Jew but to help all the poor and the sick.' The most emphatic illustration of this approach is to be found in *Megillah* 13a: 'Whoever renounces idol worship may be called a Jew.'

Talmudic legislation played a decisive role in regulating the economic life of Babylonian Jewry. In addition to laying down minute rules and regulations for every conceivable eventuality, the rabbis consistently tried to maintain social harmony and inter-class equilibrium. They did this, not by denouncing riches, as some early Christians did, but by emphasizing the merely relative value of great fortunes. Collective economic responsibility was stressed and, while there was much poverty, the numerous charitable institutions set up by the community took more or less adequate care of the needy. 'Man's right, as well as duty, to earn a living and his freedom of disposing of property were safeguarded by rabbinic law and ethics only in so far as they did not conflict with the common weal.'[5]

The Talmudic sages placed great emphasis on the value of honest labour. Even profanation of the Sabbath or idolatry was declared preferable to dependence on charity. However, as conditions progressively worsened the rabbis commiserated more and more with their people, whose 'poverty at home is worse than fifty plagues'. They often personally learned the bitter lesson that, while excessive wealth was conducive to worry and led to distraction from the more important preoccupation with study, abject poverty made a man 'lose his mind and the knowledge of his Maker'.

Under all circumstances, human life was valued more highly than wealth. Referring to the poor farmers' habit of exploiting the soil to the point of exhaustion, the rabbis cited with approval the popular proverb: 'Let the soil become meagre, but not its master.'

When conditions began to change and the lure of quick commercial profits became difficult to resist, the rabbis – taught by centuries of experience – reiterated Rabbi Isaac's advice to the investor: 'A man should always divide up his capital, and invest one-third in land, one-third in commerce, and retain one-third in hand.'

In Babylonia, law enforcement among the Jews was made possible by their enjoyment of an extensive religious–ethnic autonomy, which included the right to live in accordance with one's own laws, as administered by one's own judges, including cases involving criminal jurisdiction. It is to be stressed, however, that all the legal enactments and academic interpretations advanced by the rabbis would have remained dead letters without the general willingness of the people to follow this self-imposed religious leadership, and without some effective methods of law enforcement to counter the resistance of recalcitrant minorities or individuals.

Eventually, as both life and law became more complicated, the need arose for a professional judiciary; the social forces favouring such a development had become overwhelmingly powerful.

> Rather inconsistently, the rabbis themselves promoted this evolution by their doctrine of the judge's personal responsibility for damage resulting to either party from his errors in judgement or in fact. Curiously, errors in the interpretation of a clear-cut traditional law merely nullified the sentence without untoward consequences for the judge. If the latter provision by itself encouraged scholarly judges . . . the possibility of totally evading personal responsibility for errors by securing in advance an authorization from the exilarch inescapably led to the evolution of a judicial bureaucracy.[6]

Jewish law, as it was interpreted and elaborated in the Talmud, encompassed every aspect of life. Of the mores according to which the Jews of Babylonia – as well as most of the Jewish people then as now – endeavoured to live, special emphasis was placed on those which govern family and economic relations. Apart from providing an effective judicial and welfare system, furnishing education both to the masses and to the intellectual elite, these norms regulated religious life from birth to death, at home as well as in the synagogue.

The institution of Jewish marriage depicted in the Talmud has greatly enhanced the regenerative forces of the Jewish people. In the world of the Talmud, the whole life of the Jew, including his sexual instincts, was subjected to the rigid supervision of religion. In this respect, as in so many others, the rabbis chose the middle path. While not condemning the sexual appetite as an evil in itself they, nevertheless, effectively fought all forms of licentiousness. For them, marriage was a necessary social institution, especially vital to Judaism as the foundation of Jewish survival. In one remarkable passage, a

Babylonian rabbi even defended sensual passion as a positive good, because without it 'no one would build a house, nor take a wife and beget children, nor engage in business'. Hence Talmudic legislation neither elevated marriage to the position of a sacrament, a supernatural sanction of what otherwise would be an unforgivable sin, nor did it regard it as a mere contract in civil law.

Rigid morality was demanded in married life, and many rather intimate details of marital relationships are discussed, some recommended, others put under serious sanctions. However, while marital fidelity was taken for granted on the wife's part, husbands were free from that particular obligation. Not that the legislators wanted to encourage free sexual relationships on the part of men. The fact that husbands were not bound by marital fidelity was merely a corollary of polygamy, the recognized principle of Talmudic law being that a man might marry as many wives as he could support. Nevertheless, while polygamy was the accepted norm in the world of the Talmud, many independent developments joined to make it comparatively rare. There were, to start with, obvious economic limitations, since most Jews simply could not afford the luxury of maintaining more than one wife, especially since Talmudic law extended far-reaching protection to the wife. A second, equally vital consideration was the lack of eligible women. 'In view of the almost total absence of unmarried men, only a relatively negligible surplus of women could have been available. Female slaves also decreased in number from generation to generation. Moreover, the rabbis prohibited free relations with them, prescribing liberation and marriage.'[7]

While the permission of polygamy was by no means a commandment, incest was regarded as both a sin and a crime; the rabbis declared its prohibition to be a religious law to which one must adhere with or without reason. Marriage with heathens was also strictly prohibited, and strict and elaborate rules were set for marrying freed slaves and converted Gentiles.

Another eminently eugenic means of national preservation was the emphatic observance of family purity. Judaism, while retaining its theocratic–democratic character, developed aristocratic features. Inevitably, it seems, Persian glorification of family purity and noble descent served to fortify Babylonian Jewry in its consciousness of social stratification based on birth.

Traditions reaching back to the First Exile helped to maintain family distinctions. The Palestinians recognized the high degree of reliability of Babylonian family records, admitting that only 'pure sifted flour' had remained in Babylonia after the Return from Exile. Mar Samuel proudly asserted that, with respect to the purity of the Jewish family, 'the whole world is leavened dough in comparison to Palestine, while Palestine is leavened dough as compared with Babylonia'. So deep-rooted was this Babylonian feeling of superiority that Ze'iri, one of Rabbi Yohanan's admiring Babylonian pupils, refused to marry the [Palestinian] master's daughter, eliciting Rabbi Yohanan's caustic remark: 'Our learning is good enough, but our daughters are not.'[8]

The rabbis, however, were realistic enough to perceive that most people were far more concerned about matters other than family purity. They thus used a mixture of threats and persuasion rather than promulgating strict rules and regulations. This is a typical rabbinic injunction:

> Some marry out of lust; some marry for money; some marry for a career and some marry for the sake of Heaven. Concerning those who marry out of lust, the verse says [Hosea 5:7]: 'They have dealt treacherously against the Lord, for they have begotten strange children.' Concerning those who marry for money, the verse says [*ibid.*]: 'Now shall the new moon devour them with their portions.' Those who marry for a career will ultimately lose their position. Those who marry for the sake of Heaven will ultimately have children who will deliver Israel [*Masekhtot Derekh Eretz, Tosefta* I, 6].

As far as we can ascertain, a nobility not of blood but of learning dominated the Jewish social scene.

> For marriage, a scholar was regarded, at least by his fellow scholars, the Talmudic legislators, as more eligible than the wealthy descendant of a noble family. . . . No matter what his social origin, he who had acquired a high position in the Jewish world of learning was second to none in Jewish society. Thus family purity tended to direct natural selection into intellectual channels. Here the survival of the fittest meant primarily that of the best educated.[9]

On the subject of the woman's social status the Talmud rabbis were as clear and as realistic as they were on other subjects. Talmudic literature seldom mentions businesswomen, and the few whom we hear of must have been widows or divorced. Discussing court sessions, for example, the rabbis took it for granted that the woman could almost always be found at home. Certainly, occupations requiring protracted absences, such as those of shippers, camel drivers or sailors, are debated only in terms of males unable for this reason to comply regularly with their marital duties. On the other hand, women often assisted their husbands in business, sometimes taking over a distinct share. More regularly, a woman attended to her household chores. A characteristic enumeration of these chores states:

> These are the chores which a wife does for her husband: She grinds flour, bakes, launders, cooks, feeds her child, makes the beds, and works with wool. If she brought him one female slave, she is free from grinding, baking and laundering; two slaves, she does not have to cook or feed her child; three slaves she makes no beds and does no woollen work; four slaves she sits on the throne idly. Rabbi Eliezer says [however]: Even if she brought him a hundred slaves, he forces her to work in wool, for idleness leads to immorality. Rabbi Simon ben Gamliel says: Even if a man took a vow forbidding his wife to do any work whatsoever he must divorce her and pay her the marriage settlement, for idleness leads to boredom [*M. Ketubot* v, 5].

On the subject of women, the rabbis were not all of the same mind. 'Probably there is an uneven balance of anti-feminist utterances in the Talmudic literature, particularly in its *aggadic* portions.' Women were often considered easygoing, devoid of judgement, prone to excessive talk, indulging in sorcery, and setting their hearts on trinkets. 'He who acts on his wife's advice', declared Rab, himself married to a shrew, 'goes to hell.' Though not left uncontroverted, this utterance is typical of many irate exclamations.

At the same time, both preachers and jurists tried to buttress the woman's position within the family using all the means at their disposal.

> They taught the essential equality of men and women before the law. Although conceding the father's primacy, they pointed out the reverse order in the biblical injunction, 'Every one of you shall revere his mother and his father' (*Lev.* 19:3), and stated that the biblical lawgiver thus wished 'to teach you that both are equal'. Rabbi Eliezer praised even unreasonable extremes of filial piety, when one Domna suffered calmly when his deranged mother threw slippers at him and spat in his face in the presence of strangers.

As to the concentration of woman's activities upon her home, Salo W. Baron believes that, while this was 'perhaps prejudicial to her general economic and social standing, it nevertheless had great value for the preservation of the nation's physical and moral strength'.[10]

CHAPTER 10

Babylonia Assumes Leadership

Following the collapse of the Bar Kochba rebellion in AD 135, Rome succeeded in driving the Jewish community of Palestine into poverty, ineffectiveness and obscurity. The Roman emperor Hadrian decided that what was needed was not only the physical and material break-up of the community and its leadership but also the destruction of the Jewish religion itself, which he rightly saw as the one decisive factor in the people's refusal to assimilate or even to submit quietly to Rome's supremacy. Hadrian accordingly prohibited the practice of Judaism altogether. He forbade circumcision and Sabbath observance, and made unlawful the fixing of the calendar which was so important for the celebration of the holidays. He also prohibited study and teaching; anybody caught studying the Torah was punished by death.

But Judaism refused to die. By one of those 'coincidences' of which Jewish history seems to have more than a fair share, the Jewish community of Babylonia had by then become ready to assume leadership. It was ready to carry on, having awakened from a centuries-old slumber. Not that the Jews of Babylonia had suffered disabilities. On the contrary, they were treated fairly well by the various governments throughout the Persian and Parthian periods; their religious life was rarely disrupted or interfered with – and it was not until the first half of the third century AD that their peaceful life was briefly interrupted, as we have seen in a previous chapter. Their religious life, however, depended upon Palestine, which continued to lead the way on matters of observance, interpretation and custom. This is how one modern Jewish historian described this state of affairs:

> Until the time of Ezra, Babylonian Jews had been more progressive than Palestinian ones; by Ezra's time, Palestinian intellectual and religious activity far outstripped similar activity among the Jews who remained in Babylonia. It seems as though, after making a number of steps forward in the development of Judaism, the Babylonian community became tired and sat back to let Palestine do the rest. . . . The Babylonian Jews, like their co-religionists everywhere, were

always interested in study. Their intellectual activity, however, was not as profound or as intensive as in Palestine. When a man showed an unusual desire to continue his studies, he would go to Palestine, and sometimes would remain there. . . .[1]

Palestine did not give up leadership easily. After Bar Kochba's defeat, a great leader emerged there in the person of Judah the Prince, son of the *nasi* Simon. Among the measures which this extraordinary leader introduced in his untiring efforts to stave off the danger of Palestine's loss of leadership was his refusal to ordain scholars unless he was certain that they had no intention of emigrating. He wanted to make sure that Jewish religious leadership would continue indefinitely to depend on Palestine, and by confining ordination to that land his aim was to continue the Chain of Tradition, which he did not want to see continued in some other land. Because Jewish learning and authority, from Moses through the *tannaim* and until his own day, had originated in Palestine, Judah thought that this should and would continue indefinitely.

To some extent this position was justifiable, and certainly understandable. But it could not be maintained for long. During the third and fourth centuries the centre of gravity of Jewish life gradually and inexorably moved from Palestine to Babylonia. The declining Roman Empire, forcing many of its subjects to emigrate, offered little attraction to Palestinian Jews, while the Sassanian monarchs encouraged immigration because the new arrivals brought with them technical skills for industrial projects and experience in commercial undertakings. In Babylonia, the Jewish population increased and made steady progress, economically and culturally. In the vicinity of the capital, Ctesiphon, older and newer Jewish settlers often outnumbered their Gentile neighbours to such an extent that their rabbis seriously debated the question whether unidentified objects found there should carry the presumption of Jewish ownership with them. The city of Mahoza, again, was so overwhelmingly Jewish that – as we find in *Erubin* 6b – the question arose whether the gates in the city wall did not require a *mezuzah*.

Since simultaneously the status of Palestine Jewry deteriorated, there gradually arose a certain rivalry between the two communities. No longer was there a Temple, a Hasmonean or even a Herodian dynasty to rule Palestine, and, indirectly, world Jewry. There were patriarchs in Palestine, of course, but Babylonia boasted of exilarchs. These 'princes of captivity' had a superior claim to distinction, as

> they were supposedly direct descendants of David, while the patriarchs of the house of Hillel (incidentally also a Babylonian) were regarded as progeny only of the female line. If Judah the Patriarch combined 'learning and prestige in one place', had extensive estates, and employed a vast retinue of courtiers and a 'Gothic' (Galatian or Teuton) bodyguard, the exilarch occupied a far higher position at the royal court, and his residence resembled a township of its own.[2]

It is generally believed – and there is ample evidence to back that belief – that our world of the last decades of the twentieth century is preoccupied by the subject of ethnic–communal 'roots'. It appears, however, that the world of the first few centuries AD was no less so preoccupied – indeed one historian asserts that it was 'obsessed' with a quest for ancient origins. In such a world Babylonian Jewry had something to boast of. The Euphrates valley was dotted with ancient monuments cherished by local Jews. 'The ancient community of Nehardea genuinely believed that its synagogue had been founded by the exiled King Jehoiachim. Another synagogue was ascribed to Daniel. Babylonian Jews also pointed with pride to a building which had allegedly housed Ezra's original academy and to other noteworthy biblical sites.'[3]

Nor were these claims wholly unfounded, especially when it came to assertions regarding the unbroken continuity of Jewish life in Babylonia since the Achaemenid Empire and the contribution Babylonian Jewry made to the study and the preservation of the Torah. Rabbi Simon ben Laqish, himself a Palestinian, had his own unique way of describing this situation: 'At first when the Torah was forgotten in Israel, Ezra came from Babylonia and restored it; it was forgotten again, when Hillel the Babylonian came and restored it; once again it was forgotten, when Rabbi Hiyya and his sons came and restored it.' Rabbi Yohanan ben Zakkai himself, pondering the question as to why the Jews had been exiled to Babylonia rather than to any other country, said: 'Because their ancestors had come from there. It is like a woman misbehaving towards her husband. To whom does he send her? He sends her back to her father's house.'

In the protracted, and often open struggle for supremacy between the two, Palestine did not give in to Babylonia easily; indeed it put up a fierce and prolonged fight. In addition to the legal and official devices with which this fight was conducted, there were also mutual recriminations often seasoned with words of scorn and ridicule. Some

Palestinians continued to speak of 'the foolish Babylonians', an almost proverbial phrase reflecting nothing more substantial than the usual regional superiority complex. Rabbi Jeremiah (a native Babylonian who studied and taught in Palestine) asserted: 'These foolish Babylonians, because they live in an obscure country, express obscure thoughts.' To this envious remark Raba sharply retorted: 'Heretofore they have called us fools, now they are fools of fools, because we have taught them and they have failed to learn [*Yoma* 57a].'

As time went on, however, the rise of Babylonia could no longer be checked.

> Under the increasingly intolerant Christian Empire, the patriarchs finally found it more and more inexpedient to exercise even their supreme authority over the Jewish calendar. The Church viewed with disfavour every public broadcast of the Jewish months which made it easier for Christian sectarians to set their Easter in accordance with the Jewish Passover. . . . When such half measures as the advance proclamation of a whole cycle in the calendar failed to remedy these shortcomings, the patriarchs themselves decided in 358–9 to make a permanent astronomic computation, and thus gave up their most significant function for world Jewry.[4]

Much has been written about the Talmud, its uniqueness and its lasting influence on the survival of the Jewish people through the ages. It is worthwhile noting, however, that most scholars – Jews and non-Jews – when they speak about 'the Talmud' refer to the Babylonian version; when they want to refer to the Palestinian version they speak of the Palestinian Talmud. The rabbis of the Talmud saw their main task as erecting a 'fence around the Torah' by minute elaboration of its laws, thereby also building a fence around the people of Israel against all storms from without. This, however, did not mean that the Jews lived in seclusion. 'Everywhere their life received its special colour from the surrounding environment. But wherever the Talmudic "fence" remained erect, foreign ingredients were immediately absorbed and integrated into the total system of rabbinism.'[5]

Even this, however, is not what makes the Talmud such a unique phenomenon. As one contemporary Jewish scholar and rabbi, Judah Goldin, has put it:

> When one enters the world of the Talmud, one enters a world unlike any other. Not because nowhere else is there so serious a concern with law: no civilized culture has ever been without legalism and

casuistry: these are the basic stuff of well-ordered existence and relationships. Not because the Talmud is only a record of Halakhah, law and legal argumentation. There is, after all, a wealth of Hagada (or Agada), non-legal material, in the Talmud – legends, folklore, ethical and 'philosophical' and theosophical and theological speculation, homilies, parables, prayers, gnomic sayings, historical reminiscences, old wives' tales too: in other words, that large, unbounded expression of the human imagination reacting to the universe, in anguish, in wonder responding to the here and now and to what was and to what will be in the end of time. Taken crumb by crumb, one could perhaps find parallels in many places to this particular or the other particular saying or proverb or tale. What makes the Talmudic substance *sui generis* is (a) its non-'literary' quality, and (b) its unabashed conviction that if human character is to be refined and be given a divine dimension, then nothing is so far-reaching a *paideia* as Halakhah.[6]

Not that the Talmud lacks literary *quality*. The very seriousness towards terms, the striving towards precision, the compactness, the sharpness and the genuine alertness to style and verbal effect – all these furnish proof to the contrary. What Goldin means by ascribing a non-'literary' quality to the Talmud, he explains, is: 'In a literary work, you see things; in the Talmud, you hear voices. . . . The Talmudic rabbis were not writers of books, but teachers, by word of mouth creating and expanding the Oral Torah. We do not so much read what these great sages said as hear them in their sessions – but there are no prepared speeches. What there is, is intellect reacting to intellect.'

The second reason which makes the Talmud unique, writes Rabbi Goldin, is that the Talmud not only is focused on the Law but that, 'in a sense, Law – its study and practice – was the Talmudic *mystique*'. For this indeed is what the rabbis of the Talmud hoped: 'That they could supply the exercises which would become second nature in the World to Come, that gracious time when the righteous will be crowned and nourished by the divine splendour, as are the ministering angels. What, in the final analysis, is the Talmud if not the choreography for life in the Messianic Age. So, on that prodigious faith, one begins *now* to act out life.'[7]

Gerson Cohen, a noted Jewish scholar and historian, considers it an oddity of Jewish history that rabbinic Judaism was 'the direct outgrowth, not of Palestinian legislation and exegesis, but of the interpretation to which the Palestinian tradition was subjected in

Babylonia'. In one sense, he adds, this was all the more fortunate for later Judaism 'since Babylonian Judaism, as a completely Diaspora civilization, was the logical model for other Diaspora Jewries to imitate'.[8]

Be that as it may, the fact remains that by the fourth century AD the supremacy of the Babylonian schools became so assured and consolidated that in the Middle Ages – the heyday of rabbinic Judaism – even Palestinian Jewry adopted the Babylonian Talmud as its code of law. In the course of the fourth century, Babylonia started to assume intellectual leadership, and in subsequent centuries the Babylonian version of the Gemara – which together with the Mishnah constitute what we know as the Babylonian Talmud – became authoritative for world Jewry. The foundations on which this version was built were, of course, Palestinian – the originality of approach, the creative reinterpretation of old sources to suit new conditions, and the method itself of interpretation. These foundations, according to Baron and others, belong to the Pharisaism of independent Judah.

> But this movement itself was nourished from sources in the Babylonian Exile, and it developed with reference to world Jewry rather than to the people of Palestine exclusively. For this reason the transplantation of Palestinian law into Babylonia met with little initial difficulty. But even the segregated and autonomous Jewish settlement of Babylonia soon evolved social features of its own. To adapt the law to these, it had to reinterpret the law of Palestine while retaining its method. As life became increasingly artificial, it tended to make reinterpretations artificial too. At any rate, as in the times of Moses and Ezra, Jewish law received its authoritative formulation on foreign soil, but this time with a view to Jewish life in foreign lands.[9]

The ways in which Jewries, scattered all over the world in later centuries, put the Babylonian Talmud to use were many and varied. As new situations arose and as new needs were created, the Jews turned to the Talmud for guidance. Although in many cases they did not find exact duplicates of, or analogies to, the conditions confronting them, they nevertheless found parallels. These were of such variety and so numerous that each of these Jewish communities easily managed to apply them, or versions of them, to their own conditions. This is what led to the writing of so many commentaries to the Talmud, and to the many different codes of law based upon it.

> The Spanish commentaries and codes differed from the French, and the French from the Polish. All of them, however, hark back to the original text. The Talmud thus served as a unifying element among the Jews. It prescribed the fundamentals of their life. It helped to bind them together in action and in thought. It even united them in language, for in later Jewish writing, whether in books or in private correspondence, the language and the phraseology of the Talmud were used. Its legal discussions were not the only part of the Talmud to exercise influence on the Jews. The stories, the parables and the ethical maxims scattered among the discussions played an equally extraordinary part in shaping the Jewish character. From now on we shall meet the Talmud again and again as a force in the survival of the Jewish people. We shall see how it kept alive their hopes and courage, their culture and their faith in God.[10]

Salo Baron expresses the same belief but phrases it differently. While it became the main expression of a great crisis in the history of Jewish society and religion, he writes, the Talmud at the same time served as a powerful instrument in overcoming that crisis.

> The progressive degradation of political and social life in the late Roman Empire; the still sharper drop in the Jews' legal and political status; the decrease in the number of Jews and the protracted falling-off of whole sections of Jewry which joined the new religious movement – [all these] doubtless had far-reaching effects upon Jewish life. As a province of Rome, Palestine gradually lost its leadership, while Babylonian Jewry, happier under the rule of a rejuvenated, progressive, and relatively sympathetic Persia, took its place. Once again away from its soil, the Jewish people had, in one way or another, to live in defiance of nature. Conscious of the character of this new situation, Judaism reformulated its age-old ideology with still greater finality. In the Talmud it created a much-needed, and in many ways unique, bulwark between the Jews and the forces of nature.[11]

The immense influence which the Babylonian Talmud came to have over the dispersed Jewish communities dates from about the end of the seventh century. This period coincided with the end of Sassanian rule in Mesopotamia. Shortly after, the armies of Islam began marching triumphantly to the conquest of large segments of the then civilized world, Mesopotamia being one of their earliest achievements.

PART TWO

The Encounter with Islam (641–1850)

The dweller in Iraq saw generation follow generation without a policy, because without ideals, of rule. Sonorous loyalty to faith and Sultan supplied, as a spring to government, what neither enlightenment, nor goodwill, nor skill were there to supply. He saw mosques founded, but never a road, a school, or hospital; taxes increased or modified, but no principle of taxation conceived; *dhabit* [officer] and *qadhi* [judge] appointed, but not controlled; expedient following expedient in the government of the tribes, from brutal violence to weak surrender, but no grappling with Iraq's basic problem, the incorporation of the tribes in the state. This and the squabbles of high officials with their military backing, the half-hearted fiscal or social reforms of a few, the various personalities of governors appointed under every condition of venal caprice in Stambul – these were the phenomena spread before the Sultan's subjects in Iraq.

Stephen H. Longrigg[1]

CHAPTER II

A Deep Sigh of Relief

The hundred years or so which separate the conclusion of work on the Babylonian Talmud and the dramatic entry of Islam onto the stage of world history were a period of decline world-wide. The Sassanid Empire was crumbling under the heavy toll of unceasing internal rifts and external encroachments; the newly established Byzantine Empire was already a cultural medley and remained so despite its considerable military strength; the Roman Empire had finally crumbled, and Europe was still in its Dark Ages and several centuries away from its Renaissance. In a sense, then, the stage was comfortably set for the debut of a fresh, somewhat wild and extremely bashful new world power. This duly came during the third decade of the seventh century from the most unexpected of places.

Though in an essentially different way Islam, like Christianity before it, grew out of Judaism. Unlike Christianity, the new conquering religion did not grow directly out of Jewish roots; but its founder, Muhammed, was undoubtedly inspired by the ethics of Jehovah and taught all along that the Hebrew Scriptures were sacred. He also acknowledged the prophecy of the Hebrew Prophets, and produced a body of teachings that closely resembled those of Judaism. Early in his career, Muhammed sought acceptance by his Jewish neighbours (a considerable number of Jews had been living in Arabia for centuries); but these Jews, from whom he seems to have learned many of the things which he was to teach subsequently, did not take him seriously. Disappointed at this rejection, Muhammed fought his Jewish neighbours and by the time of his death in 632 managed to build and lead a powerful army.

It was after Muhammed's death, however, that the conquests by his followers got off to a serious start. Under a succession of caliphs (successors) the Muslim armies occupied Damascus in 635, swept Palestine in 638, invaded Mesopotamia and Persia in 641, and finished off the Sassanian Empire some three years later. Egypt, another centre of Jewish life, was conquered in 655. By the year 705, all the lands of

North Africa were vanquished and the Muslims were undisputed masters of the southern half of the Mediterranean. In 711, their armies finally crossed over to Europe and subdued the Iberian Peninsula in a four-year campaign.

There is reason to believe that the Jews of Babylonia – as well as Jews elsewhere – welcomed the new masters with a deep sigh of relief. At that point, for reasons of their own, the Sassanians had started on one of their periodical waves of harassment and persecution against their Jewish subjects. The background of this new wave had to do with the empire's crippling difficulties both on the home front and in its relations with the surrounding world. The Sassanian king, Noshirwan (531–79), is generally considered to have been the most illustrious member of the dynasty. His reorganization of the empire and the reforms and improvements he introduced contrasted sharply with the chaos that was common during the reigns of almost all his predecessors. He too, however, was unable to withstand the numerous wars in which he was engaged and the empire continued to be depleted and became increasingly weary and stagnant.

Noshirwan's successor fared even worse. He had to contend not only with the growing threat from Byzantine military might but also a Turkish invasion. It was during this monarch's time that the new wave of persecution against the Jews started. His reign also witnessed a revolt of the army against the ruler, and Sassanian Persia was never to know peace again until a cataclysmic change came in the shape of the Muslim armies; the last Sassanian sovereign, Yezdegerd III, was assassinated in exile in 651. From that time on, Islam, this new and unexpected factor in world politics, was destined to affect deeply the fortunes of the Jews everywhere, including of course those of the ancient Jewish communities of Palestine and Babylonia.

By the time Muhammed's successors and generals started on their spectacular wave of conquests, the most important centre of Jewish life as well as the most populated was situated in Mesopotamia. The ancient schools and academies still flourished; the memory of the Talmudic era was still fresh; and the office of the Exilarch, both the symbol and the main channel of Jewish self-government, was still functioning despite the many ups and downs it had undergone during the past few decades. It was, therefore, natural for the new conquerors to turn to the Exilarch of the day, having learned from their short experience as rulers in foreign lands that it would be best to make use of existing institutions rather than waste precious time trying to impose their own methods and mores.

Now the Exilarch at this time was a man named Bustanai, about whose person and shifting fortunes a considerable number of legends as well as facts were woven. Whatever truth there may be in these stories, it is fairly well established that at the time the Muslims were invading Mesopotamia Bustanai was fleeing for his life. Yezdegerd III, it is said, had deprived Bustanai of his position and was now trying to apprehend him, having sentenced him to death. It was the new Muslim rulers who saved his life and restored him to his elevated position; and his descendants continued to fill the office until its decline and final decay over four centuries later.

One legend about Bustanai's birth is worth telling here, though it is evidently rather apocryphal, as it is indicative of the seriousness with which the office of the Exilarch was taken by successive generations of Jews. The legend goes that a certain Persian king dreams that he is having all the trees of a garden (*bustan*) cut down. Just as he makes ready to strike at a tender sprig, the axe is snatched from his hand by a venerable old man and hurled at his forehead with such force that blood spurts over his face and beard. He prays for mercy and is made to promise to nurse the twig that it may shoot up into a leafy tree. On awakening he beholds the blood on his face and, convinced that the dream has significance, summons a Jew known for his skill in interpreting dreams. It so happened that the daughter of this Jew had married a scion of the Exilarch's house and was with child. Her father sees in the dream a reference to the unborn child who may be the last of the princely house of David. Upon being told this, the king orders that the mother be surrounded with every possible care, and when a boy is born he is named Bustani (or Bustanai) which means 'of the garden'. As he grows up he distinguishes himself by learning and displays extraordinary powers of intellect. Summoned before the king, he proves himself well-mannered, for though he is stung by a wasp while in the king's audience, he forbears to drive it away by so much as the movement of a finger, in deference to his royal master. The king showers gifts upon him and then and there installs him as prince of the captivity. From then on, it is said, the wasp became the design on the Exilarch's seal.

According to one version of this story, the incident with the wasp took place in the presence of no less a man than Omar ibn el-Khattab, the second caliph, who in this version is said to have ordered an older man, the Exilarch of the day, to vacate the princely office in favour of Bustanai, then a mere boy of sixteen. It is further reported that Omar bestowed upon the stripling one of the captive Persian princesses,

Izdundad by name, whom he duly married. Bustanai, of course, had other wives, and subsequently the children of these wives sought to discredit the legitimacy of their brothers whom the Persian princess had borne, on the ground that as a captive her status was that of slave. The *Geonim*, however, ruled that merely by virtue of marrying her Bustanai must have made her a free woman and a convert to Judaism beforehand. This alleged decision, by the way, is reported by a later *Gaon* in response to a query with reference to a similar case.

How much truth, if any, could have been incorporated in this legend is not of major importance to our record. What seems to be certain is that, despite the imposition of a new tax and whatever encroachment was made by the Muslims upon Jewish autonomy, the life of the Jews of Babylonia under Islam took a turn for the better. It is not known how much actual help the Muslims got from the Jews of Mesopotamia and Persia, or even if such help was in fact forthcoming or at all needed. What is known for certain is that the establishment of the Muslims as masters of these parts of the Persian Empire brought about the restoration of a temporarily suspended Exilarchate (or merely of Bustanai as Exilarch) and the reopening of the Babylonian academies.

The very expansion of the Muslim Empire opened up extraordinary opportunities for commerce and we encounter Jews in partnership with non-Jews. Agriculture, now that it was restored to its previous state following the devastation it suffered as a result of internal conflict and external wars, also attracted the Jews.

It is said that the Arab ambassadors who were sent to the court of Yezdegerd III, the last Sassanian emperor, addressed him thus in the course of their meeting with him: 'Whatever thou hast said regarding the former condition of the Arabs is true. Their food was green lizards; they buried their infant daughters alive; nay, some of them feasted on dead carcasses, and drank blood. . . . But God, in his mercy, has now sent us, by a holy prophet, a sacred volume, which teaches us the true faith.' But if the Sassanian's opinion of pre-Muhammedan Arabia and its people was so low, what was Jewish reaction to the rise of the new faith really like? Despite the wealth of stories and legends concerning the way the Jews of Arabia treated Muhammed and the scorn they allegedly heaped upon him and his mission, there are really no contemporary records of any authenticity, and accordingly we must have recourse to a few *aggadic* writings, chiefly of an apocalyptic nature and replete with ambiguities and doubtful dating. An outstanding example of these is cited by Baron, namely the apocalyptic Midrash called *Nistarot de-Rabbi Simeon bar Yohai* (*The Mysteries of Rabbi Simon bar*

Yohai), apparently written in part during the days of the Arab conquest of Palestine late in the fourth decade of the seventh century. 'This visionary author', Baron writes, 'saw in Omar "a lover of Israel who repaired their breaches" and reported that the angel, Metatron, had long comforted Rabbi Simon: "Do not fear, son of man. The Holy One, blessed be He, is only bringing the kingdom of Ishmael in order to help you [the Jews] from the wicked one." ' Another homilist – also cited by Baron – is Rabbi Eliezer. In *Pirqe de-Rabbi Eliezer*, the author extolled the similarity of the basic belief in one God in Judaism and in Islam. He pointed out that 'of all the seventy nations that the Holy One, blessed be He, created in His world' He placed His name, El, only on Israel and Ishmael.[1]

For us today it is difficult to comprehend such bursts of enthusiasm, especially since in the so-called 'Pact of Omar' a policy of intolerance against Jews and Christians was promulgated. However, what with Islam's rapid expansion and its encounter with cultures both foreign and superior to its own, that policy proved unworkable, if not positively harmful. 'Omar, for example, ordered the expulsion of all Jews and Christians from Arabia. Nevertheless, not only do we later find flourishing Jewish centres in the peninsula, but he permitted the Exilarch to enjoy dignities which were in express contradiction to his pact. Small wonder then that a Jewish visionary could hail "the kingdom of Ishmael" as a salvation and thus allay the fears of his interlocutor.'[2]

Omar's gradual retreat from the principles laid down in his own pact began early in the proceedings. Prior to embarking on his career of conquest and in a move calculated to establish a more secure base for his ambitious operations, Omar ordered the Jews of Khaibar expelled. These Jews comprised the largest and most cohesive non-Muslim group in northern Arabia, and Omar considered their expulsion sufficiently important for him to break the express safeguards included in the treaty between Muhammed and the Khaibar community. However, the caliph was soon to become so preoccupied with state affairs elsewhere that he could not pay due attention to the implementation of his own expulsion order. The result was that a great many of the Jews of Khaibar persisted there to the tenth century and beyond. Certainly there is evidence that some of the Jews of Khaibar were directed by Omar towards the new Arab encampments in southern Mesopotamia, particularly that of Kufa. This military camp was soon to develop into a major centre of trade and learning, and the Jewish community there grew by leaps and bounds, contributing greatly to the new city's intellectual and economic growth. According to Baron, 'Before long the Jews believed that Kufa had been the scene of their very early settlement in the days of the Babylonian Exile. For centuries thereafter visitors were shown remains of the tomb of King Jeconiah, allegedly buried there after his death at Nebuchadnezzar's court. In the twelfth century at any rate, Benjamin found there an elaborate mausoleum adorned by a dome, doubtless similar to those crowning many Muslim mosques.'[3]

Of even greater significance was the Jewish community in the city of Basra which rivalled Kufa as an intellectual and commercial centre. References to the Jewish community in Basra are found in the *responsa* of the *Geonim* since the early ninth century, as shown in a question put about the year 830 before the *Gaon* of Sura, Rab Moses ben R. Jacob Gaon. It appears that Basra and its Jewish community at that time boasted 'famous medical men', and later in 870 the scholars of the city turned to the *Gaon* of Sura, Nahshon ben Tzadoq, for advice on a point of law. In a sketch of the history of the Jews in Basra, David S. Sassoon states that in the ninth century the community contributed 300 gold pieces annually towards the upkeep of the Academy of Sura. 'In the same period', he adds, 'we find scholars and medical men who were born in Basra officiating in Palestine and Egypt. . . . About a hundred years later we meet Israel ben Simhah b. Saadyah b. Ephraim of Basra who presented the Bible codex of Ben Asher to the Karaite community in Jerusalem.'[4]

Joseph Wolff, a missionary, reached Basra in the year 1824 and found the Jews of the place 'liberal-minded, candid and very enquiring'. They were, he reported, 'a fine race of people whose chief object was gain'. The leading Jews of the city called upon Wolff and invited him to the synagogue although they were fully aware of the object of his mission. They even requested Bibles. He visited the synagogue, and the next day 'the prince of the Jews' and one Basri by name of Hezekiel invited him to their houses, where he had a conversation with twenty leading members of the community.[5]

Although our sources are completely and inexplicably silent about the Jews of Basra for many centuries prior to Wolff's report, it would be safe to say that the Jewish presence in that city continued uninterrupted after the Arab conquest.

CHAPTER 12

Islam and the Jews: Theory and Practice

The status of the Jews under Islam is fairly clearly defined in Muslim law and in the utterances of Muhammed and his first caliphs. In practice, however, and in day-to-day dealings and administration this status tended to vary greatly from one Muslim dynasty to the next and even from ruler to individual ruler. Theoretically the Jews – along with the Christians and the Sabians – were considered by Muslims members of a tolerated religion whose followers were to be disarmed and compelled to pay tribute in return for Muslim protection. Regarded since the days of Muhammed as believers in the one true God, they were called *ahl el-kitab* (People of the Book or Scripturalists) and considered *dhimmis* – people with whom the Muslims had made a covenant and towards whom they had an obligation. But the covenant involved duties as well as rights and the status of *dhimmi* was not granted automatically. If, for example, a Jew or a Christian or a Sabian was captured in battle, he might be killed, enslaved, ransomed, exchanged or simply set free, while the wives and children of combatants in any case had to become slaves. Each adult *dhimmi* had to pay a poll-tax, the *jizya*, of an amount fixed in the appropriate agreement; his unmovable property either became a *waqf* for the whole body of Muslims, which he continued to have the use of, or he held it still as his own. In either case he paid a land-tax for it and its crops which, in the first case, inhered in the land and had to be paid even though the land came under the possession of a Muslim. However, in the second case, on the owner's becoming a Muslim, he was exempted from the tax.

Other obligations and disabilities imposed on 'People of Scripture' included possible exactions for the maintenance of the Muslim armies, an obligation to distinguish themselves from the believers by dress, not to ride on horseback or carry weapons, and to assume a generally respectful attitude towards Muslims. A *dhimmi* was also under certain legal disabilities with regard to testimony in law courts, protection under criminal law and in marriage. On the other hand, Islam guaranteed the *dhimmis* security of life and property, protection in the exercise of their religion and defence against others. They could repair and even rebuild existing houses of worship, but not erect new ones on new sites; and in the performance of their worship they could not use an offensive publicity. Their life, public and private, had also to be of a quiet, inoffensive nature. Finally, the *dhimmis* were not considered fully fledged citizens of the Muslim state. Rather, each non-Muslim community governed itself under its responsible head – rabbi, bishop, exilarch – who acted as its link with the Muslim government.

By granting the *dhimmis* a special status, Islam had in fact introduced an intermediary 'domain' into the original division of the world between *dar al-Islam* (the domain of Islam) and *dar al-harb* (the domain of war), a division which referred to the world of the true believers and that of the infidels or unbelievers. For this third domain the term sometimes used in Muslim jurisprudence was *dar as-sulh* (the domain of conciliation), to which belonged such non-Muslims to whom toleration and protection was extended by treaty. Such treaties, written as well as informal, are said to have been concluded by Muhammed himself, and after his death the task fell mostly to the second Caliph Omar, who is said to have declared in his testament: 'I recommend to your care the *dhimmis*, for they enjoy the protection of the Prophet. See that the agreement with them is kept, and that no greater burdens than they carry are laid upon them.'

Despite the burdens involved in belonging to *dar as-sulh*, the Jews of Mesopotamia welcomed the change to Muslim rule, mainly because the new masters left them very much to themselves. The various aspects of discrimination enumerated in the so-called Covenant of Omar (*'Ahd Omar*), and which were mostly social in character, were only sporadically enforced and were often completely overlooked. In everyday practice, *dhimmis* were not only tolerated but in some areas enjoyed almost full equality before the law. In any case, what with their cultural and religious activities remaining their own concern, and with their internal affairs regulated in accordance with their own laws and customs, the Jews felt that their lot was better than it had been under the tottering, often bigoted Sassanian rulers. Even when the Muslim domain began to expand and government became unruly and uncontrollable, the principle was not changed: the state continued to be defined in religious terms and the excluded groups continued to be allowed to look after their own affairs. To quote a noted authority on the period: 'The extension of internal autonomy to the Jewish communities under Islam made possible the continuance of a Jewish way of life, or at least the semblance of it, the cultivation of Jewish learning, and patterns of behaviour which remained rooted in Talmudic literature, though they underwent an evolution and modification.'[1]

Loopholes, oversights and omissions are found in all laws and treaties, and the Covenant of Omar was no exception. The Jews of Mesopotamia and other parts of the now greatly extended Muslim domain took every advantage of these. To give one rather extreme example from the religious sphere, Muslims who converted to Judaism (or Christianity), a *dhimmi* who blasphemed the Prophet and a Muslim who was guilty of the same 'crime' were all guilty of a capital crime punishable by death. It was repentance, however, rather than destruction that was the real aim, and the unfortunates who were caught in any of these instances were summoned three times and given the opportunity to repent; only if they persisted would they be put to death. In other related instances, namely of forced conversion of a *dhimmi* to Islam, the converts were often given express permission to return to Judaism or Christianity.

Jews were also permitted to defend their own religion against verbal or written attacks by Muslim debaters, and we have evidence of Jewish polemical and apologetic literature, often quite outspoken in its critique of Muslim fundamentalists. At times Jews were even accused of meddling in purely Muslim religious controversies, while quite a few Jewish polemics against the dominant faith were allowed to circulate, without causing immediate reprisals from the Muslim administration.[2]

There were some crucial instances, too, of measures which the Muslim legislator intended to be discriminatory against *dhimmis* but which they had reason to view as salutary to themselves. For example, in order to uphold Muslim morality the law punished a Muslim's illicit relations with an unmarried *dhimmi* woman with extreme severeness. This was perfectly welcome to the Jewish leadership, which traditionally did its best to prevent such relationships lest the Jewish minority be gradually submerged in the community of Islam. Another example is provided by Muslim behaviour concerning living quarters and neighbourhoods. Although Muslim law never called for segregated quarters for the different faiths, certain limitations were imposed, such as that a synagogue or church should not exceed in height a neighbouring mosque, and that even Muslim private houses should not be dwarfed by those of their *dhimmi* neighbours. These regulations, too, proved more than acceptable to the Jewish leadership, which for social as well as ritualistic reasons preferred to keep non-Jews away from self-selected Jewish quarters. Rabbinic law even considered it a serious transgression on the part of a Jewish owner to sell or let his property in the Jewish quarter to a non-Jew. In his reply to an enquiry from a Kairawan Jew, an unnamed Babylonian *Gaon* wrote: 'A Jewish houseowner must not let his house to a Gentile for living quarters. This prohibition applies not only to a powerful and evil Gentile, who might do harm to the Jew, but also to one who is not known for his violence. For we have the general rule that the average Gentile is violent.'

Not that there was no friendly intercourse between members of the various faiths. Salo Baron, who quotes the above rather severe *responsum*, points out that business and cultural interests brought Muslims and non-Muslims closer together than is indicated in the usually accepted sources.

> Certainly the influential Jewish court bankers and counsellors must have been in constant touch with Muslim officials. Scholars, too, frequently associated with their colleagues of other faiths, professionally as well as socially. Only thus was it possible for the famous Jewish physician, Isaac Israeli, to receive instruction from a distinguished Muslim doctor, and in turn impart his knowledge to Muslim as well as Jewish pupils, some of whom achieved fame in their own right. And master–pupil relationships at that time approximated close family ties! . . . Ordinary Jews, too, often attended non-Jewish festivities and family celebrations, and entertained Muslim friends in their homes. . . .'[3]

The most striking example of this Muslim–Jewish 'complicity', whereby a purportedly discriminatory measure against *dhimmis* was welcomed by its alleged victims, was perhaps in the sphere of taxation. There are numerous records of acts of humiliation connected with the payment of taxes by the *dhimmis*. But the Jewish community never sought to free itself from state taxation. 'Its enlightened leadership', Baron reports, 'fully realized that the *dhimmis*' fiscal contributions were their main *raison d'être* from the standpoint of the Muslim state and society.' A story about the Baghdadi Jewish banker Netira, though apocryphal in character, well reflects this awareness. The story goes that when the Caliph al-Mu'tadhid expressed his wish to relieve the Jews of all special taxes, Netira consented only to a reduction of the tax to its original size, pleading: 'Through the tax the Jew insures his existence. By eliminating it, you would give free rein to the populace to shed Jewish blood.'

In no field, however, did the wide discrepancy between written law and real life become clearer than in the business of appointing Jews and other non-Muslims to public office. As far as the Jews were concerned, during the first phases of the Muslim conquest they had little to offer by way of administrative or even financial experience, having been kept out of such employment by their Persian masters for a long time. However, the caliphs began enlisting the services of Jews as counsellors and organizers of tax collection, and when the Christians were suspected of sympathy towards Byzantium – which was posing a growing danger to the Muslims – the Jewish share in these and other administrative activities tended to increase. Records, however, are few and somewhat wanting even when they are available, since they usually concentrate on the powerful and the exalted officials and neglect the lower echelons of officialdom, where Jews no doubt had a sizeable share. Both Muslim and Jewish sources speak almost solely about prominent communal leaders and officials, while poems composed in honour of some benefactor or patron of the arts obviously fail to refer to lowly employees.

With regard to private enterprise, the records speak mainly of banking and commerce. One of the more interesting stories about such Jewish activities concerns the rise to power and influence of a Baghdadi Jewish family. It all starts with the career of two bankers, Aaron ben Amram and Joseph ben Phinehas, who started out by being employed by al-Khaqani, a minister of the Caliph al-Muqtadir, to run certain financial errands. Some fifteen years thereafter, about the year 892, Joseph's son-in-law Netira rendered a service to the Treasury by helping track down a high-ranking embezzler. This was in the days of the Caliph al-Mu'tadhid, whose minister was on record as having written to his caliph: 'Not because of any sympathy on my part for Judaism or Christianity did I take the unbelievers into civil service, but because I found them to be more faithfully attached to thy dynasty than Muslims.' It appears that on that occasion Netira behaved with such magnanimity towards the caliph and his chief advisers that the monarch rewarded him with great gratitude. As a result, a story started circulating about Elijah's appearance to the ruler in his sleep in an attempt to prevent a threatening anti-Jewish decree. The decree having been withdrawn, the chronicler of the tale goes on to recount:

> And Israel lived in peace and without disturbance during the remaining nine and a half years of Al-Mu'tadhid's reign. They wore black clothes like the Abbasid family, the Gentiles lived in good relations with them and enjoyed no superior status above them. Only some of the Sufi mystics behaved haughtily towards them and maltreated them, but these were severely punished by the authorities. After Al-Mu'tadhid's death, his son Al-Muqtadir [the chronicler here skipped Al-Muqtafi's reign, 902–8] ascended the throne. Netira remained with the Caliph in the same post for more than eight years until his death, may God have mercy on him. He was succeeded by his sons, Sahl and Isaac, since he had had no other children, male or female.

Obviously this chronicle leaves many questions unanswered and its author is frequently in error. There is, however, a good deal of outside testimony to show that the tale contains a solid kernel of truth. Thanks to research conducted by Professor Walter Fischel, we now know a good deal about the banking firm established by the two partners Aaron and Joseph and the nature of the mercantile transactions it engaged in. The two, we are told, derived their wealth from their services to the state and the chief minister, and the fortune they amassed was invested in commerce and trade. It was because of these commercial activities that the two are referred to in the Arabic sources as *tujjar*, merchants. The services of the 'sons of Netira' and the 'sons of Aaron' continued uninterrupted through the reigns of three caliphs. The last of these, al-Muqtadir, was himself rather unfriendly to 'unbelievers'. But being a man of good sense and sound judgement – as he was described by an Arab historian of the period – he could not very well dispense with the services of Jewish financiers, especially when he was also reputed to be 'addicted to sensuality and drinking, and profuse in his expenditure'.

But even without reference to this piece of historical 'gossip', the bankers were indispensable to high officials, the caliph and his prime minister because, for one thing, they required applicants to remit deposits to their bankers. These remittances were often of obscure origin, consisting of bribes and other unlawful income and the depositors were, therefore, anxious to keep such matters secret. One financial scandal connected with the name of a famous vizier (prime minister) offers a good example of this type of banker's activity. The vizier, Muhassin ibn al-Furat, deposited considerable sums of money with Aaron ben Amram throughout his term of office. After his downfall, he confessed to having banked the sum of 160,000 dinars – and when the Caliph al-Mu'tadhid summoned the bankers and asked them to reveal the state of his discredited vizier's account with them they mentioned the same sum. The money was then duly confiscated and transferred to the caliph's private account. An enquiry revealed that the vizier had increased his wealth by transmitting confiscated money to his own secret account with the bankers instead of to the public exchequer. It is curious to note that no action of any kind seems to have been taken against Aaron and his son as a result of these shady transactions; but the whole affair could not have been pleasant for them.

A far simpler and legitimate banking activity the brothers engaged in was the transmission of funds by such modern means as letters of credit and bills, in addition to cash payments. We first hear of the custom of paying debts by such means in the tenth century, and it is quite feasible that Jewish bankers and merchants had a considerable share in originating this method of payment. These Jewish businessmen were, after all, dispersed all over the Muslim Empire and beyond, and in this way they must have become a link between countries in commercial as well as intellectual spheres. We know from Jewish sources that the gifts and contributions sent by pious individuals and communities for the upkeep of the Babylonian academies in the *Geonic* period were conveyed by such bills or cheques, and that such payment facilities accompanied the questions addressed to the *Geonim* by outside individuals and communities on legal and ritual matters. It is worth noting, in this connection, that this method of transferring money was not quite in keeping with Talmudic rules and regulations; however, owing to its convenience and general acceptance the *Geonic* authorities managed to find some Talmudic justification for it and raised no objections to its use.

The third and last major type of service rendered by these Jewish bankers was perhaps the most unpleasant of them all; it concerned the supply of funds for special projects, such as military purposes. In such cases, the vizier used to turn to these bankers for loans. There is evidence to show that the main importance of these bankers in the economy of the empire was their ability to supply funds and loans in considerable quantities. We hear of the Vizier al-Furat summoning Joseph ben Phinehas and asking him to advance money to the officials of the Ahwaz province for two months. The banker hesitated, pleading that two months was too long a period for such a loan and that he could not afford it. After long negotiations the vizier managed to persuade Joseph to grant the loan for one month.

Another more instructive example is provided by certain transactions between al-Furat's successor, the Vizier 'Ali ibn 'Isa, concerning a loan for the consolidation of the public budget. The letter sent by this vizier to the Jewish bankers reads in full:

> Do you want to avoid my inflicting penalties on you that may affect you and your heirs for ever? I shall only refrain from doing so in consideration of a matter that will cause you no damage whatsoever. At the beginning of each month I need an amount of 30,000 dinars, which must be paid within the first six days to the infantry troops. However, I am usually not in possession of such a sum, either on the first or on the second day of the month. I want you, therefore, to advance on the first of each month a loan of 150,000 dirhams, an amount which you, as you know, will get back in the course of the month from the Ahwaz revenue. For the administration of the Ahwaz revenue belongs to you, and these funds (due from Ahwaz) are a permanent advance of money to you, to which I am going to add (as security) the sum of 20,000 dinars that are payable every month by Hamid ibn 'Abbas. This will be the compensation for the first instalment, and I shall be relieved of a heavy burden.

From this letter, in which threat and admonition are used to good effect, and from Arabic and various Judeo–Arabic sources, we can safely conclude that these 'royal bankers' performed tasks analogous to those of our modern 'national banks'. The need for these bankers was very real. The taxes, which came from all parts of the empire, were paid in different coins (when they were paid in cash) and were transferred by letters of credit; loans were to be obtained for government expenditure in times of emergency; bribes and other illicit sources of the viziers' income had to be channelled through safe and trusted hands. All these tasks appear to have been performed by the banking firm of Aaron ben Amram and Joseph ben Phinehas to the satisfaction of a succession of viziers and caliphs. Their services were so indispensable, that when in 908 the Caliph al-Muqtadir invoked the now almost forgotten Muslim rule forbidding the employment of non-Muslims in the government administration, he decided to exempt bankers and physicians.

When Netira, who became related to ben Phinehas by marrying one of his daughters, died in 916, his son Sahl inherited his post. But in the later years of the reign of al-Muqtadir the role of the banking house of Netira was eclipsed by the firm of ben Amram and ben Phinehas, the latter being Sahl's grandfather. As we have seen, this firm served the Vizier ibn al-Furat first as a private bank and later as a royal bank, both in Baghdad and in Ahwaz. With such great financial power and influence, did these Jewish bankers manage to influence events, especially those affecting their community? Did they constitute some sort of pressure group? Are we to take at face value the few tales told in Judeo–Arabic documents about the beneficial effects on the fortunes of Babylonian Jewry from the good relations these bankers had with the seat of power and the help they no doubt could and did furnish to the administration in its hour of need? Opinions vary greatly on this point. One scholar, writing recently, believes the answer to these questions must be negative. 'They [the Jewish bankers] had neither the resources the tax-farmers had nor could they aspire to political power as those other great financiers did. The tax-farmers had become chiefs of the administration in their provinces, had guards and retainers, and, what is more important, their profits were much greater.'[4]

CHAPTER 13

Baghdad's Jewish Population

One of the most significant developments in the life of the Jews of Mesopotamia following the Muslim occupation was the entrenchment and institutionalization of the *Gaonate*. Though not a new institution, being related to the academies of Sura and Pumbeditha in the first place, the *Gaonate* in the seventh and eighth centuries acquired an importance and played a role in Jewish life which was world-wide in its influence.

As we have seen earlier, the *Gaon* was someone who presided over a school, a *yeshivah* or academy where Law was taught. As time passed, however, the *Gaonate* became a great deal more than a mere academic institution and came to depend less and less on scholarly attainment; some of the *Geonim*, in fact, continued to enjoy pre-eminence within the framework of the academy despite the fact that they were intellectually inferior to some of the scholars in their employ.

> Like the earlier Palestinian Patriarchs or like the Exilarchs, the Geonim enjoyed their dignity and authority not necessarily because of their excellence, but because of family connections. The office was in effect hereditary. Geonim like Exilarchs levied taxes, appointed judges and communal officers for the districts over which they had jurisdiction. What in preceding centuries had been essentially a scholars' forum was now almost literally a Sanhedrin, whose chief not only expressed views but expected his decisions to be enforced, whose personnel's influence was not dependent on talent or erudition, but on established prerogative.[1]

One of the main activities of the academies of Sura and Pumbeditha – and accordingly one of the most significant functions of their heads, the *Geonim* – was answering queries coming from Jewish communities far and near. These answers were given in a form later to become known as *teshuboth* (*responsa*), and many of these, sent to communities throughout the Diaspora, have survived. The questions coming in were extremely diversified and touched upon the whole range of law and upon the conclusions to be drawn from the extended discussions in the

Talmud, or upon the plain meaning of a Talmudic phrase, *halakhic* or *aggadic*. Some of these queries were about a word or point in the Scriptures, some turned on the order of prayer, others focused on a point of dogma, and still others dealt with points of history. Copies of the answers were mostly kept by the senders, and where these were lost or destroyed scholars have found some of the originals, which were no doubt cherished and preserved by the recipient communities or individuals. Moreover, the *teshuboth* were often read in public, in synagogues and schools, and the recipients permitted transcripts to be made and carried from one seat of learning to another. Subsequently these were assembled by various hands and copied and distributed in volumes according to subject, author or place of origin, and it was upon their authority that the early and later codes were constructed.

The rapid growth and the sheer scope of these replies – later to be known under the general title of '*responsa* literature' – can only be fully grasped against the background of Jewish life in those days outside Mesopotamia, Palestine and, to a lesser extent, Egypt. There Jews lived mostly in small groups in far distant places. They were also on the whole new arrivals, mostly fugitives from Roman persecution, or adventurous souls out to try their luck in new lands. It would seem that these Jews, who in the first stages of their settlement were usually too busy eking out a livelihood and building a home for themselves to bother too much about such things, eventually began to feel isolated as Jews. They and their children no doubt wanted to know where they came from, their history, their obligations as Jews, their heritage and their identity. They wanted to know what legal guides and aids they had to help them and their communal leaders and rabbis overcome everyday problems which they had to face and resolve.

Another difficulty was posed by the Talmud itself – a work too unwieldy for the average Jew to make practical use of in order to arrive at concrete conclusions and workable decisions. The earliest compendious code, prepared to help the uninitiated, followed the same unsystematic order of the Talmud; it was compiled by Rabbi Yehudai, a blind scholar who succeeded to the *Gaonate* of Sura in 760. A contemporaneous work of a different order, known as *she'iltoth* (questions, problems), was compiled by Rabbi Aha of Shabha, who left Babylonia for Palestine in protest against the appointment of a younger colleague as master of Pumbeditha. This latter work consisted of a series of weekly discourses following the order of the Torah, in which legal matter was interwoven with homilies. On the basis of these two works there arose the so-called 'Great Halakhoth', which passed through various stages of compilation and was to enjoy such popularity that students were loath to consult the Talmud at first hand.[2]

If such was the case in Babylonia and Palestine it is not difficult to imagine how far more difficult it used to be in the Dispersion. Even where the order of the synagogue service was concerned there was much uncertainty in those far-away Jewish communities. At the request of the community of Lucena, in Spain, for instance, a brief arrangement of the daily blessings was prepared by Rabbi Natronai, the *Gaon* of Sura, around the middle of the ninth century. The first complete Order of Prayers, however, was prepared some two decades later by Natronai's successor to the Sura *Gaonate*, Rabbi Amram – also for the benefit of the communities in Spain. Though the liturgical pieces were reproduced in full in this new Order, the real purpose of the work was to incorporate all the regulations appertaining to the synagogue service, thereby answering to the needs of these distant communities. The material was thus culled both from the Talmud and from the homiletical Midrashim. Cited in the work, too, were the service customs obtaining in the two schools, as well as that followed in Rab's old synagogue at Sura. Pumbeditha too provided guidance and instruction for the Spanish communities, as when the *Gaon* of Pumbeditha, Rabbi Paltoi, sent them some time in the fourth or fifth decade of the ninth century a copy of the Talmud and a collection of Talmudic explanations.[3]

It was thus that a unifying influence was exercised by the Babylonian seats of learning, thereby helping the farthest communities of the West to be brought under the sway of an age-old tradition of which the Talmud was the authoritative expression.

Spain, of course, was not the only country in the West that had Jewish communities in those days. There were communities in what is now France, Germany, North Africa, Italy, the Mediterranean islands and southern Russia. It would not be too exaggerated to say that these communities would probably have been lost completely had the Jews of Babylonia not come to their aid by providing them with what was the only means for survival as Jews. Materially as well as spiritually, the conditions in which these Jewish communities lived were disheartening in the extreme. Most of the lands in the Western part of the world had at one time been part of the Roman Empire and had thus been influenced by the culture of the Greeks and Romans. By the middle of the seventh century, however, all that became a thing of the past.

> In the course of the centuries, barbarian nations invaded this territory, and Greek–Roman culture was all but forgotten. There

were almost no schools for children, let alone for adults. The Jews who lived in these lands were influenced by these conditions. They had no incentive for study, since the little they knew about the Bible and Jewish life was far more than their neighbours knew about the Bible and Christian life. But, since Judaism is impossible without knowledge, there was grave danger that Judaism would be forgotten among the Jews as Greek–Roman culture had been forgotten among the Christians. Nevertheless, though reduced in numbers and living in the midst of the deepest ignorance, many Jews and Jewish communities scattered throughout the then known world survived, largely because of the moral courage and intellectual guidance given them from Babylonia and Palestine, where Jewish life and thought were active.[4]

In recent years, our knowledge of *responsa* literature has been enormously enhanced thanks to the work done in sifting, collecting and publishing the huge number of documents and papers 'buried' at the *geniza* discovered in the synagogue of Fostat, Cairo, which was built in the year AD 882. These documents provide ample evidence to show that, from around AD 800 the Jews of the Muslim world looked to the Talmudic academies of Babylonia for information and guidance on subjects as disparate and varied as theological interpretation, current affairs, historical problems and everyday behaviour. The transmission of this material was greatly facilitated by the fact that, throughout the ninth, tenth and eleventh centuries, the Jewish communities in the territories conquered by Islam were in closer contact with one another than they had ever been in the past. Moreover, since the seat of the central Arab government was Baghdad, communication became comparatively easy and steady within the orbit of the capital, just as the problems and enquiries of the various communities were easily relayed to the two leading centres of learning.

Although neither the Exilarchate nor the *Gaonate* was a product of the Islamic era in Babylonia's history, these two institutions flourished and became renowned during the period of Muslim supremacy. However, while the Exilarchs and their office grew in pomp and external appearances (while retaining their usual administrative responsibilities *vis-à-vis* the authorities), it was the *Geonim* and their academies that gained substantially both in status and function. The Exilarchs continued to appoint judges, impose and execute penalties, see to the collection of taxes, and generally act as symbol and vehicle of the internal autonomy which the Jews had enjoyed in the Persian period but which was significantly extended under Islam. From the beginning of the Islamic era, which coincided roughly with the completion of the work on the Talmud, until the eleventh century the chief glory of Babylonian Jewry resided in the two ancient academies of Sura and Pumbeditha and the work of their successive heads. (Sura maintained its supremacy even after the academy of Pumbeditha was later transferred to the capital Baghdad, though the head of the latter school attained equality with that of Sura, both now being called *Gaon*.)

The Talmud was completed during a time of oppression and danger. When the crisis passed, and especially following the fall of the Sassanians and the establishment of Muslim rule, the scholars were able to continue their work in tranquillity. However, with only a few additions to make to the text, they now devoted themselves wholly to mastering, interpreting and practically applying its contents and conclusions. Considering that the Talmud was a difficult, intricate and in places rather cryptic work, the *Geonim* had to spend a good deal of time preparing answers to queries coming in from almost the four corners of the world. Some of these academy heads took great pains to research the answer. We have already referred to the work done by Rabbi Amram *Gaon* on the prayer book at the request of the communities in Spain. Another great *Gaon*, Rabbi Sherira of Pumbeditha, was approached by scholars of the North African city of Kairawan seeking information on the origin of the Mishnah and the Talmud. His answer known as *Iggereth Rab Sherira Gaon*, was so well ordered and comprehensive that it remains of great value to students until this day. Because of its unusual length, moreover, it became known as an *iggereth* (epistle) rather than a *teshubah*(answer, *responsum*).

A good deal of the information available to us today about the Babylonian Jewish community and about the Jews of Baghdad at this time derives from the *responsa*. For instance, in his *Iggereth* Sherira *Gaon* relates that when Rab Isaac *Gaon*, in the year 655, headed a procession into the presence of the fourth caliph, 'Ali ibn abi Talib, he was followed by 90,000 Jews, an enormous crowd by any standard and evidence of the density of the Jewish population of Baghdad. Another indication of this density which tends to confirm Sherira's report is evidence gleaned from documents and correspondence found in the Cairo *geniza*, and elsewhere, of the fact that Babylonian Jews emigrated to Egypt in such considerable numbers that they established a separate community and synagogue in Fostat under the name *Kanisat el-'Irakiyyin* or *el-Bablim*. Through the centuries members of this community were to play some leading roles in the life of Eastern Jewry in general and in Egyptian Jewry in particular; and as early as the year 750 one of them, known by his Arabic name of Abu 'Ali Hasan al-Baghdadi, was the leader of his community.

It was during the eighth century that Baghdad became the centre of gravity not only of the Muslim Empire but also of Babylonian Jewish life and learning. In his *Iggereth*, Sherira mentions another native of Baghdad, Rab Isaiah Ha-Levy ben Rab Abba, as occupying the *Geonic* seat of Pumbeditha in the years 796–8. Rab Hai *Gaon*, Sherira's son and successor and an equally eminent scholar, used to include in his *responsa* many bits of information about Baghdadi Jews and their customs. In his book, *A History of the Jews in Baghdad*, David Sassoon cites two of these details. In one of his answers, Rab Hai writes: 'In Baghdad they erect their tabernacles within the synagogues.' In another, the enquirer is told that the Jews of Baghdad used to provide a temporary grave for their dead, and after a time they carried them 'many parsangs' to the wilderness on the western side of Persia. He also writes that in the case of the death of a noble lady the body would be sent to Piri Shabur, also in Persia.

There are numerous such references to Baghdad and its Jews. In one of these, which deals with Baghdad as a seat of justice, the *Gaon* writes: 'In this city, where we now are, namely in Baghdad, no witness is accepted at the non-Jewish courts unless he is intelligent, grown-up, wealthy and free from any suspicion of robbery, falsehood and untruth; and he must also be observant in his religion so as to belong to those who are known as El-Mu'addilin.' The Arabic *mu'addil*, singular of *mu'addilin*, can be freely rendered as 'just', 'balanced' or 'fair-minded'; Sassoon sees this *responsum* as 'an eloquent witness to the mutual high esteem in which Jews and Muslims held each other', no doubt because it indicated that Muslim judges honoured the testimony only of Jews who respected and observed the commandments of their own religion.[5]

Shortly after its emergence as a capital and metropolis, Baghdad gradually became the seat, first of the Exilarch and then of the *Geonim* themselves. The first significant change occurred when the Exilarchs, who up till then had resided in Nehardea, Sura or Pumbeditha, removed their courts from these residences of the *Geonim* to the metropolis. This move was natural in the sense that, being mainly secular-political representatives of their community, their proper place was in the vicinity of the temporal rulers rather than in the shadow of the spiritual guides and the elected leaders of their congregations. Nevertheless, this change of abode proved to be an impediment to the smooth and expedient relationship between the lay and the religious leaderships of Babylonian Jewry. The *Geonim* of the two great academies, situated as they were one to the south and the other to the north, had to make the long journey to the capital to attend some of the more important services, celebrations and initiations. We have a description of one of these services from Rabbi Nathan Ha-Babli. The service at the synagogues was attended by the Exilarch, accompanied and assisted by the two *Geonim* of Sura and Pumbeditha; all took an active part in the service and in the reading of the Law. The names of the Exilarch and the two *Geonim* were specially mentioned in a prayer appropriate to the occasion. Fragments of such a prayer, and of the sermon delivered on the occasion, survive partly in the documents of the Cairo *geniza*, and according to Sassoon the whole service must have made 'a lasting impression on all who had the privilege of being present'. As to the purpose of these annual services, the available sources indicate that this, apart from the spiritual side, 'was to renew the relations between the Exilarch and the Academies, to solve political questions which arose between Babylonian Jewry and the government, to define the administration and organization of communal life, and, finally, to advert to the relations between the Jews of Babylonia and the Jews abroad.'[6] The questions and discussions varied in volume and in importance according to the respective status and abilities of the leading men.

There were other occasions on which the *Geonim* had to leave their academies and travel to the capital, as when a new Exilarch was elected and installed. We have a description of one such ceremony, supplied by the same Ha-Babli cited above. On such an occasion the two *Geonim*, the prominent members of the academies and the lay heads of the community gathered at the residence of one of the most prominent members of the community, where they officially elected a descendant of David to the elevated office. The Exilarch, whose election and installation are described by Ha-Babli, happened to be of the house of Netira, but the description of the position and the esteem in which he was held both inside and outside the community applies to all those who held the office. The installation service and the annual Sabbath service, together with the festivities and banquets accompanying the religious ceremonies, were of considerable importance in the communal life of the Jews. Great honour was lavished on the person of the Exilarch by his co-religionists when he appeared in the streets of Baghdad on his way for an audience with the caliph or his ministers. Officials of the government, too, treated the Exilarch with the same measure of honour and respect.[7]

Ha-Babli's eye-witness account was written in the ninth century. We have a similar account, written almost three centuries later by a Jewish traveller, which imparts an even more colourful impression of the office of the Exilarchate under Islam. Benjamin of Tudela in Navarre was in Baghdad about the year 1168, and his account throws much light on the life of the Jews of that city in the twelfth century, his itinerary having taken place during the reign of the Abbasid Caliph al-Mustanjid (1160–70). Following are extracts from the standard English translation by Marcus Nathan Adler, with certain slight changes:

> In Baghdad there are forty thousand Jews, and they dwell in security, prosperity, and honour under the great Caliph, and amongst them are great sages, the heads of the Academies engaged in the study of the Law. At the head of the great academy is the chief rabbi, Rabbi Samuel the son of Ali. He is the 'Head of the Academy which is the Excellency of Jacob'. He is a Levite, and traces his pedigree back to Moses our teacher.[8]

The *Gaon* Samuel ben Ali held office *c.* 1164–93, and after the death of the Exilarch he became the real ruler of the Jews in the Islamic East. Benjamin lists the names of nine other scholars who devoted their time to teaching and communal administration, and goes on to say:

> These are the ten scholars, and they do not engage in any other work than communal administration; and all the days of the week they judge the Jews their countrymen, except on Monday, when they all appear before the Chief Rabbi Samuel, the Head of the Academy Excellency of Jacob, who in conjunction with the other scholars judges all those that appear before him. And at the head of them all is Daniel, the son of Hisdai, who is styled 'Our Lord, the Head of the Exile of all Israel'.

Daniel, the Exilarch, was in office from about 1160 to about 1174; and Benjamin reports that he 'possesses a book of pedigrees going back as far as David, King of Israel'. The Jews, he continues, call him 'our Lord, Head of the Exile', and the Muhammedans call him 'Sayidna ben Daoud (our Master, descendant of David)' who, we are told, 'has been invested with authority over all the congregations of Israel at the hands of Amir al-Muminin, the Lord of Islam (the Caliph)'.

> For thus Muhammed commanded concerning him and his descendants; and he granted him a seal of office over all the

> congregations that dwell under his rule, and ordered that everyone, whether Muhammedan or Jew or belonging to any other nation in his dominion, should rise up before the Exilarch and salute him, and that anyone who refuses to rise up should receive one hundred stripes. And every Thursday when he goes to pay a visit to the great Caliph, horsemen – non-Jews as well as Jews – escort him, and heralds proclaim in advance: 'Make way before our Lord, the son of David, as is due unto him', the Arabic words being *amlu tariq la-Sayidna ben Daoud*. He is mounted on a horse, and is attired in robes of silk and embroidery with a large turban on his head, and from the turban is suspended a long white cloth adorned with a chain upon which the seal of Muhammed is engraved. Then he appears before the Caliph and kisses his hand, and the Caliph rises and places him on a throne which Muhammed had ordered to be made in honour of him, and all the Muhammedan princes who attend the court of the Caliph rise up before him. And the Exilarch is seated on his throne opposite to the Caliph, in compliance with the command of Muhammed to give effect to what is written in the Law: 'The sceptre shall not depart from Judah, nor the rulers' staff from between his feet, as long as men come to Shiloh; and unto him shall the obedience of the people be.'

This last verse is taken by Benjamin from Genesis 49:10, which Jews have usually interpreted to mean that there will always be a Jewish ruler somewhere till the Messiah comes. Going into more detail, Benjamin writes:

> The authority of the Exilarch extends over all the communities of Babylon, Persia, Khorasan and Sheba, which is el-Yemen, and Diyar Kalach [Beker] and all the land of Mesopotamia, and over the dwellers in the mountains of Ararat and the land of the Alans [in the Caucasus], which is a land surrounded by mountains and has no outlet except by the iron gates which Alexander made, but which were afterwards broken. Here are the people called Alani. His authority extends also over the land of the Sawir, and the land of the Turks, unto the mountains of Asveh and the land of Gurgan [near the Caspian Sea], the inhabitants of which are called Gurganim who dwell by the river Gihon, and these are the Girgashites who follow the Christian religion. Further it extends to the gates of Samarkand, the land of Tivet, and the land of India. In respect of all these countries the Exilarch gives the communities power to appoint rabbis and overseers who come unto him to be consecrated and to receive his authority.

The overseer referred to here is the *hazzan*, who in those days was an important official of the synagogue. Benjamin of Tudela goes on to report that these overseers bring the Exilarch 'offerings and gifts from the end of the earth'. The Exilarch, we are further told, 'owns hospices, gardens, and plantations in Babylon, and much land inherited from his fathers, and no one can take his possessions from him by force. He has a fixed weekly revenue arising from the hospices of the Jews, the markets and the merchants, apart from that which is brought to him from far-off lands.'

> The man is very rich, and wise in the Scriptures as well as in the Talmud, and many Israelites dine at his table every day. At his installation, the Exilarch gives much money to the Caliph, to the princes and the officials. On the day that the Caliph performs the ceremony of investing him with authority, the Exilarch rides in the second of the royal equipages, and is escorted from the palace of the Caliph to his own house with timbrels and fifes. The Exilarch appoints the Head of the Academy by placing his hand upon his head, thus installing him in his office. The Jews of the city are learned men and very rich.

In speaking of the Exilarch's great wealth, Benjamin was referring to the time of his itinerary. Daniel the Exilarch, however, complained in a letter dated 1161 of his poverty; but that was seven years before Benjamin came to Baghdad. The statement, too, that the Jews of Baghdad were 'very rich' must be taken with a sizeable pinch of salt. Turning to another aspect of Jewish life in the city, Benjamin writes:

> In Baghdad there are twenty-eight Jewish synagogues, situated either in the city itself or in al-Karkh [the business section of greater Baghdad] on the other side of the Tigris; for the river divides the metropolis into two parts. The great synagogue of the Exilarch has columns of marble of various colours overlaid with silver and gold, and on these columns are sentences of the Psalms in golden letters. And in front of the ark are about ten steps of marble; on the topmost step are the seats of the Exilarch and of the princes of the House of David. The city of Baghdad is twenty miles in circumference, situated in a land of palms, gardens, and plantations, the like of which is not to be found in the whole land of Babylon. People come thither with merchandise from all lands. Wise men live there, philosophers who know all manner of wisdom, and magicians expert in all manner of witchcraft.

CHAPTER 14

Messianism and Karaism: Rabbinic Judaism Challenged

Speculation, the probing of things secret and mysterious, mysticism, and finally messianism – these are but different though widely and radically divergent degrees of the same phenomenon. The Jews of Babylonia, before as well as after the close of the Talmudic era, were constantly exposed to such influences, and though they were fully occupied with legal deductions and biblical and mishnaic interpretation, they could not withstand the lure of what was taking place in their midst and on their borders. Though they tended clearly to disdain probing into things secret, to try to lift the veil from 'what is above and what is below, what was in the beginning, and what will be in the end', some of their best intellects showed clear signs of restlessness. The common people were the first to come in contact and be affected by the crude superstitions of Chaldaic lore and custom, but even the learned could not entirely shake these off. This was true also of the wild speculation then rife among the sects on the borders of Christianity, and later of the no less intensive, almost feverish religious, juridical and theological disputations which plagued Islam at a fairly early stage.

> The very soil was impregnated with a succession of religious systems in which, as in Manicheism, mystic notions were blended, for the elect to take hold on. Jewish mysticism in the times of the Gaons revelled in the contemplation of the divine majesty, which took on grossly anthropomorphic forms. Those of sober mind were hostile to the fantastic writings of this genre. Nevertheless the boast of mystic profundity and of intimate intercourse with the prophet Elijah secured in 814 the headship of the school at Pumbeditha to the aged Joseph ben Abba. His successor Abraham ben Sherira (816–28) was reputed to be able to prognosticate events from the soft murmur of palms on calm days.[1]

From this to the claims of the composers of apocalypses and even to those of the false Messiahs the distance was not so great. Indeed, in the

Geonic period many new apocalypses were composed, similar in form and style to those of the Maccabean and Roman periods. Dealing with eschatology (the doctrine of the last things) and comprising such works as the *Book of Jubilees*, the *Book of Enoch*, the *Book of Zerubbabel* and others, apocalypses were written mostly anonymously by a class of visionaries who directed their hopes to a future in which the present temporal and religious world order would give way to a supernatural and eternal world brought about by divine intervention through some universal catastrophe. In these booklets, the eschatological future is always depicted as being connected with the coming of a heavenly Messiah, an event which is invariably claimed to occur just a little ahead of the date of writing. To this consummation, man cannot contribute it any way; no action of his can serve either to speed it on or to retard it. The event has been predetermined from the beginning in the counsels of God, and all that the faithful are bidden to do is to have patience and trustingly await the miraculous deliverance and the reward that is theirs.

The *Geonic* period also witnessed the revival of religious mysticism, a phenomenon well known to Islam in its post-conquest days, and which took the form of a systematic effort to experience the immediate presence of God. The phenomenon was not quite new to Judaism; it was known in Talmudic times though in a different form – the mysteries of creation, the lore of God's chariot-throne. But the rabbis regarded these matters as deep secrets into which only the most soberly pious could be initiated. With the passage of time, and starting with the eighth century, what used to be committed as secret doctrine to a privileged few became the manifest pursuit of the many. The mystics now developed a regular technique of contemplation, and they recorded their inner experience in documents which furnished detailed descriptions of the progress of the soul through various levels of the spiritual world until it arrives at the very chariot of God and knows the unspeakable bliss of the Divine Presence.[2]

What distinguishes Jewish mysticism from its Muslim and Christian counterparts is a clear tendency towards messianism. This form of mysticism sees the whole of creation engaged in a struggle for redemption from evil and seeks salvation in the establishment of the universal kingdom of God. With the spread of this messianic streak, people's souls became accessible to anyone who appealed to their imagination. And these were not in short supply, especially in times of hardship. There were those who claimed to 'calculate the end' by deftly manipulating the obscure numbers in the Book of Daniel.

In the more distant provinces of Persia, in the eighth century, Jewish masses were stirred by a false Messiah who came from Ispahan and who held out the promise of restoration of the Holy Land and bade his followers abandon their possessions. This pretender to the messianic dignity, who was a tailor by profession nicknamed Abu Issa, managed to gather an army of Jews, who though poorly equipped trusted in their leader's miraculous powers and started their march to Palestine. One version of Abu Issa's story has it that, faced with an army of non-Jews, he roped his followers off and announced that the enemy could not get inside the circle. The miracle duly worked, we are told; but in a battle which was finally fought with their enemies the Jews were badly beaten and scattered, while Abu Issa chose to die by his own hands.

A disciple of Abu Issa's, Yudghan of Hamadan, was not daunted; he proclaimed himself a prophet and a forerunner of the Messiah, and some of his Jewish followers acclaimed him as 'shepherd' (*al-Ra'i*). According to one report, he was a shepherd by profession. In the end Yudghan was also defeated and killed. It is noteworthy that most of these pretenders, and their followers, used to make light of various rabbinic precepts, some of them even ruling that the observance of the Sabbath and festivals was not obligatory in exile. They were also generally given to ascetic exercises and abstained from meat and wine and increased the number of daily prayers.

Common to all these movements was one form or another of anti-Talmudism, and opposition to the line of traditional development which the Talmud connoted. But this undercurrent of anti-rabbinism and anti-Talmudism was itself not new. Already during the Amoraic period there were some murmurings against the sages and their work of interpretation and preservation of the Oral Law. 'What good have the sages ever done us?' was a complaint heard in certain quarters long before the completion of the Talmud. Exactly what the resentment was directed against is not clear, for – as we are told in *Sanhedrin* 99b f. – even as the complainers and critics disapproved of the law which forbade the eating of ravens, so they objected to the permission to eat dove's meat.

These anti-rabbinic tendencies, which characterized all the apocalyptic, mystical and messianic movements, failed to leave a lasting mark or in any serious way affect the authority of the Talmud – with the exception of one, Karaism, with which we will deal in this chapter and which managed to survive up till our own day though its effects on Jewish life and Jewish theology remains at best marginal. Rabbinic Judaism, in short, managed to weather one crisis after another, starting with the rise of various messianic pretenders before the Muslim conquest and continuing with an assortment of sectarian movements which emerged under the impact of Muhammed's successful challenge to the existing political and religious order. Salo Baron remarks on the relative paucity and historical insignificance of these movements, calling the phenomenon 'amazing'. He explains: 'With all the research hitherto done by modern scholars, intensely interested in any form of Jewish heterodoxy as well as in yearnings for the return to Zion, only about half a dozen non-Karaite heresiarchs and less than a score of messianic pretenders, including all the former, are known to us by name in the long and crucial period of seven centuries following the religious consolidation of the Babylonian Talmud.'[3]

During this 700-year period, one of the main tasks of the Babylonian Jewish leadership was to guard important Jewish principles and precepts from outside influences, especially those emanating from Persia. For the truth is that, along with whatever indigenous echoes excited their imagination, the Jews of Babylonia and of Persia were exposed to ample stimulus from a variety of non-Jewish sects, particularly from the far-off provinces of Persia.

> The old Persian Empire [writes one modern Jewish historian] had for centuries been the battle ground of numerous conflicting cultures. The ancient religion of Babylon still exerted its influence, surviving in various sects, such as the Mandeans, and transmitted through other channels. The religion of Zoroaster had reigned supreme for centuries. Persia was the home of Manicheism which, despite all persecutions, still had numerous adherents and spread its powerful influence far beyond the boundaries of Persia. The tenets of Mazdak outlived the destruction of its believers and continued as an important spiritual factor. The Neoplatonic and Gnostic doctrines, which very early asserted their influence through the medium of the above sects, had been, as it were, personally introduced in the middle of the sixth century through the exiled philosophies of Byzantium. Among these agencies must also be counted the ancient paganism or the so-called Sabeism of Harran, whose adherents were also largely represented in Mesopotamia, not to speak of the great Jewish and Christian centres and perhaps Hindu influences. All these variegated elements, often in a modified or mutilated form, found expression in a motley multitude of Shiitic sects with a weird mixture of all possible doctrines and practices which were artificially harmonized with the official religion by means of allegorical interpretation.[4]

It was this Shiite deposit, the writer goes on to demonstrate, that assisted the political anarchy of the eighth century; it also found receptive temperaments in certain contemporary Jewish circles.

The various messianic movements, and the variety of signs of active dissent which surfaced in Mesopotamia and Persia from the seventh century onwards, were based on a strange mixture of ideas and motives. There was, to start with, a desire among a fairly large number of Jews to throw off the yoke of their new Muslim masters – a desire which was somehow bound up with rebelliousness against the Jewish establishment of the day. Secondly, one of the things advocated by the messianic pretenders was a relaxation of the laws of *kashrut* (dietary regulations) as well as some other basic changes and revisions of what was then accepted as normative Judaism. Among these was the call to increase to seven the number of times a man must pray every day, and even the recognition of both Muhammed and Jesus as prophets.

These were rather radical departures from Judaism and some Jewish scholars find it astonishing that they should have found supporters among the common people. Solomon Grayzel has written:

> It merely proves that the influence of ideas current among non-Jews was great among the Jews, and that the power of the Talmud was still weak, since the Geonim had not yet gained control over the spiritual life of the people. Thus the freedom of movement and of contact with their neighbours had served to weaken Jewish unity as long as Jewish knowledge and faith had not counterbalanced the influence of the environment. For generations after the downfall of the false prophets, a considerable number of Jews still believed in them and their principles. In the course of time their followers were either absorbed by the Muhammedans or returned to the Jewish fold. The net result was a loss in Jewish numbers.[5]

But the loss could not have been great quantitatively nor, with the exception of Karaism, was the rift with these sects and movements either long or lasting. As Shahrastani, a contemporary Muslim student of religion, remarks after listing the names and surveying the teachings of a number of Jewish heterodoxies, all Jews, regardless of their sectarian divergence, believed in monotheism, the uniqueness of the Torah revealed to Moses, the observance of the Sabbath, and the coming of the Messiah, 'the shining star, which will illumine the world'.

The *Gaonate*, whose origins can be traced back to the last two decades of the sixth century but which some historians insist on dating only from the year AD 657, no doubt constitutes the most significant development in Jewish history and in the life of Jews world-wide. It is no wonder, therefore, that historians speak of this episode as 'the *Geonic* Period' in Jewish history – a span of just less than five centuries generally fixed as starting with the appointment of the first *Gaon*, the head of the academy of Pumbeditha, in 589 and as ending in 1038 with the death of the last of the *Geonim*, Rab Hai *Gaon*. During this period, calculations show that forty-nine *Geonim* headed the Pumbeditha academy, and forty-two headed the academy of Sura. After Hai's death, the two institutions of *Gaonate* and Exilarchate were combined in the person of the Exilarch, with the result that neither office ever again managed to maintain more than a semblance of its past glory. The man who assumed the enhanced function after Hai's death was the scholarly Exilarch Hezekiah, who perished shortly afterwards as a result of a wave of anti-Jewish persecutions.

Throughout its years of existence the *Gaonate* sustained a number of grave setbacks, beginning as early as the year 767 with the outbreak of the Karaite schism and continuing with periodic fierce clashes between the two supreme authorities, the *Geonim* and the Exilarchs. In order to understand better the Karaite movement, we must try and view it in the context of Jewish religious history as a whole.

In the evolution of Jewish religious thought there had always been two main trends. One of these regarded Judaism as a living, organic tradition, continually growing and developing yet in essence always the same, and represented in every age by its rabbis and teachers; the other viewed it as fixed and immutable, with its final expression in a specific code of law. During the period of the second Temple these two trends were represented respectively by the Pharisees and Sadducees. The former were distinguished from the latter by their adherence to the Oral Law, and were noted for their skilful interpretation of the Torah. The Pharisaic line was continued by the rabbis of the Talmudic period and henceforth by their successors, who together form the tradition of Rabbinic Judaism. It is thus accurate to say that the entire subsequent development of Judaism bears the indelible stamp of Pharisaism.

The other leading trend in Judaism, whose proponents were known as Sadducees, derives its name from the priestly house of Zadok, the ancestors of the Hasmoneans, and is thus connected both with the Hasmonean dynasty and with the Temple hierarchy. The Sadducees' distinctive doctrine was a rejection of the Oral Law and consequently of the work of the rabbis. They emerged at a time in which the contrast became sharply polarized between the non-priestly, popular, rabbinic type of Judaism developed since the days of Ezra and which was close to the life of peasants and artisans, and the more conservative, almost fundamentalist tendencies of a powerful and wealthy priesthood, whose interests coincided with those of the aristocracy and the landowners. It was only natural, therefore, that with the destruction of the Temple the Sadducees should have lost both their ideological and social centre and lapsed into near oblivion.

Although they were virtually finished as a distinct sect in Judaism, the trends which the Sadducees represented continued. Although dormant throughout the Talmudic period, this trend was none the less awaiting an opportune moment to rise to the surface. This was duly furnished by the world-shattering events which had been taking place since the middle of the seventh century with the creation of the Muslim Empire and the fierce controversies that erupted among peoples and sects living in such proximity to the then established centre of Jewish life – Babylonia. These heated controversies were strangely analogous to those that had raged among the Jews throughout their history. They concerned such topics as the genuineness of certain traditions allegedly going back to Muhammed, and they also touched upon the fundamentals of the relation between tradition and Scripture. Watching their close neighbours debating fine points of difference about a *hadith* (a saying reported to have been uttered by Muhammed) and travelling hundreds of miles to verify its authenticity generations after their prophet's death, many an enquiring Jew started wondering about their own Oral Law and whether some of its traditions were not equally doubtful and even spurious. The time, so it seemed to some members of the growing Jewish intelligentsia, was ripe for doctrinal readjustments and for throwing off the shackles of a confining tradition, whose divine origin they now seriously questioned.

It was at this juncture that a personality appeared on the scene that was to sound the keynote for breaking away from tradition and going back to 'fundamentals', namely the Scriptures themselves. According to one tradition emanating from rabbinic sources, the occasion for the rebellion against the rabbis and all they stood for was a dispute over a succession to the office of the Exilarch in the year 767. The story goes that one 'Anan ben David was in the line of succession to the Exilarchate. The two *Geonim*, however, had reason to suspect his orthodoxy, as he had lived for some time in Persia, the centre of a number of Jewish heresies. They therefore chose as the new Exilarch 'Anan's younger brother Hananiah, a man of inferior scholarship and apparently a far more pliable person. The election, as was customary, was duly confirmed by the caliph and Hananiah was installed as

Exilarch in 767. It was 'Anan's refusal to accept this decision that set in motion a chain of developments which resulted in the rise of Karaism, a considerable force in Jewish life and thought which persisted for a number of centuries and spread to every important part of the Jewish world.

The following rabbinic account of the rise of Karaism is curiously preserved for us in a book written by a Karaite, Elijah ben Abraham, and entitled *The Rift between the Karaites and the Rabbanites* (*Hilluk ha-Karaim veha-Rabbanim*). It is possible that the account is an extract from Rab Saadia *Gaon*'s lost Arabic polemic, *Refutation of 'Anan*, written about the year 905, when Saadia was still in Egypt and but twenty-three years of age. Generally speaking, the facts given here are accurate, and the tone itself seems to justify the opinion that the Karaites and the rabbinites – like the Protestants and the Catholics in a later period – 'disliked each other so cordially that it was difficult for either side to write dispassionately'.[6]

> 'Anan [so the rabbinite's account goes] had a younger brother whose name was Hananiah. Now 'Anan was greater than his brother in knowledge of the Torah and older in years, but the schools of the generation were not willing to set him as Exilarch because of the unmitigated unruliness and irreverence which characterized him. The sages, therefore, turned to Hananiah his brother because of his great modesty, shyness, and fear of God, and made him Exilarch. Then 'Anan became incensed, he and every scoundrel that was left of the Sadducean and Boethusian breed, and he secretly determined to make a schism in Judaism because he feared the government of the day. These heretics appointed 'Anan as their Exilarch.
>
> This matter was made known to the authorities on a Sunday and it was ordered that he be put into jail until Friday, when he was to be hanged. There, in the prison, he met a certain Muslim scholar who was also imprisoned and was to be hanged also on that very Friday, for he had rebelled against the religion of Muhammed. The Muslim gave him a piece of advice, and this is what he said to him: 'Are there not in the Torah commands which may permit of two interpretations?' 'Anan answered: 'There certainly are.' Then he said to him: 'Take some point and interpret it differently from those who follow your brother Hananiah; only be sure your partisans agree to it, and don't fail also to give a bribe to the Vizier. Perhaps he will give you permission to speak. Then prostrate yourself and say: "My lord King, have you appointed my brother over one religion or

two?" And when he will answer you: "Over one religion", then say to him: "But I and my brother rule over two different religions!" Then you will surely be saved, if you will only make clear to him the religious differences between your faith and the faith of your brother, and if your followers agree with you. Talk like this and when the King [al-Mansur, 754–75] hears these things, he'll keep quiet.'

'Anan thereupon set out to deceive his own group and said to them: 'Last night Elijah appeared to me in a dream and said to me: "You deserve to die because you have transgressed against that which is written in the Torah." '

Through his sharp sophistry he taught them these things, and in order to save himself from violent death and to win a victory he spent a lot of money bribing his way until the King gave him permission to speak. Then he began saying: 'The religion of my brother is dependent, in making the calendar, on astronomical calculations of the months and year, but my religion is dependent on the actual observation of the new moon and the signs of the ripening grain.' Now since that King made his calculation, too, through actual observation of the new moon and the signs of the ripening grain, he was pacified and reconciled to 'Anan.[7]

Written as it was some 140 years after the event, this narrative must be treated with scepticism. What we learn from it, however, is that after being thrown into prison for insubordination, 'Anan's neck was saved only when he proclaimed himself leader of a new religious denomination, a separate sect – a phenomenon which the government of the day tolerated amongst the *dhimmis*. It is widely thought, incidentally, that the Muslim scholar referred to here was none other than Abu Hanifa, the founder of one of the great schools of Muslim jurisprudence. It remains a moot point, however, whether 'Anan, whose quarrel with the Jewish establishment of the day started as a political struggle for succession, had ever thought of establishing a new sect and of starting a conflict relating to control over the whole domain of Jewish law. According to Baron, 'Anan – like Abu Hanifa – may merely have intended to establish another school of jurisprudence, rather than a sect, and that this was why he evidently refrained from injecting any serious dogmatic deviation from orthodox Judaism.[8]

It is interesting to note that almost all the accounts we have of the rise of the Karaite schism and of the great debates which accompanied it date from at least 130 years after the event. This is true not only of the accounts left by the rabbinites but also of the various defences and pleas written by the Karaites themselves. One such apologia, written at some date between the years 960 and 1000, is by the Jerusalem Karaite Sahl ben Masliah Ha-Kohen; it is included in an openly missionary and propagandist pamphlet entitled *Tokahat Megullah* (*An Open Rebuke*). It is a rather fierce attack on the rabbinic tradition as a whole, and it goes to the core of the Karaite ideology by advising the individual Jew to turn directly to the Bible for guidance and, on the basis of his own reasoning, to determine the laws which he must observe.[9]

One of the more curious aspects of the rise and growth of Karaism was the apparent reluctance of the Jewish establishment of the day to react to it. The first rabbinite leader on record as reacting to the Karaite schism was Natronai bar Hilai *Gaon*, who headed the academy of Sura nearly 100 years after 'Anan challenged the rabbinites – and this only in the form of a *responsum*. Answering some unknown enquirer, the *Gaon* was brief and rather summary in his verdict. 'Anan, he wrote, had instigated his followers to ridicule the words of the Talmudic sages; he promised his followers: 'I shall prepare for you a Talmud of my own'; and he and his followers were heretics who should be 'banished, not allowed to pray with Jews in the synagogue and be segregated until they mend their ways and pledge themselves to observe the customs of the two academies'. Another *Gaon*, Hai ben David of Pumbeditha (890–97), is reported to have translated 'Anan's work into Arabic or Hebrew; but neither he nor his father, who collaborated with him in the project, could find 'anything of which they could not trace the source in the doctrine of the rabbinites'.

This somewhat startling conclusion may have meant nothing more than that the rabbinites wanted it to be noted that 'Anan utterly lacked originality. The evidence, however, points to something far more significant. The rabbinite leadership was either no match for 'Anan and his new doctrines or it simply did not consider the schism to be a serious threat to the established order. The fact that the rabbinites evinced little concern about the new schism, and the lack of any serious reaction to it for close on a century, belies the idea that the rise of Karaism shook the Jewish community to its foundations, and that the danger of a complete breakdown was averted only by the intervention of the militant and superlatively gifted Saadia *Gaon*.[10]

Baron goes even further and calls this idea 'part of a scholarly mythology which has grown up since the days of Pinsker and Graetz'. He raises a major issue in Babylonian Jewish historiography when he adds:

> Blinded by the flashes of light thrown on the theretofore obscure Karaite history by newly discovered documents, spurious as well as genuine, the generation of scholars living between 1850 and 1880 proceeded to rewrite in a 'pan-Karaite' vein the entire cultural history of the Jewish people in the crucial centuries after the rise of Islam. Before long all the revolutionary discoveries of that period in Hebrew philology, Bible exegesis, and philosophy were ascribed to Karaites or, at best, to Rabbinites reacting to the rise of the new sect. These exaggerations of literary history have . . . been effectively disproved by more recent painstaking research which, at times, went to the opposite extreme of denying even some indubitable pioneering merits of Karaite authors. But there remained the residual conviction of the great impact of Karaite propaganda on all Jewish life and letters of the period. This view, too, requires considerable qualification.[11]

However, even if Baron's radically dissenting version of this episode in Babylonian Jewish history is completely valid, and historians like Graetz and Pinsker grossly overestimated the importance of the Karaites, the fact remains that by the time Saadia wrote his first attack on Karaism some 140 years after the outbreak of the schism the Karaites were not only still there but were growing in numbers and in intellectual vigour alike. The source of this vitality seems to have resided in one of the Karaites' main articles of faith, namely their refusal to bow to authority of any kind, not excluding that of their leaders. It was the boast of 'Anan's followers and heirs that no two of their number agreed. 'Anan himself had undermined authority by his ambiguous ruling: 'Search the Scriptures diligently, and lean not upon my opinion.' Anyone might interpret Scripture according to his own lights, and no one's ruling need be accepted by others. 'Anan, however, continued to be venerated by later generations among those who attached themselves to his movement, and he was looked up to as the 'principal teacher'. Although in the course of time the 'Ananites disappeared, making way for men who governed their lives in accordance with newer teachings, 'Anan remained the Karaites' first teacher and his person was invested with a legendary halo.

The movement started by 'Anan ben David in 767 was not originally called Karaism, a term derived from the word *Mikrah* (Scripture). The term was coined only in the third decade of the ninth century, with the emergence of a second prominent Karaite, Benjamin of Nehawend. This man exercised such an influence, and his contribution was so crucial, that some historians believe that were it not for him the movement would have disintegrated completely; so much so, indeed, that when Arab chroniclers spoke of the Karaites they referred to them as 'the companions of 'Anan and Benjamin'. It was in the days of Benjamin's leadership that his followers came to be called 'Children of Scripture' (*Bene Mikrah*), and subsequently 'Scripturists' or 'Scripturalists' (*Karaim*). With his profounder understanding and his milder approach, Benjamin helped consolidate the movement; he abandoned his sect's traditionally unquestioning opposition to the rabbinites and did not hesitate even to adopt a number of rabbinic ordinances or accept rabbinic interpretations of the Law which 'Anan had rejected. 'I have compiled for you this Code', he declared in the introduction to *Benjamin's Portion*, which he wrote in Hebrew, 'that you may judge your Karaite brethren. I cite in every instance the Scriptural source. As for those laws which the Rabbinites follow, but for which I was not able to find support in the Scriptures, I wrote them as well, that you might follow them if you so choose.' Thus Benjamin, true Karaite that he was, left his followers free to disregard his own authority.

Another outstanding Karaite leader and theoretician was Daniel ibn Musa al-Qumisi, who rose to prominence at the end of the ninth century. Austere and somewhat more limited in intellectual range than Benjamin, al-Qumisi in his later years became radically opposed to 'Anan and the 'Ananites. In contrast to Benjamin, he rejected reason as a means of deciding religious law. He spurned the allegorical method so widespread in his day and adhered strictly to the simple, natural sense of the Scriptural text. He was, however, far from consistent on this point. To give one example: taking literally such biblical phrases as 'I am the Lord that healeth thee' (Exodus 15:26), many 'Ananites roundly rejected medical treatment of any kind, and al-Qumisi agreed with them. However, he rejected Benjamin's vision of a divine government of the world through intermediary 'angels' – a rejection which did not result from an excess of rationalism. Indeed, a later Karaite intellectual, al-Qirqisani, censures al-Qumisi for his inconsistency in employing rigorous logical reasoning to the interpretation of Scripture and yet being 'dissatisfied with rationalism to such an extent that he reviles both it and its devotees many times in his work'.

With al-Qumisi the first period in the history of the Karaite sect came to a close. However, despite the movement's persistent efforts to arrive at a measure of fixity in matters of religious observance, it was hesitant about committing itself to the reign of authority. As a matter of fact, neither in 'Anan nor in Benjamin, nor in their various successors, do we reach a crystallization of authority or a recognized legal code. Nevertheless, by the middle of the tenth century or thereabouts the writings of such teachers as Benjamin and al-Qumisi formed part of an equipment which the Karaites had as they moved to more favourable centres. 'A beginning had been made; a literature was being produced, both in Aramaic and in Hebrew; the movement had a distinct identity; it had already included a few forceful personalities. It could afford, therefore, to adopt a more aggressive tone.'[12]

Al-Qirqisani taught that 'intellect is the foundation upon which every doctrine should be built', and that 'all knowledge should be derived by means of reason only'; he even advanced a purely psycho-physiological explanation of dreams, whose divinatory functions are so frequently stressed in Scripture. However, only a few among the Karaites dared to deny physical resurrection, or to interpret it in the sense of Israel's future deliverance from exile. In view of their extreme nationalism, moreover, the early Karaites gave even freer rein to messianic speculation than their rabbinite contemporaries; we even know of one Karaite messianic pretender, Solomon Ha-Kohen, who proclaimed himself the Messiah about the year 1121.

All this, however, could not affect what seems to be the central point of conflict between the Karaites and the rabbinites, which was the reason why normative Judaism could not accept the tenets of Karaism. The point, as Rabbi Goldin suggests, was that the Karaites' anti-Talmudism amounted to a denial of history. As Goldin asserts:

> We fail utterly to understand the movement if we see in it a form of anti-nomianism. Not only 'Anan but also every Karaite of note was preoccupied with law. What finally petrified Karaism was in truth a combination of factors, not the least of which was its failure to appreciate that Talmudic law had been an organic product. No *tour de force* could take its place. Before long Karaite protagonists, too, had to appeal to an inherited corpus of teaching, which, they insisted, was Scripture made explicit. . . . An undeveloped historical sense afflicted the schismatics in practically every period. . . .[13]

The ultimate fate of Karaism, however, is not representative of its state in the tenth century. At that point in Jewish history its threat to the unity of Jewish life was serious and the silence of the *Geonim* was poor strategy.

CHAPTER 15

Saadia's Legacy

The challenge posed by the Karaites to some of the basic tenets of Judaism seems to have remained unanswered for a considerable number of years, either because the rabbinites did not take it seriously or for lack of interest and stamina. But a response had to come, and it finally came with the appearance on the scene of a young man by the name of Saadia ben Joseph. It is a curious fact of Jewish history at that phase that Saadia (whom the Arabs knew as Saad ibn Yusuf al-Fayyumi) was born not in Mesopotamia but in Egypt, although he and his works are justly considered part of the cultural and religious heritage of Babylonian Jewry.

Born in the district of al-Fayyum in upper Egypt in 892 AD, Saadia left his native land in 915, travelled in Syria and Palestine, and finally settled in Iraq, where, in 922, he became a leading member (*Aluf*) of the academy of Sura. Six years later, due to his brilliance as a scholar and the volume of work he had managed to produce, Saadia was appointed *Gaon*. He died, still holding the office, at the age of fifty.

In order fully to appreciate Saadia's work, as well as some of the reasons which led to his unprecedented appointment to the *Gaonate* of Sura, it must be kept in mind that the Karaites did not present the only challenge to Judaism in those days. Baghdad in the final decades of the ninth century was the capital and metropolis of an empire not only great politically but intellectually as well, and the Jews there could not help being affected. In the Introduction to his major philosophical work, *Kitab al-Amanat wal-I'tiqadat* (*The Book of Doctrines and Beliefs*), written in 933, Saadia draws a grim picture of the confusion he saw reigning in the religio-intellectual life of his Jewish contemporaries. He lists four categories of men, classifying them on the basis of doubt and certainty, error and truth:

> Some there are who have arrived at the truth and rejoice in the knowledge that they possess it. . . . Others have arrived at the truth, but doubt it; they fail to know it for a certainty and to hold on to it . . .

> still others confidently affirm that which is false in the belief that it is true . . . others again base their conduct on a certain belief for a time, and then reject it on account of some defect they find in it; then they change over to another belief and renounce it in turn because of something in it which seems questionable to them; then they go over to yet another belief for a while, and drop it because of some point which, in their opinion, renders it invalid. . . .[1]

In other words, there were those who possessed both truth and certainty; others who possessed truth but lacked certainty; a third category of men who lacked truth but possessed certainty; and finally those who lacked both truth and certainty.

That this confusion was the lot of both Jewish and Muslim intellectuals in the Baghdad of the tenth century is amply illustrated by a story told by a Muslim historian who lived there in those days. This historian, called al-Humaydi, relates the experience of a Muslim theologian from Spain who visited Baghdad, identified as Abu Omar Ahmad ibn Muhammed ibn Sa'idi. We are told that this theologian, upon his return to Spain, was asked by a fellow theologian whether he had an opportunity of attending, during his stay in Baghdad, one of the assemblies regularly held by the Mutakallimun, a school of Muslim theologians who generally opposed their orthodox counterparts. Sa'idi's answer was:

> 'Yes, I attended twice, but I refused to go there for a third time.' Upon being asked why, he said: 'For this simple reason, which you will appreciate: At the first meeting there were present not only people of various [Islamic] sects, but also unbelievers, Magians, materialists, atheists, Jews and Christians – in short, unbelievers of all kinds. Each group had its own leader, whose task it was to defend its views, and every time one of the leaders entered the room his followers rose to their feet and remained standing until he took his seat. In the meanwhile, the hall had become overcrowded with people. One of the unbelievers rose and said to the assembly: "We are meeting here for a discussion. Its conditions are known to all. You, Muslims, are not allowed to argue from your books and prophetic traditions since we deny both. Everybody, therefore, has to limit himself to rational arguments." The whole assembly applauded these words. So you can imagine that after these words I decided to withdraw. They proposed to me that I should attend another meeting in a different hall, but I found the same calamity there.'[2]

Obviously this depiction of the state of intellectual and religious life among the Muslims of those days must be taken with some reservations. But there seems to be no doubt whatever that disruption of the kind described by Sa'idi was rampant among Jews as well as Muslims in the Baghdad of those days. The fact is that, between the latter decades of the eighth century, which witnessed the birth of Karaism, and the first decades of the tenth century, when Saadia launched his single-minded campaign against error and doubt and for what he saw as truth and certainty, Jewish life found itself threatened from several sects and circles besides that of the Karaites. In addition to these, there existed a number of minor but apparently active and influential sects and groups which presented a variety of challenges to the Jewish establishment of the day. Al-Qirqisani, the Karaite, describes some of these in *Kitab al-Anwar* (*The Book of Lights*). There was, for one, the Maghariyya sect, which seems to have owed its existence to the influence of the Philonic tradition; like Philo, they indulged in an allegorical interpretation of the Bible, and their Angel doctrine echoes in some way Philo's Logos conception. Another group of Jews had strong leanings towards the Manichean religion. The spokesman and theoretician of this group was the formidable Hiwi al-Balkhi (middle of the ninth century), who wrote a book in which he propounded 200 questions against the teaching of the Pentateuch; he even denied the unity of God, His omnipotence and omniscience. He denied free will and the possibility of miracles, and went so far as to object to circumcision. What was surprising, and rather disturbing to the leaders of Babylonian Jewry, was that his book created quite a stir, and his ideas found many adherents and were even taught to schoolchildren.[3]

Belatedly perhaps but with due determination, the rabbinites finally decided to meet these growing challenges. They must have realized, in the process, that the most effective method of fighting the enemy was by employing his own weapons, so they set out to widen the range of their studies by going beyond the subjects covered by Talmudists. In Rabbi Epstein's words, 'While the onslaught of the Karaites led the rabbinites to pay greater attention to biblical exegesis, Hebrew grammar and philology, the challenge of rationalism gave a strong impetus among them to the cultivation of philosophy, logic, and the physical sciences.' It is not at all unlikely that Saadia's appointment to the *Gaonate* of Sura in 928 was motivated partly or even largely by the need to meet these challenges. After all, not only was Saadia not a native Babylonian but he did not have any of the family connections that had usually been indispensable to aspirants to that office, which for two centuries had been in the almost exclusive possession of three families.

No less significant than the reality of the challenges was the fact that by the tenth century Sura had only a distinguished past to boast of. The dearth of outstanding scholars had brought the institution to a low ebb, and when Yom Tob Kahana, the *Gaon* who was a weaver by trade and who held the office for only two years, died in 928, the Exilarch David ben Zakkai thought of closing the school altogether – a step which would have pleased the ambitious head of the now Baghdad-based rival academy of Pumbeditha, Kohen-Tzedek II (917–36). However, a nominal head was appointed to the office in the person of Nathan ben Yehudai, whose sudden death soon afterwards was taken as a warning that it would be sinful to terminate the existence of the venerable seat of learning. The choice now before the Exilarch was narrowed down to two candidates – Tzemah ben Shahin and Saadia. According to one widely accepted account, ben Shahin was a learned man of a distinguished family, and ben Zakkai sought the advice of Nissi Naharwandi, who had just declined an offer of the *Gaonate* of Sura on the ground that the head of the academy was called 'Light of the World' while he, Naharwandi, was blind.

Naharwandi advised the Exilarch to appoint ben Shahin and not Saadia, even though the latter was a great man and a distinguished scholar. 'He fears no man, however,' he explained, 'and kotows to no one because of his great wisdom, his spirit, his eloquence and his fear of sin.' But the Exilarch had already made up his mind and Saadia was duly named *Gaon* of Sura and induced into office in the presence of Kohen-Tzedek II and the scholars of the Pumbeditha academy. This was a decision that the Exilarch was going to regret having made.

Saadia al-Fayyumi was already a known name in the Jewish world of learning when he was named *Gaon* of Sura. For a number of years his name had figured prominently in literary and intellectual circles. At the age of twenty, while still in Egypt, he had compiled a Hebrew lexicon and a rhyming dictionary, for which – he said in a highly instructive introduction to the dictionary – there was a contemporary need. What prompted him to prepare the work, he added, was that Jews were rapidly forgetting how to express themselves properly in their own language. It is interesting to note here that the foundation for Saadia's vast erudition had already been laid in the land of his birth, where there had been a revival of Jewish communal life and of Jewish learning since the Muslim conquest of Egypt in 655. The largest and most flourishing Jewish settlement was in the capital Fostat (Old Cairo) and was presided over in the middle of the ninth century by a Babylonian Jew, Abu 'Ali Hasan al-Baghdadi, referred to above. What must have irked young Saadia and led him to his attempts at a Hebrew revival was that the Jews of his native land spoke the language of the governing Arab classes, while his younger contemporaries were eagerly absorbing the dominant culture. By that time the Karaites, too, had penetrated some Jewish circles in Egypt and were propagating their views, which again aroused Saadia, who composed his first anti-Karaite work, *Kitab al-Rad 'ala 'Anan* (*The Refutation of 'Anan*), when he was twenty-three years old.

Saadia was never to abandon his battle against the Karaites, and he fought sectarianism of any type, which he thought undermined the survival of the Jewish people. He did not hesitate to engage in controversies, nor did he deal with them kindly. One of these is especially worth mentioning, since among other things it brought Saadia fame and renown. The controversy originated in an action taken by the head of a Palestinian academy concerning the Jewish calendar. It is worth noting here that following the Muslim conquest of Palestine the 'lot' of the Jews there was greatly improved. In the words of one of their leaders, Yehudai: 'When the Ishmaelites came, they left them [the Jews] free to occupy themselves with the Torah.' Palestine thus regained some of its ancient status as the seat and arbiter of Jewish learning. The revival was such that heads of the higher Palestinian schools of learning began to style themselves *Gaons*, like their Babylonian counterparts. In two crucial spheres, too, the Babylonians deferred to the Palestinians, namely in matters pertaining to the letter of Scripture and in the regulation of the calendar. This latter subject was a sensitive and rather intricate point of unceasing controversy. In the old days, when the empirical method prevailed of accepting the evidence of anyone who chanced to see the new moon in a clear sky, it had been the prerogative of the Palestinian patriarchal court to sanctify the new moon. Similarly, when owing to a discrepancy between the solar and the lunar calendars the vernal season would have occurred at too early a date, it had been the rule of the patriarch to postpone the Passover festival by intercalating a thirteenth month before the month of Nisan. In later times, when observation gave way to astrological calculation, the intricacies of computation often seemed to be attended by mystery, and the teachers of Babylonia had to travel to Palestine to get instruction. As late as AD 835, the Exilarch recognized as ancient custom for himself and the heads of the academies and for all the Jewish people to accept the calendar as sent out by the authorities in Palestine. Later, however, owing partly to the ascendancy of Babylonia and partly to the uniformly established method of computation, the practice fell into disuse and the Babylonians made themselves independent of the Holy Land.

Things went smoothly until, in the autumn of 921, one zealous Palestinian *Gaon* and dignitary, Aaron ben Meir, came out with what he regarded as an improvement in the calendar and sought thereby to re-establish the ancient authority of the Palestinian establishment. Accordingly, the improved calendar was proclaimed from the Mount of Olives, in keeping with a now discarded custom. It is quite possible that, were it not for Saadia's firm objections, the Babylonian authorities would have yielded on this point. In the event, when the news reached Saadia, who was then sojourning in Aleppo, he immediately started remonstrating with ben Meir by letter and a fierce controversy developed.

To start with, it turned out that ben Meir had previously visited Baghdad and won the adherence of the *Gaon* of Pumbeditha, apparently in return for the support he extended to him against a rival. By the time Saadia arrived, however, that particular internal quarrel had been resolved, and he was able to persuade the authorities to address a joint letter to the author of the new calendar, asking him civilly to withdraw his proclamation that the coming Passover would fall on Sunday instead of Tuesday. Ben Meir, however, would not yield, insisting that the calculations of the Babylonians were in error. To this Saadia replied to the effect that the Palestinians' claims were baseless. Incriminations and recriminations were thus hurled and the tone of the missives grew in bitterness. Meanwhile, some Jewish communities celebrated the holidays according to ben Meir's calendar, others according to the dates set by the Babylonians, and the confusion which ensued was noticed even by non-Jews. The rift, breaking at a time in which the Karaites seemed particularly active, must have persuaded Saadia even more that ben Meir's dissenting plans had to be defeated. In the course of the controversy, he proved his mettle, meeting invective with invective and – what was far more important – demonstrating his vast learning and his grasp of an intricate subject. At the request of the Exilarch, whose support he enjoyed, Saadia composed a *Book of Seasons*, in which he effectively refuted ben Meir's assertions. The work was widely circulated among Jewish communities far and near, and it came to be recited annually in the month preceding the new year. Saadia emerged victorious from a controversy which, though it must have made him enemies, won him a number of admirers in high places.

A few years after this controversy Saadia was named *Gaon* of Sura, and for two years all went well as far as relations with the Exilarch were concerned. But the almost inevitable rupture came soon enough, the occasion being a lawsuit which involved a settlement of a large estate consisting of property and a large sum of money which fell to some men through inheritance and which they desired to divide. This led to a dispute between the heirs, who in the end agreed to pay the Exilarch ten per cent of all the estate in return for removing all complaints against themselves and to settle the case. Since all such legal papers had to be confirmed by the heads of the academies of Sura and Pumbeditha, the Exilarch after signing the documents ordered the parties to go to the two *Gaons* who would confirm them. They went first to Saadia, who after examining the papers asked them to get first the signature of Kohen-Tzedek II, the *Gaon* of Pumbeditha. However, when they came back with the required signature affixed on the papers, Saadia refused to sign them. The Exilarch became insistent, sending his son Judah with an explicit order to the *Gaon* to sign. 'Tell your father', Saadia told Judah, 'that it is written in the Torah [Deut. 1:17]: "Ye shall not respect persons in judgement." '

Threats ensued, and during one of his missions Judah even raised his hand to strike Saadia. Finally the exasperated Exilarch deposed the *Gaon* of Sura and appointed Joseph ben Jacob bar Satia to the vacant office. He then pronounced the ban on Saadia, who retaliated by excommunicating the Exilarch and appointing his younger brother Hasan as successor to the Exilarchate. Obviously a great survivor and with a lot of money and influence, David ben Zakkai remained in his office, either because Hasan died or owing to the caliph's support. For seven years, Babylonian Jewry was divided into two opposing camps, with the majority of the wealthy and prominent families siding with Saadia, while the Exilarch was aided and abetted by his influential friends. Saadia lived in retirement in Baghdad, writing some of his most important works, including *The Book of Doctrines and Beliefs*. After seven years, the people wearied of the strife and, when the Exilarch declined to sustain an appeal by Saadia on the part of a Suran litigant and had him flogged, there was universal clamour for reconciliation. The two men were brought together on the eve of Purim in the year 937, and after a touching ceremony embraced. Saadia returned to his post and directed the work of his academy for five more years. He died in 942, reportedly of melancholia.[4]

Tenth-century Baghdad, where Saadia *Gaon* wrote his major

philosophical work while in forced retirement in 933, was a place torn between religious and intellectual extremes. Conflicting philosophical creeds abounded, and the impact of works translated from Greek since the middle of the eighth century was becoming visible. Saadia himself depicted the situation in moving terms in the Introduction to *The Book of Doctrines and Beliefs*:

> When I considered these evils, my heart grieved for my race, the race of mankind, and my soul was moved on account of our own people Israel, as I saw in my time many of the believers clinging to unsound doctrines and mistaken beliefs while many of those who deny the faith boast of their unbelief and despise the men of truth, although they are themselves in error. . . . I felt that to help them was my duty, and guiding them aright an obligation upon me.[5]

The great philosopher-poet Abu el-'Alaa al-Mu'arri, a contemporary of Saadia's, was similarly troubled by the intellectual confusion. 'Muslims, Jews, Christians and Magians,' he lamented, 'they all are walking in error and darkness. There are only two kinds of people left in the world; the one group is intelligent, but lacking in faith; the other has faith, but is lacking in intelligence.' What Saadia, as a teacher of his people and as a member of 'the race of mankind', tried to do was to introduce some order into the general confusion. In this monumental undertaking, his sole guide was reason, by way of which, he felt, man would ultimately apprehend the existence and nature of God.

Saadia's belief in the power of reason was such that he felt that man would have acquired knowledge of God even without revelation, which according to him hastened the process and acted as a guide during this quest. In what amounts to a hymn to reason, Saadia writes in Book Four of *The Book of Doctrines and Beliefs*:

> By virtue of it man preserves the memory of deeds that happened long ago, and by virtue of it he foresees many of the things that will occur in the future. By virtue of it he is able to subdue the animals so that they may till the earth for him and bring in its produce. By virtue of it he is able to draw the water from the depth of the earth to its surface; he even invents irrigating wheels that draw the water automatically. By virtue of it he is able to build lofty mansions, to make magnificent garments, and to prepare delicate dishes. By virtue of it he is able to organize armies and camps, and to exercise kingship and authority for establishing order and civilization among

men. By virtue of it he is able to study the nature of the celestial spheres, the course of the planets, their dimensions, their distances from one another, as well as other matters relating to them.[6]

Throughout this book, Saadia takes a position of strict rationalism. Judaism, he argues, is in harmony with the dictates of reason. Revelation may give us some truths which we could not prove by logic alone, but it never teaches us anything unacceptable to logic and good sense. Many of the basic tenets of religion can be demonstrated by reasoning, and Saadia duly offered such rational proofs for the existence and unity of God. The great advantage of revelation, he argued further, is that it provides certainty – since we might make errors in the use of logical proofs – and that, moreover, it makes the truth available and clear to the simple and uneducated who have not the time, talent or maturity for philosophical study. It is precisely for the benefit of such minds that the Bible was written in a concrete and vivid style. Saadia, in short, undertook to establish a rational, Jewish creed and to demonstrate the soundness of the religious heritage. *The Book of Doctrines and Beliefs* is unanimously considered to have been the first comprehensive and systematic attempt ever made to give a rational basis to Jewish religious doctrine and practice, a landmark in Jewish religious and philosophical thinking, the like of which was not undertaken until Maimonides wrote his epoch-making *Guide for the Perplexed* two and a half centuries later.

That Saadia proclaimed the supremacy of reason (*'aql*), that his thinking was so totally dominated by an uncompromising rationalism, does not mean that he was not aware of a certain anti-rationalist strain within Jewry that would forbid philosophical enquiry. 'How can we undertake to pursue knowledge by means of speculation and enquiry with the object of attaining mathematical certainty seeing that our people reject this manner of speculation as leading to unbelief [*kufr*] and the adoption of heretical views [*zandaqa*]?' To this hypothetical objection, so carefully worded by the author himself, Saadia has a ready answer equally well formulated:

Our answer is that only the ignorant speak thus. Similarly one will find that the ignorant people in our town are of the opinion that everyone who goes to India becomes rich. So, too, some of the ignorant people in our nation are said to think that the eclipse of the moon occurs whenever something resembling a dragon swallows the moon. Some of the ignorant people of Arabia are said to hold the opinion that unless a man's camel is slaughtered over his grave, he will have to appear on foot on Judgement Day. There exist many more ridiculous opinions like these.

Responding to another objection, namely 'that the greatest of the Sages of Israel prohibited [speculation], and particularly the speculation on the origin of Time and Space, when they declared, "Whosoever speculates on four things should better not have been created: on what is above and what is below, what was in the beginning, and what will be in the end." [*Hagigah* 2:1]', he writes:

> Our answer is this: It cannot be thought that the Sages should have wished to prohibit us from rational enquiry seeing that our Creator has commanded us to engage in such enquiry in addition to accepting the reliable Tradition. Thus He said, 'Know ye not? Hear ye not? Hath it not been told you from the beginning? Have ye not understood the foundations of the earth?' [Isaiah 40:21] The pious men said to each other, 'Let us choose for us that which is right; let us know among ourselves what is good' [Job 34:4], and, indeed, the five men, namely Job, Eliphaz, Bildad, Zopher and Elihu, had long discussions on this subject.[7]

It is impossible not to marvel, reading these remarks, at the matter-of-fact, relaxed and rather devastating way in which Saadia dismisses beliefs and attitudes that were widespread even in those days of intellectual unrest. It is also interesting to note the inroads and influences which Greek thought and philosophy had on his writing.

Two more outstanding features of Saadia's work are worth mentioning, namely the orderly, methodical fashion in which he expressed his thoughts and the fact that his works, wide-ranging and varied though they were in their scope, were all intended to fill a pressing need and addressed to a popular rather than a specialized audience. Although in many instances only fragments of his writings have been preserved, even these reveal his lucidity of manner and outlook. As Judah Goldin has remarked:

> Saadia's codifications of the law became models for future codifiers.... Before he undertook to treat details, he prepared an introduction to the subject matter as a whole. The very fact, incidentally, that he recognized the purpose and value of introductory discussions is a commentary on his approach to the craft of teaching and writing. His introductions not only outlined the principal ideas of the books, but also furnished him with an opportunity to discuss problems which might occur to a reflective student.[8]

Thus, in his introductory analysis of the Pentateuch he speaks of 'three kinds of education, of which one is stronger than the others'. After examining the several kinds of education, he sums up:

> And God has revealed, in this Book which is dedicated to the education of His servants, the three methods. . . . He commands piety and prohibits sin; He announces the reward of good actions and the punishment of evil actions; and finally He gives the history of those who lived on earth before us – the salvation of those who have been virtuous and the punishment of those who have been wicked.[9]

That Saadia's various works were all intended to fill a popular need is perhaps best illustrated by the fact that his very first effort was the compilation of a Hebrew lexicon, followed by a rhyming dictionary. Seeing how sectarianism was endangering the unity of Jewish life and the Jewish heritage, he then addressed himself to the task of combating the 'Ananites and systematically refuting their anti-Talmudism. And this is true of all his other works.

> In his prayer book he omitted reference to authorities as he discussed the laws of worship, since his audience was the folk at large, not the small scholarly circle. When he saw how his generation, ignorant of Hebrew, was forgetting the Bible, he translated it for their benefit. Where mere translation would still leave difficulty, he paraphrased. The philosophical speculations of the age challenged the teachings of traditional Judaism; he undertook in his *Doctrines and Beliefs*, therefore, to establish a rational Jewish creed and to demonstrate the soundness of the religious heritage.[10]

Some students of the period consider Saadia's translation of the Bible to be his crowning achievement. This Arabic version of the Scriptures, accompanied in certain books or parts of books by a commentary, was in its way an epoch-making undertaking. The translation was intended for the common people, the Jews living in the vast Muslim Empire and fast absorbing the Arabic language and Arab culture. Discarding the habitual forced interpretation so often indulged in by the rabbis, Saadia in his translation and commentaries broke the ground for a rational, systematic exposition. The work, which students of Judeo-Arabic culture still hold in awe, yielded stores of information to successive generations of biblical scholars as a whole. What made these scholars especially grateful to Saadia was that, apart from rendering the Bible into Arabic, Saadia composed an independent treatise in which he made suggestions as to the meaning and import of some ninety words which are found but once in the Bible, 'having neither brother nor friend' but still capable of being understood with the aid of the later Hebrew or the cognate Arabic.

As a philosopher, too, Saadia has justly been called 'the father of medieval Jewish philosophy'. Not only was he the first to undertake a systematic philosophical justification of Judaism, but he was the first also to develop the notions of Islamic theology and philosophy in an independent manner. This latter accomplishment was of crucial importance because, as Julius Guttmann explains in his history of Jewish philosophies of religion, the same needs which brought about the development of the Muslim philosophy of religion produced its Jewish counterpart:

> This Islamic background determines the character of medieval Jewish philosophy from beginning to end. Even more than Islamic philosophy, it was definitely a philosophy of religion. Whereas the Islamic Neoplatonists and Aristotelians dealt with the full range of philosophy, Jewish thinkers relied for the most part on the work of their Islamic predecessors in regard to general philosophic questions, and concentrated on more specifically religio-philosophic problems.[11]

In this Saadia was no exception. For his fundamental theses, he relied on the Kalam (speech, scholastic theology), inclining toward its rationalist Mu'tazilite version which approximated the Jewish position both in its strict and uncompromising treatment of the concept of God's unity and in its insistence on the doctrine of free will. 'Saadia followed the Mu'tazilite convention even in the formal structure of his book by having the chapter on God's justice follow the chapter on the unity of God. But apart from this he handled the traditional scholastic themes with great freedom.'[12]

Preoccupied as he was with what appear to be purely theological problems, Saadia had his feet firmly on the ground. To be sure, the Torah by virtue of its intrinsic worth is both eternal and immutable; but it is not unrelated to life. In fact, the Torah is of little use to those who proclaim that 'the best thing for man to do is to devote himself to worship of God, fast during the day, and spend the night in praise of God, and relinquish all worldly occupation'. In the first place, the eternity of the Torah is bound up with the eternity of the Jewish people, and with their very existence as a people. 'Israel is a nation only by virtue of its Torah', and since God through His prophets guaranteed the eternity of Israel, the Torah, too, must of necessity endure to eternity. Secondly, the Torah has little meaning if it is to be divorced from human and social activities. If life is renounced for the sake of worship of God, Saadia insists, then we have no chance to obey or disobey many of the religious observances decreed therein. 'How shall the hermit observe the laws of correct weights and measures? . . . Which part of the civil law will he fulfil with truth and justice? . . . And so it is with regard to the laws of sowing, of tithes, of charity and similar precepts. . . .'[13]

Nor was Saadia an uncompromising doctrinaire, although as we have seen he knew how to take a firm stand when matters of principle were involved. An Arab historian, Ibn al-Hiti, relates a story about Saadia attending the funeral in Aleppo of the Karaite leader Salmon ben Yeruhim, who among other things had accused the rabbinites of abandoning the Ten Commandments and whom Saadia had fought tooth and nail during his lifetime. Saadia, says al-Hiti in what may be an apocryphal report, attended the funeral 'with his garment torn, girded with a rope and barefoot'. As if to lend credence to the story, Saadia in al-Hiti's account is further reported to have declared on the occasion: 'We both derived much profit from our controversies.'

He was equally magnanimous in his attitude to the man who had sought his personal downfall and caused him so much distress, the Exilarch David ben Zakkai. When David died, in 940, Saadia used his influence to have the deceased Exilarch's son Judah installed in the office. But Judah held the Exilarchate for barely seven months; he died, leaving a boy of twelve years, and Saadia took his erstwhile enemy's grandson to his house and reared him with fatherly care. Two years later Saadia died, and the boy Solomon eventually became the next Exilarch.

Saadia left a great and many-faceted legacy. There was almost no field of Jewish literature and thought that did not interest him intensely, and in many of these he was the true pioneer. Perhaps the best and most eloquent tribute to his work was the one made by Maimonides, who in many ways followed in the steps of his eminent precursor and predecessor. 'Were it not for Saadia,' wrote Maimonides in his *Iggeret Teman* (*Epistle to Yemen*), 'the Torah would almost have disappeared from the midst of Israel; for it was he who made manifest what was obscure therein, made strong what had been weakened.'

CHAPTER 16

The Last of the *Geonim*

It is generally agreed among students of this phase of Jewish history that the *Gaonate* as well as the supremacy of the Babylonian schools ended in the year 1038 with the death of Rab Hai *Gaon*. This is only partly true, as later research into fragments and shreds of evidence discovered in the Cairo *geniza* and elsewhere shows that the institution of the *Gaonate* continued to function up to the middle of the fourteenth century. The decline, in fact, had started even before the days of Saadia, whose fame and stature seem to have checked only for a short while the fall to which it was destined. One of the main reasons for the decline was the tension and conflict besetting relations between the Exilarchs and *Gaons*. These differences centred on points of relative power and prerogatives as well as on the style of life and the exercise of authority on the part of those in power. Within the academies themselves, too, mutual recriminations and strictures became a feature of daily life. Many of the rabbis and scholars received their public appointments from the temporal rulers and held office in the vicinity of the central authorities, with which they usually identified and which they refrained from criticizing, while the more independently minded among the *Gaons* as well as some of the scholars tended to voice disapproval of the Exilarchate and the ways in which it was conducting the community's affairs. The rise of the Karaites, too, contributed to the decline, inasmuch as the controversies which they provoked led to increasing preoccupation with philosophical issues and with a new type of biblical exegesis and bible studies. Other contributing factors were the emergence of a number of active Jewish centres in North Africa, Spain and the East, which weakened the Diaspora's dependence on the Babylonian centre, and the negative effects this had on the financial position of the academies themselves; the general worsening of the economy which naturally affected the Jewish community as a whole; and the steady deterioration of the central government in Baghdad as the Abbasid caliphs fell prey to an assortment of foreign blackmailers, usurpers and conquerors.

Nevertheless, the *Gaonate* did not end with the death of Saadia. It is true that his successor, Joseph bar Satia, did not distinguish himself in any way, while those who assumed the *Gaonate* of Sura after him failed to perform any better, with the exception of Samuel ben Ḥofni, the grandson of one of Saadia's main rivals, Rab Kohen-Tzedek. Samuel followed in the footsteps of Saadia and produced a new Arabic version of the Scriptures, likewise accompanied by commentaries which were no match, however, for the master's clear and succinct interpretations. He was succeeded by Saadia's aged son Dosa, who held the office for about four years (1013–17). By the end of the fourth decade of the eleventh century the ancient academy of Sura, whose foundations had been laid by the great Rab, virtually ceased to function after an active and fruitful existence of eight centuries. Some historians speculate that the institution was transferred to Egypt, probably in honour of its most illustrious *Gaon* of recent times, Saadia, whose native land Egypt was.

Ben Hofni's Bible exegesis was rationalistic enough, however, to lead to opposition from many quarters, including Hai *Gaon*'s strong objections to his interpretation of phenomena like the serpent in the Garden of Eden, Bil'am's ass, the story of the witch of Endor, and other biblical accounts. Like Saadia, he wrote an introduction to the Talmud, *Kitab al-Madkhal ila al-Talmud*, only fragments of which survive. He also left a number of treatises which deal with certain aspects and branches of the law, such as one in which he codified the laws pertaining to the status of the minor in religious life, the laws of *tzitzith* and the Benedictions. It is possible, however, that these treatises are in fact parts of a larger and more comprehensive work which covered the whole range of ritual law, which is known to bibliographers by the title *Kitab al-Sharayi'* (*The Book of Precepts*). Of considerable interest, too, is ben Hofni's contribution to the philosophy of religion in his book, *Kitab Naskh el-Shar' wa-Usul el-Din wa-Furu'uh* (*Book on the Abrogation of Law and the Origins of Religion and its Branches*). In this book, which survives in its Arabic original but which does not seem to have been translated into Hebrew at any time, ben Hofni presents a coherent system of religious philosophy, arguing against those philosophers of religion who believe in the eternity of the universe but deny the Divine Creation. He also condemns anthropomorphic theories, and refutes the claims of Muslim theologians who maintain that the language and the inimitable style of the Koran constitute conclusive proof of its divine origin.

Ben Hofni was Sura's last *Gaon* of any standing and erudition. In the academy of Pumbeditha (now in Baghdad), shortly after Saadia's death, the *Gaon* was Aaron ben Joseph Ibn-Sarjado, who had been one of Saadia's leading opponents and who attained the *Gaonate* only through his wealth and influence, taking over after the death of Hananiah ben Judah in 943. As Rab Sherira, Hananiah's son and later *Gaon* of Pumbeditha, reports, Aaron did not belong to the class of scholars but to that of merchants. He bore himself majestically and would tolerate no opposition or contradiction from his subordinates; he became so insufferable that Nehemiah ben Kohen-Tzedek finally led a revolt against him, accusing him of untruthfulness, gross meddling with the administration of the academy's funds, favouritism towards students, and general malfeasance. At this point the Exilarch, David ben Zakkai's grandson Solomon, stepped in to recover the donations received from the community in Spain and diverted by Aaron for his own uses.

At this stage we hear a great deal about the financial straits in which the academies, and the communal administration as a whole, found themselves. The truth is that conditions were becoming exceedingly precarious, endangering the very existence of the schools. One province after another had fallen away from the empire and was in the hands of independent local rulers, while the capital Baghdad itself fell prey to a succession of domineering and ambitious chiefs who managed to turn the caliphs into mere puppets. The country as a whole was ravaged, and the Jewish seats of learning found themselves deprived of their landed property and were virtually dependent on pious donations and gifts from Jewish communities abroad. At this time a Jewish scholar from Baghdad lamented: 'Naught is left to us but the writings of our fathers.'

Under these conditions internal strife tended to intensify. Aaron and Nehemiah had followers and supporters, and the latter was generally considered to be the worthier of the two. When Aaron died in 960, Nehemiah succeeded him, with only Sherira, the *ab beth din* (president of the court) withholding recognition.

Sherira, whose position made him next in rank to the *Gaon*, eventually assumed the *Gaonate* of Pumbeditha after Nehemiah passed away in 968 – and emerged as one of the most illustrious heads this institution was to know. For thirty years, up till his death at the ripe old age of one hundred or more, he worked assiduously to check the threatening decline. Although he helped in the spread of Torah and Talmudic studies among the Jewish communities abroad, Sherira held that the parent institutions in the East must not be allowed to disintegrate. 'For how could the body be healthy if the head hurt?' However, despite the visible weakening of the Babylonian centre that had already started some time before he assumed the *Gaonate*, queries in matters of law kept coming to him from the farthest corners, and in the hundreds of *responsa* which have survived Sherira displays the same rationalistic influences we note in some of his more recent predecessors following Saadia's lead. For, although he generally follows the rulings of the Talmud, he considers the homilies (*haggadoth*) less binding, maintaining that these were to be accepted only when supported by reason and Scripture.

Sherira's fame, however, rests on his *Epistle* (*Iggereth Rab Sherira Gaon*), which he addressed to the scholars in Kairawan in reply to their request for a history of the Oral Law, information about the redaction of the Mishnah and the Talmud, the extent of rabbinic literature, and the chronology of the *tannaim*, *amoraim*, *saboraim* and *Geonim*. Quite undeterred by the enormity of the task, Sherira set out to compose a comprehensive and workmanlike outline of the whole history of post-biblical Judaism; this remains until now the best and most authoritative source of information on the subject. Using documents and papers preserved in the archives of the two academies as well as his own experience and memoirs, he produced a work which Talmudic scholarship, ancient and modern, looks upon as the corner-stone of rabbinic research. This is not in the least surprising since Sherira managed with masterly erudition to establish the unbroken Chain of Tradition by listing the names and careers of the bearers of this tradition from remote beginnings down to his own day.

In addition to his justly acclaimed *Epistle*, some of Sherira's commentaries on the Talmud, and fragments from other works of his, have been preserved in the works of earlier lexicographers and Talmud commentators. These, and the numerous *responsa* sent by the academy under his presidency, shed more light on the significance of his contribution. They also show him as a true and faithful representative of the age in which he lived, reflecting as he did the intellectual atmosphere of those days. One quotation from a Talmudic commentary reveals his attitude to the *Aggadah*. In holding that most of the *Aggadah* is to be interpreted allegorically, Sherira emerges as a landmark figure in *aggadic* studies, as these words – often cited by teachers of the following generations – clearly show: 'Things derived from the Scriptures which are current under the names of Midrash and Aggadah are mostly not to be taken literally, and therefore not to be relied upon. Yet, whatever agrees with the Scriptures and is based on logic has to be accepted.' It is clear, incidentally, that Sherira's pronouncements on *aggadic* problems stemmed from the hostile propaganda current in his day against the Talmud, the *halakhah* and the *Aggadah* on the part of the Karaites.

It appears that the greater part of the *responsa* sent forth from the academy during Sherira's presidency were composed jointly with his son Hai, and it is, therefore, difficult to establish which of these were the father's and which the son's. Be that as it may, Sherira placed his son as next in rank. But owing to some personal intrigues and enmities, the *Gaon* was denounced before the caliph, and both he and Hai were cast into prison, to be released only through the intervention of friends. In 998, broken in health, Sherira retired in favour of his son, now almost sixty years old (he was born in 939). It is said that on the Sabbath of Hai's installation a signal honour was paid to father and son in that, by suitable selections from the Scriptures, it was brought home to the people that God had placed in the seat of the retired master as worthy a successor as Joshua had been to Moses or as Solomon to King David. Sherira himself had a very high opinion of his son's keenness and erudition. 'Our son Hai', he wrote in his famous *Iggereth*, 'is very diligent in teaching them [the students] and in explaining to them, and those who do not know how to ask he shows the way of raising questions, and makes this method of study popular with them.'

Unanimously viewed as the last *Gaon* of eminence, Hai worthily summed up a whole creative period in the history of the Jewish people; and his literary activities and scholarly influence are said by many to have surpassed those of any of his predecessors. Like his father, he lived to be about a hundred, having served as *Gaon* for forty years (998–1038), disseminating knowledge near and far and issuing decisions and explanations which were accepted by Jewish communities everywhere. He mastered many tongues – Hebrew, Arabic, Aramaic, Greek, Persian – turning them all to good account in elucidating obscure points in the Talmud or Scripture. Like his father, he displayed a special interest in secular studies, and we find him consulting Christian clerics as well as Muslim scholars about various biblical and theological problems. He enjoyed the friendship of the head of the Eastern Church, whose seat was Baghdad, and sought information from him as to how a difficult verse in the Bible was rendered into the Syriac version. His chief work is his commentaries on the Talmud, of which parts were studied and taught in Spanish and Italian schools. Next in importance were his *halakhic* compendia on various subjects of law and ritual, some in prose, others in verse. One example is his *Kitab al-Shar' wal-Bai'*, which codifies details of the civil law and which was translated into Hebrew by Isaac ben Reuben of

Barcelona under the title *Mekah u-Memkar*. Another of his treaties, written in Arabic like all his other works, is called *Kitab al-Iman* (*Book of Faith*) and it too was rendered into Hebrew by the same Spanish scholar. Hai *Gaon*'s other works include a lexicon, *Kitab al-Hawi* (*The Compendium*) which, though used a great deal by early authorities, is not accessible to us. He conducted a correspondence with nearly all the prominent Jewish scholars of his day, and we possess over 1,000 answers to queries on a wide range of subjects, including many of philosophical as well as theological moment. Among many other decisions, he laid down the rule, followed by scholars and rabbis up till this day, that when the Palestinian Talmud clashed with the Babylonian the latter alone was authoritative.

Liturgical tradition includes Hai's name among the poets of the synagogue, and ascribes to him the composition of the litany, *Shema' koli asher yishma' be-koloth*, which is to be found in the prayers of the Jews of Spain, North Africa and Yemen as well as Baghdad. In all these communities the *Gaon*'s fervent prayer is still repeated on the eve of Yom Kippur – a worthy monument to the memory of the great teacher of Baghdad.[1]

CHAPTER 17

The Dark Ages of Iraqi Jewry

There is a sense in which it would be true to say that the loss of influence over the other Jewish communities of the world by the Jews of Babylonia was due in large measure to quarrels among the Muslim peoples themselves. For over a century, the lands which the Muslims had conquered remained under the rule of the Abbasid dynasty and constituted an empire both in name and in reality, united under one caliph. By the middle of the ninth century, however, the Abbasid dynasty was facing collapse, being surrounded and infiltrated by a body of predominantly Turkish soldiery. Originally, these troops had been brought as a bodyguard by the eighth Abbasid caliph, al-Mu'tasim, son of Harun al-Rashid by a Turkish slave, in a bid to counterbalance the influence of troops from Khorasan; but the haughtiness of the Turkish soldiers and the yearly import of more of them began to pose an even greater danger to the Abbasids. So much so that in 836, in an effort to prevent a native uprising in Baghdad against his bodyguard, al-Mu'tasim removed his seat of government from the capital to Samarra, some sixty miles farther up the Tigris. It was in Samarra that the Caliph al-Mutawakkil was murdered by the Turkish soldiery at the instigation of his own son. This marked the start of the period of decline for the empire. After al-Mutawakkil we find caliphs made and unmade by troops, mostly Turkish, under generals who were usually former slaves striving for mastery. Eight caliphs ruled in Samarra, most of them deposed, imprisoned and murdered following a number of putsches perpetrated by the military, who were mostly slaves over whom the women of the court came to exercise great influence.

In the midst of this confusion and unrest, a rebellion was staged by the Zanj (Ethiopian) slaves led by one 'Ali ibn Muhammed and resulted in a great deal of fighting and bloodshed which lasted fourteen years (870–83). When, towards the end of the century, Baghdad was restored as the capital under the Caliph al-Mu'tadhid (892–902), the situation did not improve materially, and real power continued to slip into the hands of the military. The year 908 saw the rise and fall within the same day, 17 December, of the Caliph Abdullah ibn al-Mu'tazz. His successor, al-Muqtadir, ruled for twenty-four years, but his reign was marked by the rise and fall of thirteen prime ministers, some of whom were put to death. A succession of caliphs following al-Muqtadir – who likewise met a violent death – fared no better, being no more than titular rulers dominated and dictated to by foreign conquerors and intruders each bearing the pompous title of *amir al-umaraa* (prince of princes) which was bestowed on them by the caliph himself. One of these went so far as to have his name joined with that of the caliph (al-Radhi, 934–40) in the Friday prayer. Al-Radhi, who though not deposed did not escape death at the hands of the soldiery, is considered by Arab chroniclers 'the last of the real caliphs', meaning that he was the last to deliver the Friday oration at the mosque and conduct certain affairs of state. With him vanished the last vestiges of power and dignity that used to be associated with his office, and 'the prince of princes' became well established as the actual ruler of the Muslim state.[1]

It was during this period of confusion, bordering on total anarchy, that most of the crucial developments in the history of the *Gaonate* occurred. During the reign of David ben Zakkai as Exilarch, it is important to remember that his office had dealings with up to ten caliphs, all of them mere puppets and many of them corrupt to a degree that denouncing some *Gaon* or Jewish dignitary to them or to their ministers must have been an extremely simple transaction. It is worth noting, in this connection, that the great six-year-long feud between the Exilarch and Saadia *Gaon* took place during the reign of al-Radhi, and that only three years after Saadia's death the Caliph al-Mustakfi (944–6) virtually surrendered all his authority to Ahmad ibn Buwaih, thus ushering in the Buwaihid period of Iraqi history which lasted from 945 to 1055.

The coming of the Buwaihids opened an even darker chapter in the history of the Abbasid caliphate. Incredible as it may sound, it managed to survive in one form or other for just over three centuries more. Al-Mustakfi, neither in the mood nor in a position to fight, received ibn Buwaih one day in December 945 and made him his *amir al-umaraa*; he also gave him the honorific title of *Mu'izz al-Dawla* (one who cherishes the state). Ahmad ibn Buwaih was one of three sons whose father, Abu Shujaa' Buwaih, was the chief of a warlike horde who claimed descent from the ancient Sassanid kings. During their 110 years of supremacy, the Buwaihids made and unmade caliphs at will, and the position of the empire deteriorated even further. Baghdad ceased to be the centre and hub of the Muslim world, and likewise its Jewry began to lose its intellectual and religious hold on Jews in other parts of the world. The year which many historians fix as marking the end of the *Gaonate*, 1038, occurs during the reign of the last Buwaihid-controlled caliph, al-Qayim (1031–75). In 1055, the Saljuq Tughril Beg entered Baghdad and put an end to Buwaihid rule, opening yet another chapter in the history of Islam and the caliphate.

The Buwaihids were Persian Shiites notorious for their religious fanaticism. The Saljuqs were Turks. About the year 956, a chieftain named Saljuq made a surprise appearance, settling in the region of Bokhara at the head of his clan of Turkoman Ghuzz. They embraced Sunni Islam, and then slowly but surely Saljuq and his sons after him fought their way westwards and southwards until, on 18 December 1055, one of Saljuq's grandsons, Tughril Beg, stood at the head of his wild Turkoman tribes at the gates of Baghdad. Al-Qayim, seeing that the military governor of the city under the last Buwaihids left the capital without much ado, hastened to receive the Saljuq invader. For nearly 203 years (1055–1258) the Saljuqs ruled most of Islam's eastern domain, and their era is considered one of the most notable in the history of Islam. This is not surprising, if only because Salah el-Din (Saladin), the liberator of Jerusalem and the man who defeated the mighty Crusaders, was himself a Saljuq.

As far as Baghdad was concerned, the Saljuq supremacy came to an effective end in 1194, when at the instigation of the Caliph al-Nasser (1180–1225) Takash, a member of the Turkish dynasty of the Khwarizm Shahs, fought and defeated Sultan Tughril, entering Baghdad and thus ending the Saljuq line in Iraq and Kurdistan. But neither Takash nor his successors were to prove of any help to the last Abbasid caliphs, and in 1258 the Abbasid dynasty finally gave up the ghost, after a little over five centuries of reign, of which less than one of them can be said to have been really theirs.

Chingiz Khan, also known as Genghis Khan, is reported to have described himself as 'the scourge of God sent to men as a punishment for their sins'. The realm of the Abbasids during this Mongol conqueror's lifetime (1155–1227) was perhaps the most deserving of such punishment. Here is how Philip Hitti depicts Baghdad society during the last century of Abbasid rule:

> The large harems, made possible by the countless number of eunuchs; the girl and the boy slaves (*ghilman*), who contributed most to the degradation of womanhood and the degeneration of

manhood; the unlimited concubines and the numberless half-brothers and half-sisters in the imperial household with their unavoidable jealousies and intrigues; the luxurious scale of high living with the emphasis on wine and song – all these and other similar forces sapped the vitality of family life and inevitably produced the persistently feeble heirs to the throne. The position of these heirs was rendered still more feeble by their interminable disputes over a right of succession which was never definitely determined.[2]

It was Chingiz Khan's grandson Hulagu, however, who was to mete out his grandfather's terrible punishment. Sweeping before him all those petty princedoms which were striving to grow on the ruins of the empire of the Khwarizm Shahs, Hulagu sent an invitation to the Caliph al-Musta'sim to join in the campaign against the Ismaili Assassins. But the caliph failed to respond, thereby making the mistake of his life. By 1256 all the Assassin strongholds were overrun – and in true Mongol fashion not only were the Assassins crushed but even babies were ruthlessly slaughtered. In September 1257, as he was winding his way down the Khorasan highway, Hulagu sent the caliph an ultimatum demanding his surrender. Al-Musta'sim's reply was too evasive for the conqueror's taste, and in January 1258 Hulagu's mangonels were effectively storming the walls of the capital.

A series of desperate attempts were then made on the part of the inhabitants to stave off the coming disaster. The caliph's chief minister ibn al-'Alqami, accompanied by the Nestorian catholicos, appeared to ask for terms; warnings were issued citing the fate of others who had dared violate 'the city of peace' (*Madinat al-Salam*), which was the name by which the capital was also known. One appeal claimed that 'if the Caliph is killed the whole universe is disorganized, the sun hides its face, rain ceases, and plants grow no more'. But Hulagu refused to receive the minister and his companions, and paid no heed to the ominous warnings and threats, especially since his own astrologers had advised him differently.

By the tenth of February [Hulagu's] hordes had swarmed into the city and the unfortunate caliph with his 300 officials and *qadis* [judges] rushed to offer an unconditional surrender. Ten days later they were all put to death. The city itself was given over to plunder and flames; the majority of its population, including the family of the caliph, were wiped out of existence. Pestilential odours emitted by corpses strewn unburied in the streets compelled Hulagu to withdraw from the town for a few days. Perhaps he intended to retain Baghdad for his residence and, therefore, the devastation was not as thorough as in other towns. . . . For the first time the Muslim world was left without a caliph whose name could be cited in the Friday prayers.[3]

Of the fortunes of the Jewish community of Baghdad during those havoc-stricken days we know very little. We know that Hulagu deigned to spare the Nestorians, whose patriarch received special favours probably owing to the fact that the Mongol conqueror had a Christian wife. We know also that certain mosques and schools were spared or rebuilt, and it is quite likely that Jewish institutions and houses of worship received similar treatment. One thing we know for certain. Although the Jews suffered alongside other inhabitants from the general anarchy and destruction, Hulagu and his successors subsequently employed members of a Jewish family as their physicians and ministers, and a Jew by the name of Sa'd el-Dawla was eventually named governor of Mesopotamia on their behalf.

After the death of Hai *Gaon* in 1038 the Exilarch Hezekiah, a descendant of David ben Zakkai, took over the *Gaonate* as well, and we know from shreds of information in various documents that he was still in office in 1055. He, too, was denounced to the caliph and thrown into prison, where he probably died, while his two sons escaped to Spain. By that time the Babylonian centre was all but eclipsed, and Samuel ben Joseph, nicknamed al-Baghdadi, who was then in Spain, was being mentioned as Hezekiah's successor. But for some reason Samuel did not return to Baghdad; instead, a native of Spain, Isaac ben Moses, was finally put in charge of affairs there. There is then a gap between Isaac ben Moses – who hailed from Denia and who was known as ibn Sakni – and the next *Gaon* about whom we do have some information, Solomon ben Samuel *Gaon*. He was probably in office until about the middle of the twelfth century, and a number of documents from the Cairo *geniza* show that at that time the *Gaonate* in Baghdad was in close connection with the Jewries of Persia, North Africa, Spain and Central Europe. 'Ali abu Samuel, who took office either before or after Solomon *Gaon*, is considered the most important of the *Geonim* of the post-*Geonic* period in Baghdad.

'Ali's son Samuel, known as ibn al-Dustur, was a minor when his father died, and this is supposed to be the reason for the assumption of the *Gaonate* by an outsider. Solomon ben Samuel had prepared his son to be next in line, but the latter's early death resulted in the dignity falling to the lot of Samuel ben 'Ali. This *Gaon* became famous through his dispute with Maimonides, his correspondence with scholars, and descriptions by travellers. Benjamin of Tudela, who visited Baghdad about 1170, reports that in Samuel's time there were ten academies in the city, the first and most important being under the guidance of the *Gaon* himself while the second was headed by his brother Hananiah ben 'Ali ha-Levy. Another traveller, Rabbi Pethahiah of Ratisbon, visited Baghdad a couple of years later and wrote about the *Gaon* that, among many other things, he could trace his genealogy back to the Prophet Samuel, that he had no sons, and that he had a very learned daughter well versed in the Bible and the Talmud. This young lady, we learn further, used to give lessons in the Scriptures to the students, addressing them through a window. She herself was within the building while her disciples were outside, below, and could not see her. The *Gaon*, we are further told, had authority over the whole of Mesopotamia, the districts of Mosul and Damascus, and the cities of Persia and Media. His jurisdiction extended even to Europe; a *responsum* of his in reply to a query from Rabbi Moses of Kiev is still preserved.

As to Samuel's objections to Maimonides's work, little is known about this. What is certain is that these two leaders could not see eye to eye in many important theological and ritual questions. Maimonides's views concerning bodily resurrection after death, for example, gave rise to many attacks against him; his critics stirred up unrest and ill-feeling among the Jews of Yemen; and in 1189 one of them approached the *Gaon* of Baghdad for guidance. The *Gaon*'s reply was lost, but we have the following description of it in Maimonides's own words in one of his *responsa*:

> This year [1191] some correspondence written by our colleagues and friends of Baghdad reached us. They mention that a Yemenite enquirer asked about these problems of the Gaon who officiates at present in Baghdad, Rab Samuel ha-Levy, and he compiled for them a dissertation on the resurrection of the dead. And he put my opinions concerning this problem partly in a mistaken way, and partly in a form which can be justified. He defended me, but very little help can be derived from his penmanship. After this exchange of letters, the Gaon's dissertation in its original form was sent to me. I saw in it all the homilies and Aggadoth which he compiled. Yet it is well known that scholars cannot be required to relate such homilies

and wonderful deeds verbatim as women are accustomed to tell them in the house of mourners, but the aim is to explain their subjects till they are clear to the intelligent, or at least nearly so. And more wonderful still are some strange ideas mentioned by him pretending that they are philosophical views on psychology.

These rather sharp remarks made by Maimonides about his influential critic are understandable, though they do not in the end amount to much since Samuel *Gaon* was known to be fairly well versed in contemporary philosophy. The *Gaon*'s treatise against Maimonides's views on the resurrection of the dead did, indeed, create such a stir that a Baghdadi scholar – probably named Daniel – found it necessary to compile a refutation of his critique.

Samuel ben 'Ali *Gaon* died about 1207 on the same day as his daughter, and one *paitan* (religious poet) was moved to exclaim: 'God has forbidden to slaughter a lamb and its young one on the same day. How could death be so cruel as to snatch away simultaneously both father and daughter?'

A succession of *Gaons* followed Samuel ben 'Ali, his immediate heirs being his two sons-in-law 'Azariah and Zekhariah ben Berakhiah. The latter, who in Samuel's lifetime had already attained prominence as *ab beth din* (president of the religious court), was known for his great scholarship and learning. However, having spent a very short time in the office, little is known about his conduct as *Gaon*. Another *Gaon*, Eleazar ben Hilal, called ibn Fahd, is also mentioned as officiating about this time. From a decree signed by the caliph, el-Nasser Bidinillah, and recorded by the Arab historian ibn al-Sa'i, we learn that Daniel ben Eleazar ben Nathanel (Hibatullah) was appointed in 1209 to succeed Eleazar ben Hilal. The decree, which was publicly proclaimed in the synagogues of Baghdad, was apparently made at the request of the candidate himself, since the power of appointment rested in the caliph.

The next *Gaon* in Baghdad was Isaac ibn Shweikh, whom the famous al-Harizi praises as a liturgical writer. Another poet, Eleazar el-Babli of Baghdad, was personally acquainted with this *Gaon* and took part in some lively grammatical and lexicographical skirmishes with him. Four *Gaons* by the name of Isaac followed one another – Isaac ibn Shweikh, Isaac ben Israel, Isaac el-Awani, and a fourth who is not clearly identified but who was active in the years 1210–29. This last *Gaon* was succeeded by Daniel ibn abil-Rabi' ha-Kohen, about whom only very scanty information is available from the work of a contemporary poet. Others are mentioned in the work of certain poets of the time, but none are clearly identified as *Gaon*; and what tends to add to the confusion is that the term with the passage of time became a family name.

By the middle of the thirteenth century, we can no longer find concrete information of any kind concerning the *Gaonate* and conditions in Mesopotamia as a whole. We cannot even tell whether the *Gaonate* ceased to exist altogether and, unless some new discoveries are made or some evidence comes up somewhere, we will remain in the dark in this matter. What seems certain, however, is that after the Mongol conquest in 1258, the Babylonian centre fell into a period of deep slumber. Other centres were fast arising and consolidating themselves. As Marx and Margolis put it: 'The creative work of Babylonian Jewry was done. Its achievement passed on as a heritage to the communities of the West. In the halls of learning of North Africa and Europe reverberated the discussions of Rab and Samuel, of Rabban and Joseph, of Abaye and Raba. There men rehearsed codes and commentaries and theological treatises of the Gaons of Sura and Pumbeditha, who had blazed the path and given direction to Jewish life for centuries to come.'[4]

CHAPTER 18

Lasting Imprint

Joseph ben Judah ibn Aknin, a twelfth-century Judeo-Arabic author who is generally identified with Maimonides's famous pupil and disciple of the same surname, left us a work in which he provides a painstaking description of what a person who wishes to secure a Jewish and general education ought to study. In an ethical work entitled *Tub el-Nufous* (*A Cure for Sick Souls*), he gives a detailed programme of study which he claims a brilliant student could complete before he was twenty. Apart from such obvious subjects as reading and writing; Torah, Mishnah and Hebrew grammar; poetry; Talmud; 'philosophic observations of religion'; logic, mathematics, geometry, optics, astronomy, mechanics and the natural sciences; and astrology and music, he also lists 'philosophical studies' and metaphysics. In the middle of the thirteenth century, Jehudah ben Samuel ibn 'Abbas includes in his school curriculum: reading, (Arabic) translation of the Pentateuch, the historical books of the Old Testament, certain specific treatises on Hebrew grammar, Talmud, and ethical works including *A Cure for Sick Souls*. These, however, were included in the religious curriculum. When the pupil had completed them, he 'tasted the honey of science', beginning, curiously enough, with medicine, followed by 'Indian' arithmetic and music. After this the pupil commenced the study of Aristotle's logic as interpreted by ibn Rushd (Averroes, the Muslim philosopher), and finally he took up natural science and metaphysics.

Both ibn Aknin and ibn 'Abbas lived and studied in Arabic Spain, but the situation in Baghdad schools and academies did not radically differ from that in their Spanish counterparts. Philosophy, however, as distinct from theology and the philosophy of religion, was never one of the strong points of Babylonian Jewish intellectual life. Apart from Saadia al-Fayyumi, who was born in Egypt though he reached intellectual maturity and produced the bulk of his work in Sura and Baghdad, only a few Babylonian Jewish thinkers engaged in the study of philosophy proper. These, and their more prominent successors in

Spain in the twelfth and thirteenth centuries, were all thoroughly influenced by their Muslim contemporaries. In the heyday of Muslim philosophy there were three categories of philosopher – the Mutakallimun (from Kalam), the Neoplatonists and the Aristotelians. For the most part, the Babylonian Jewish philosophers were the pupils and followers of the Mutakallimun, who in turn were divided into two main schools, the Mu'tazilites and Ash'arites. In Chapter 71 of *A Guide of the Perplexed* (*Dalalat al-Hayirin*) Maimonides refers to this phenomenon:

> You will find that in the few works composed by the Geonim and the Karaites on the unity of God and on such matter as is connected with this doctrine, they followed the lead of the Muhammedan Mutakallimun. . . . It also happened that at the time when the Muhammedans adopted this method of the Kalam, there arose among them a certain sect, called Mu'tazila. In certain things our scholars followed the theory and the method of these Mu'tazila.

There was, however, a marked difference between the rabbinites and the Karaites though both came under the influence of the Mutakallimun, especially the Mu'tazilites.

> The Rabbinites being staunch adherents of the Talmud, to the influence of which they owed a national and religious self-consciousness much stronger than that of the Karaites, who rejected the authority of tradition, did not allow themselves to be carried away so far by the ideas of the Muhammedan rationalists as to become their slavish followers. The Karaites are less scrupulous; and as they were the first among the Jews to imitate the Mu'tazila in the endeavour to rationalize Jewish doctrine, they adopted their views in all details, and it is sometimes impossible to tell from the contents of a Karaite Mu'tazilite work whether it was written by a Jew or a Muhammedan.

There is, however, another side to this coin. Some scholars have suggested that the origin of the Mu'tazilite movement itself was due to the influence of learned Jews with whom the Muhammedans came into contact, especially in Basra, an important centre of the school.[1]

One Babylonian Jewish philosopher who was a true Mu'tazilite and 'moves in the path laid out by these Muhammedan rationalists' was David al-Muqammas, who lived in Baghdad and preceded Saadia. His chief work is known by the title *Twenty Chapters*, fifteen of which were discovered in the original Arabic in 1898. Al-Muqammas is said to have associated with Saadia, who is claimed to have learned much from him – which, if true, makes these two thinkers contemporaries although Saadia may have been the younger in age. His work, parts of which also survive in Hebrew translation, deals partly with science and philosophy, their definition and classification. Science, according to al-Muqammas, is divided into two categories, theoretical and practical. Theoretical science aims at knowledge for its own sake, while practical science seeks an end beyond knowledge, namely the production of something. This type of science we call art. Thus geometry is science in so far as one desires to know the nature and the relationship to each other of solid, surface, line, point, square, triangle and circle. But if his purpose is to know how to build a square or circular house, or to construct a mill or dig a well, or measure land, one becomes an artisan.

Theoretical science, according to al-Muqammas, is threefold. First and foremost stands theology, which investigates the unity of God, His laws and His commandments. This is the highest and most important of all the sciences. Next comes logic and ethics, which help men to form opinions and guide them in the path of understanding. The third and last type of theoretical science is physics, the knowledge of created things.

In the ninth and tenth chapters, after discussing the divine attributes, al-Muqammas sums up the results of his investigations. God, he maintains, is one not in the sense in which a genus is said to be one, nor in that in which a species is one, nor as the number 1 is one, nor yet as an individual creature is one; He is one in the sense of a simple unity in which there is no distinction or composition. He is one and there is no second like Him. He is first without beginning, and He is last without end. He is the cause and ground of everything caused and effected.[2]

The best known of the Babylonian Jewish followers of the Mu'tazilites was Joseph ben Abraham, euphemistically surnamed al-Basir (the seer) on account of his blindness. Al-Basir was a Karaite who lived in the early decades of the eleventh century. Unlike Saadia, who only tacitly accepts the views and methods of the Mu'tazilites, al-Basir was an avowed follower of the Kalam, and in his works treats only of those questions which are common to Jew and Muhammedan alike. He avoids, for example, such important issues as those centring on the question of whether it is possible that the law of God may be abrogated – a question which meant so much to his rabbinite predecessor, Saadia. Another fundamental difference between the two is that al-Basir shows himself as a more loyal follower of the Kalam by openly adopting the atomic theory, which Saadia opposed. This theory comprised the underlying premise of the Kalam, which maintained that all existence is composed of atoms, which form the substance, characterized by certain properties which are called accidents. These latter are constantly changing since their duration is only momentary. Since no object can be conceived without its properties, and as these are constantly created, it follows that all existence must have been created. Having thus established creation, the Kalam school further argued that this created universe must have been fashioned by an outside force, namely God. Saadia, as well as other non-Karaite Jewish philosophers, did not adopt the atomic theory, preferring a variety of the Aristotelian conception of matter and form. Nevertheless, they all had in common the view that God's existence is proved by establishing the fact of creation and necessitating a creator.

Al-Basir also maintained, along with his Muslim contemporaries, that God's creation was a pure act of grace. However, having done this and communicated to us a knowledge of Himself and His will, it was then God's duty to guide us in the right path, by sending us prophets. The commandments and prohibitions, therefore, must never be contrary to the knowledge of reason, since the former are means of guidance and the latter a protection against destructive influences. If commandments and prohibitions did not have this rational basis, we do not see why God should have imposed them upon us.

Another article of faith of the Mu'tazilites which al-Basir adopted whole-heartedly was the argument that, having given us reason to know His being and having announced His truth through the prophets, it was God's duty to reward those who knew him and were obedient, eternally in the next world, and to punish eternally the unbeliever. If a person has merits and sins, they are balanced against each other. If the sinner repents of his evil deeds, it is the duty of God to accept his repentance and remit his punishment.[3]

One of the most remarkable developments in the cultural sphere which resulted from the Islamic conquests was the shift from Aramaic to Arabic as the vernacular of the Babylonian Jews. It was a change of radical importance. In Baghdad and Basra, the centres of Islamic culture and literature, educated Jews developed a voracious appetite for literature in Arabic, 'not only the imported part of it, but also the Koran and Muslim poetry, philology, biography and history', as Abraham Halkin asserts. He continues:

> Thus they became citizens of the great world. This naturalization in the culture of their environment was of prime importance. The vocabulary of the Islamic faith finds its way into Jewish books; the Koran becomes a proof-text. The Arabs' practice of citing poetry in their works is taken over by Jews. Jewish writings teem with sentences from the works of scientists, philosophers and theologians. Indeed, Arabic literature, native and imported, becomes the general background of all that the Jews write. And all this goes on for a long time with no hostility toward the foreign learning, no suspicion of its negative or dangerous effects, no awareness that it is the same 'Greek wisdom' which Talmudic sources warned Jews to study only when it is neither day nor night.[4]

With a cultural and mental transformation of such dimensions it was inevitable that the dominant language should soon prevail. At first, works in *Halakhah* during the Muslim period – *responsa* and codifications – were written in the Aramaic dialect which we find in the Talmud. But Arabic soon encroached on this field as well, challenging the supremacy of Aramaic and actually superseding it. The influence of the environment did not stop at the language, however; it also affected the method of presentation. Jewish writers on theological and philosophical subjects began to show a greater interest in systematization, in summaries, introductions and lexicography. *Gaons* and rabbis who composed their *halakhic* works in Arabic include Saadia, Hefes ben Yasliah, Samuel ben Hofni, Hai *Gaon*, and hosts of others whose works are mostly lost to us. By the tenth century the great majority of Babylonian Jews used Arabic as their vernacular, and the language established itself thoroughly in the life and culture of the Jewish population as a whole.

Another lasting facet of the cultural heritage of Babylonian Jewry was the decisive role it played in the rise and efflorescence of Judeo–Arabic culture in Muslim Spain. In a very valid sense, the legacy left by Spanish Jewry – what later came to be known as 'the Golden Age of Jewish culture' – would not have been possible were it not for the contribution made by the scholars and rabbis of Sura, Baghdad and Pumbeditha, some of whom actually made their way to Spain and settled and worked there. As one student of Spanish–Jewish history has put it, from a cultural viewpoint 'the Jewish settlement of Spain was, in a sense, a colony of Babylonian Jewry'.[5] Compared to the close ties between the Spanish communities and the academies of Babylonia, we are further told,

> the influence of the Jewish population in Palestine upon them was small. . . . The Palestinian Talmud never won acceptance from Spanish Jewry. They studied the laws in the Babylonian Talmud and the decisions of the *geonim* of Babylonia. . . . [The Jews of Spain] followed Babylonian Jewry in every aspect and even imitated them in the pronunciation of Hebrew.[6]

The transference of Babylonian Jewish influence, and in a sense of the centre of Jewish learning as a whole, from Iraq to Muslim Spain was effected in many well-known ways, including emigration. The story is told, for instance, that during the reign of the Umayyad Caliph Abdul Rahman III in Cordoba (912–61), a vessel from the East was seized by the caliph's admiral. The ship, which was headed for the Spanish coast, carried among others a Babylonian Jewish family of three: Moses ben Enoch, his wife and his young son. Fearing dishonour, the young mother threw herself into the sea, while the boy and his father were taken captive and brought to Cordoba where, in accordance with the ways of those days, they were ransomed by the influential Jewish community there.

Moses ben Enoch (Hanoch) happened to be one of the most learned teachers at the Babylonian academy of Sura, who had been sent on a fund-raising mission to Jewish centres in Spain and North Africa. In the event, he came to Spain at a highly opportune moment. The Western caliphs were eager to see their Jewish subjects become independent of the hegemony of Eastern Jewish learning and to stop sending funds to the lands of their arch-enemies, the Eastern caliphs. Accordingly, with the help of Hasdai ibn Shaprut, a cultured Jew who was Abdul Rahman's trusted adviser, Moses ben Enoch was persuaded to stay in Cordoba and was installed as the head of the Talmudical school there. With his appointment, he launched upon an extensive educational scheme. Being first and foremost a teacher of *Halakhah*, his fame spread throughout Spain and students from the various Spanish communities came to Cordoba to study at his academy. Ben Enoch's success was so thorough and so impressive, indeed, that in the end it led to the weakening of the cultural ties between Spanish and Babylonian Jewries, and the long-standing ambition of the Western caliphs to make themselves and their peoples less dependent on the East was realized. 'As the religious centre at the western edge of the Mediterranean basin rose to ever greater eminence,' writes Ashtor, 'the old centre in Babylonia faded away. Its condition at that time was at the nadir.'[7]

Moses ben Enoch's Spanish career was by no means the first of its kind. Indeed, it was almost the last of a series of such emigrations – and not the most important. The movement, in fact, had started towards the end of the eighth century, 150 years before ben Enoch's appearance. In the last quarter of that century, a teacher of considerable prominence came to Muslim Spain from Babylonia. His name was Natronai bar Habibae, and he came to Spain because his candidacy for the position of Exilarch had failed. Disappointed, Natronai left Babylonia in 773, setting out on the road to the other end of the Mediterranean where, according to reports reaching him, a large and prosperous Jewish community had sprung up.

> He went to Spain, where he was received with great honours, and at the request of the community leaders and scholars he taught them about the more involved problems of the Halakha. The name of this illustrious scholar was not forgotten by the Andalusian Jews, and later generations told how the expelled exilarch came to the Jews of Spain and set the Talmud down in writing for them as he knew it – by heart.[8]

While it is true that the religious–cultural ties between the Jews of Spain and those of Babylonia weakened considerably during the era of Moses ben Enoch and of his son, Enoch ben Moses, these ties were not completely severed:

> The Jews living between these two points [Babylonia and Muslim Spain] sent the writings of Spanish authors to Babylonia, and copies of the *responsa* of the heads of the Babylonian academies – in which they commented on complete tractates of the Gemara – were brought to Spain. Nonetheless, by the time of Rabbi Moses and his son they no longer turned to the *geonim* of Babylonia with every difficult problem, which earlier was the practice of Andalusian Jewry; they also sent fewer contributions.[9]

What led to this weakening of ties was not merely the existence in Spain of noted rabbis and scholars. Ashtor writes:

> There is no doubt that the Omayyads [who reigned in Cordoba] looked favourably upon the burgeoning of Spain as a Jewish cultural centre and the consequent break in the close ties with the Babylonian schools. They were not opposed to such ties *per se*; but, in former times, the relations between their subjects and the *geonim* in Babylonia had distinctly implied an acknowledgement of another authority – and this was not to their liking.[10]

It is almost in the nature of a commonplace to say that for a period of 800 years or so, from the days of Rab to the days of Hai, Judaism was guided by the thought and the spiritual vigour of the Jews of Babylonia. Indeed, it would be true to say that the achievements of this Jewry, crowned by the conclusion of the Talmud and continuing through several centuries until the middle of the eleventh century and beyond, have had an influence which continues to be felt up till our own day. Even though Babylonian Jewry began to lose its grip after 800 years of continuous intellectual leadership supplied mainly by the academies of Sura and Pumbeditha, the impact they made has not been affected in any material way. This is not the place, however, for delving into the reasons for the progressive loss of influence suffered by this Jewry, though this has already been dealt with in previous chapters. Suffice it to say here that, apart from those factors which sprang from the life and conduct of the Babylonian Jews themselves, there were certain historical forces at play which were to change the whole aspect of life in the Muslim Empire, and with it the life and fortunes of the Jews themselves.

These forces, over which the Jewish community did not and could not possibly have had any control, included the constant quarrels that characterized the life of the empire itself and its peoples. The impact of these outside forces soon began to be felt. To start with, contact became difficult between the Babylonian centre and Jews who lived in the western lands of the declining caliphate. Another difficulty was the interruption of the easy flow of commerce between East and West, and as a result of their loss of control over the distant parts of their empire the caliphs lost a lot of income and resorted to imposing heavy taxes, and also enforced other laws which weighed heavily upon their subjects. The Jews of Babylonia, along with the Muslims and the Christians, became poor, and the academies and the Exilarch could not obtain enough funds either from their local supporters or from donors abroad.

Evidence of this deterioration in the economic conditions of the Jews is to be found in a letter, sent by Sherira *Gaon* towards the end of the tenth century to friends abroad, in which he complains that he and his colleagues had to withhold nourishment from their children owing to lack of funds from abroad and the great poverty prevailing at the seat of the *Gaonate*. He begs of his addressees to continue the tradition set by their fathers of supporting the institutions of the *Gaonate* and save them from impending collapse. From the tone of the letter it would seem that the communities abroad no longer sent their queries to Baghdad or

Sura on matters of law and theology, and that this threatened the institution of the *Gaonate* itself in addition to the great material loss it obviously entailed. 'Our old scholars sit desolate,' he writes, 'our young students are sighing in desperation, our teachers are complaining. We feel bitterly, for it seems to us as if the whole world is heading toward destruction.' Sherira's main fear, however, is that the downfall of the *Gaonate* which may result from its economic plight would spell misfortune to the study of the Torah and to religious life as a whole. He also reveals that complaints had reached him from friends and supporters abroad that the wisdom and the learning of the academy had diminished, implying that this was probably the reason why many communities and donors had discontinued their regular contributions. To this he retorts:

> Indeed it is so; behold our glory is dimmed, our learning decreased, our Midrashim are desolate, we are left a few out of many, the Mishnah school [Midrash Tannaim] is almost forsaken. Previously any lad, even if he was blind, was brought to the Midrash ha-Mishnah, but nowadays no one brings his son, and we have to use sticks so that some students should enter in order that the Mishnah should not be forgotten entirely. Most parents send their sons to other occupations where they can earn a living. From generation to generation, from year to year, the situation gets worse and worse.

There may well be some exaggeration in these gloomy descriptions; yet the trend was there and unmistakable; and economic and political conditions even led to emigration with Jews of all descriptions and from the various occupations – merchants, scholars, farmers and just plain adventurers – deciding to seek their fortunes where they were needed by growing Jewish communities to the west – Egypt, North Africa, Spain. At no time was the movement so extensive as to affect the continuity of Jewish life in Babylonia in any material sense, but over several generations the toll tended to be felt, and Babylonian Jewry became a mere shadow of its former self.

Although, as we saw in Chapter 17, the *Gaonate* continued to exist well after Sherira's death, it would be fair to say that by the year 1000 Babylonia was fast losing its hold on the Jewish mind. This, however, can in no way detract from the value of its contribution to Jewish life and the many-faceted religious, cultural and literary heritage this Jewry left and which continues to give spiritual nourishment and moral strength to Jews everywhere. Some elements of this heritage, which some like to link with what is called 'the miracle of Jewish survival', have been listed by a modern Jewish historian under a few headings not necessarily arranged according to either importance or lasting impact.

One of these is the literary heritage. Both in volume and in scope the actual books produced during the period of Babylonian Jewish supremacy were extremely impressive. All growing out of the Bible, these works fell into the following literary categories: law; Midrash; poetry, which was mostly in the form of prayer; stories and parables; philosophy; and grammar. 'Through these the first half of Jewish history bequeathed to its succeeding ages a number of important principles by which the Jews continued to be distinguished from other peoples.'[11]

The supremacy of knowledge is another of the elements of this heritage. One of the primary ideas which Babylonian Jewry – and Eastern Jewries as a whole – left as an inheritance to the Jews of the West is that learning is the foundation of Jewish life. The idea was that an ignorant man cannot be a pious one, for such a man does not understand God's word or the basis of human behaviour. Not that physical strength and wealth were under-estimated, but they were considered secondary to the good life. Leadership must, therefore, rest in the hands of the scholar. 'Subsequent communities of Jews sometimes wandered away from this ideal, and the Jewishness of such communities was always in danger. The usual Jewish community, the self-respecting one, never failed to encourage study among adults as well as children and to show the utmost respect for the learned man. To study the Torah, which meant all of Jewish learning, became one of the foremost Jewish ideals.'

Another idea transmitted by Eastern Jewry to the West was that man's whole life must be dedicated to God. 'It was not enough to *think* of Godliness; it was necessary to *act* in such a way as to devote every minute of the day to holy living. A man's character is developed by his actions. Consequently, the more exacting the actions he imposes upon himself the better his character will be. *Mitzvot*, religious commandments, became the bases of Jewish life.'

The principle of the unity of Israel is another of the primary ideas comprising the heritage of the Jews of Babylonia. The force and the lasting impact of the saying, 'All Israelites are brothers', can hardly be exaggerated.

> Other peoples might depend upon national territory to keep them united. But the Jewish people was considered a unique people in that its unity depended, not upon race or land, but upon a common

devotion to the One God and to the laws and ideals developed throughout Jewish history. . . . The hope of restoring a Jewish nation to Palestine never died in Jewish hearts; but Jewish unity never depended upon the realization of this hope.

In the field of community life, the Jews of Babylonia developed a form of community which was taken over and continued by the Jews of the West. 'The same officials and the same public institutions as existed in Sura were established in Rome, Toledo, Cologne and Cracow. In time they became modified to some extent, but till the nineteenth century the general forms remained unchanged. Every Jew was a member of the community; rich and poor had rights and duties which they could not be denied.'

Finally, Eastern Jewry in general, and the Jews of Babylonia in particular, bequeathed to the Jews of the West an ideal of the future world which inspired hope. 'They called it the Days of the Messiah. In His own good time God will redeem the world from oppression and wickedness. Humanity will then recognize the greatness of the Jewish contribution to civilization, and peace will reign supreme. That time will come when Israel deserves it; hence its coming or its delay depends upon the actions of each individual Jew.'

CHAPTER 19

100 Years of Turmoil

The slaughter perpetrated in the winter of 1258 by Hulagu's hordes in Baghdad alone was of such dimensions that the number of victims has been estimated at anything between 800,000 and 2,000,000. According to one Arab historian, the *dhimmis* of the capital, Christians and Jews, were spared; in fact, he claims that 'none was spared except *ahl el-dhimma* . . . and those of the inhabitants who sought refuge in their houses and in the residence of the Wazir ibn al-'Alqami, in addition to a group of merchants who acquired *dhimmi* certificates for huge sums of money. . . .' However, while this account may be partly or even largely true as far as life and limb were concerned, the Jews of Baghdad suffered along with their Muslim compatriots from the destruction and the pillage which accompanied the Mongol invasion.

We know little about the conditions in which these Jews lived during the first three decades of Mongol rule. According to one Arab historian writing some seven centuries later, the number of Jews in Baghdad on Hulagu's entry was 3,600 tax-payers, and they had sixteen houses of worship. But this figure cannot stand the test of comparison with other accounts, which give the impression of a community numbering at least 40,000 souls. By the end of the thirteenth century, Arab chroniclers were speaking of 100,000 Jews living in Baghdad – a figure which again cannot be accepted since these writers were generally hostile to the Jews and were trying to exaggerate Jewish power and influence under the Mongol-appointed Jewish governor Sa'd el-Dawla, who governed Iraq under Argun Khan for over two years, 1288–91.

One of the few factual accounts we have about the demographic and political conditions of the Jews of Baghdad relates to the year 1168, ninety years before the Mongol invasion. This was the year the Spanish Jewish traveller Benjamin of Tudela visited the city. In his *Travels*, Benjamin speaks of Baghdad and its Jewish community – and especially the institution of the Exilarchate – in superlatives. He also praises the Caliph al-Mustanjid (1160–70) as being 'kind unto Israel'. He gives the number of Jews in the capital as 40,000, and of the synagogues as twenty-eight. According to this account, the Jews enjoyed favourable political conditions under this caliph. They lived in the eastern part of Baghdad and in al-Karkh, situated on the other side of the river Tigris. He described Baghdad as

> the great city and the royal residence of the Caliph Amir al-Muminin al-'Abbasi, who is the head of the Muhammedan religion whom all the kings of Islam obey, occupying as he does a position similar to that held by the Pope over the Christians. The Caliph has a palace three miles in extent and with a great park full of trees and animals. The whole compound is surrounded by a wall, and in the park there is a lake whose waters are drawn from the Tigris. Whenever the king wishes to indulge in recreation, to rejoice or to celebrate, his servants catch all manner of birds, game and fish, and he goes to his palace accompanied by his counsellors and princes.

Benjamin describes the palace and the caliph at great length, both because he must have been very highly impressed by what he saw and because al-Mustanjid was said to have dealt kindly with his Jewish subjects, many of whom could be found in his entourage. The caliph is also credited with a knowledge of languages and of Jewish law, reading and writing Hebrew – attributes which seem exaggerated at best but which we have no way of verifying or refuting. Be that as it may, the work of another traveller, who visited Baghdad only a few decades later, depicts a totally different scene. This was Rabbi Pethahiah of Ratisbon, who visited the city during the reign of the Caliph al-Nasser (1180–1225), and who gave a picture of decline and degradation which does not fit Benjamin's account. Instead of the seat of wealth and learning, of a thriving Jewish community full of religious vigour, industrious, free and happy, depicted by Benjamin, we learn from Ratisbon that the community was full of sinners, bereft of the pious, forsaken, and its members pleasure-seeking and corrupt. The synagogues and the houses of learning, too, were either in ruins or relegated to some profane purpose.

We are thus quite in the dark as to both the size of the Jewish community in Baghdad and its socio-economic and educational conditions at the time Sa'd el-Dawla was named governor. What we know about Sa'd el-Dawla himself is that he was born in Abhar, Persia, scion of a Jewish family with close connections to the Mongol rulers and enjoying great wealth and prestige. At an early age he was sent to Baghdad to pursue his studies; he learnt medicine and soon became a famous physician, the most renowned in the city. He was also known as a great public figure, nimble in the arts of diplomacy and administration. In 1284 he was appointed a member of the Diwan (Bureau) of administration, and four years later he was named governor of Mesopotamia by Argun Khan. In this capacity he worked diligently in promoting the interests of his royal master, whose seat of power was in Tabriz, and is said to have raised Baghdad to a great height of wealth and importance. It appears, too, that in gratitude to his loyalty, integrity and skill the khan decided to elevate him to the dignity of Counsellor of the Empire, a position equivalent to that of wazir or prime minister.

Sa'd el-Dawla's strictness as governor and counsellor, however, proved to be too burdensome for the various public servants and the soldiery of the day, the overwhelming majority of whom were Muslims. At first he was praised by his contemporaries, and it is said that poems composed in his praise and collected by one of his aides filled a whole volume. However, when the first opportunity arose, the jealousy and the enmity – which were directed as much against the Mongol overlords as against Sa'd el-Dawla himself – began to find expression. When Argun Khan became seriously ill, and his great counsellor and physician failed to cure him, those who had feared and flattered him in his days of power and influence immediately turned against him, penning a petition to the khan complaining about the growing power of the Jews. Eventually, they took the first opportunity to overthrow him. They first attacked some of his aides, including his Mongol friend who bore the title of 'prince'. The death of the khan himself, which followed soon after these events, led to the muder of the wazir and an attack on the Jews of the city. The mob, not content with Sa'd el-Dawla's death, turned the Jewish quarter of the city into a horrible scene of murder and plunder.

Quoting Arabic and Persian sources, the British Orientalist Edward G. Browne provides interesting additional information about Sa'd el-Dawla's spell of power which sheds some light on the position of the Jews during that period. We learn from these sources that the wazir earned Argun's confidence by his knowledge of languages, such as Turkish and Mongolian. The significance of the minister's position and influence, and his identification with the Jews of his day, is reflected in these lines by a contemporary Arab poet:

> The Jews of this our time a rank attain,
> To which the Heavens might aspire in vain;
> Theirs is dominion, riches to them cling,
> To them belong both Councillor and King.

The exaggeration here is as gross as it is evident, and it is difficult to believe that a statesman of the shrewdness with which Sa'd el-Dawla is usually credited could so openly have identified himself with the Jews and showered them with such favours. Be that as it may, it would seem that jubilation was common among the Muslims of Baghdad after the wave of murder and destruction which followed the wazir's death. This is attested by the following lines, written by another contemporary poet after the events just described and referring to the Jews of Baghdad:

> Grim captains made them drink Death's cup of ill,
> Until their skulls the blood-bathed streets did fill,
> And from their dwellings seized the wealth they'd gained,
> And their well-guarded women's rooms profaned.

We will never know if these lines were written by a bragging Muslim, an envious Christian or even a Jew trying to bring home some point or other. We do know, however, that in spite of these terrible events some of the succeeding Mongol rulers went on appointing Jews to high positions and responsible places of trust. Some of these dignitaries, it is true, could not resist the temptation and abandoned Judaism in favour of Islam. Some of these Jewish converts to Islam are mentioned in the works of Arab historians and foreign travellers. The lot of the Jews and the Christians of Baghdad tended to fluctuate; under one of the khans the old distinguishing signs and the special tax which some Abbasid caliphs introduced were again imposed on them. The position of the Jews of Baghdad worsened, however, even compared to that of their co-religionists in other parts of the Mongol Empire, especially in Persia. This was no doubt another indicator of the general decline in the fortunes of the community, a decline which was gradually to develop into near collapse.[1]

Of the rest of the history of Babylonian Jews under the Mongol khans we know only bits and pieces. It appears that only some two years after Sa'd el-Dawla's tragic end an economic crisis compelled the regime to turn to another Jewish physician–financier for help. This man, who was reputed to be something of a historian and philosopher, had converted to Islam either shortly before or immediately after his rise to power and prominence. Eventually, he too attained to the lofty position of wazir and was given the honorific name Rashid el-Dawla or Rashid el-Din. Like Sa'd el-Dawla before him, his position gained him enemies in high places, being personal physician to the khan as well as his adviser and chief minister. When Uljaitu Khan (also known as Muhammed

Khadabandah Khan) fell ill, his physician failed to cure him and rumours spread by his enemies had it that he himself poisoned his master. When the khan died, in 1316, Rashid el-Dawla was formally accused of causing the khan's death and was executed. Subsequently and under Uljaitu Khan's successors a number of Jews were forced to convert to Islam, and some of them attained high positions in the empire. Among these were Sadid el-Dawla, whose name alone indicates that he occupied high office.

In 1336 the Mongols' hold on Iraq came to an end, and they were succeeded by the Jala'iris, a minor Mongol tribe. It was to the head of the tribe, Hasan Jala'ir, that the fate of the country fell following a partition of the empire. In 1339 Hasan, now a Muslim, made Baghdad the winter capital of his state, which included the provinces of Jezirah, Azarbaijan and Jibal as well as Iraq. The Jala'iris 'restored to Iraq, if little prosperity, some self-respect . . . and gave peace from aggression and some patronage to the arts'; but in 1383 the Mongol Sultan, Ahmad, again united the country with Tabriz into a single state and gave it ten years of peace under his viceroys.[2]

We know next to nothing about the Jews of Iraq in those turbulent times. The peace which the Jala'iris and Sultan Ahmad gave the country was again disturbed, this time by a catastrophe the like of which it had not known since Hulagu led his hordes into Baghdad. In 1401, during the reign of Qara Yusif, ruler of the Turkoman kingdom of the Black Sheep, Tamerlane (Timur the Lame), last and greatest of the Mongols, conquered Baghdad. Thousands were massacred; mosques, schools and dwellings were demolished. 'If the scenes and losses were less dreadful than those of the ruin of the Khalifate,' notes Longrigg, 'it was that Baghdad in 1401 had not the same pride to be humbled, the same materials for atrocity.'[3] During these developments, and the events which followed Timur's death in 1405, the brief return of the Jala'iris and the subsequent supremacy of the Turkomans under Qara Yusif's son, the little we know about the fortunes of the Jews there amounts to the fact that the synagogues of Baghdad were destroyed along with its mosques and churches, that Jewish property was similarly looted, many Jewish lives lost, and a number of Jews converted to Islam. By this time, neither the name *Gaon* is mentioned nor the title *resh galutha* (head of the exile) is recorded; what we hear about is the title *nasi* (prince, president), and specifically of one *nasi*, Sar Shalom ben Phinehas. It is believed that during nearly 100 years of turbulence, conquest and massacre Baghdad had little Jewish population to reckon with, if at all.

In the 1460s bitter enmity developed between the Black Sheep dynasty and a growing rival, similar in origin and in race – the White Sheep dynasty of Diyarbakr. In 1467, with Uzun Hasan of the White Sheep dynasty defeating Jihan Shah of the Black Sheep kingdom, his rule spread over Iraq and Persia.

> The change made little difference to Iraq, and the struggle of ambition rent the provinces of the White Sheep as of the Black. . . . Prince followed prince, intrigue and violence rent the loose and mutinous empire. The arms and diplomacy of Stambul, of Diyarbakr, of Isfahan were involved on this side or that, but none could secure peace or control. And when in 1499 a precarious agreement was reached between the warring cousins, it was to be torn up not [for once] by their own hands, but by the new monarch of a Persia revived and reinspired.[4]

It is generally thought that it was during the reign of Uzun Hasan and his successors of the White Sheep dynasty that the Jews began to come back to Baghdad. It is also thought that after 1492 a number of Jews who had been expelled from Spain found their way to the city.

CHAPTER 20

Recovery and Reassertion

Our sources on the Jews of Iraq in the fourteenth and fifteenth centuries are so scant that what we learn about them comes our way by sheer accident. As indicated in Chapter 19, the persecution of the Jews of Baghdad after the downfall of Sa'd el-Dawla was of such dimensions that it probably put a temporary end to the Jewish presence in that city. According to David S. Sassoon, however, there is evidence that the continuity of the Jewish settlement there was not interrupted. In the year 1341, we learn, the *nasi* of the community was a man named 'Azariah ben Yahalalel ben 'Azariah ben David, a descendant of the Exilarchs and the son of the previous *nasi*. It was 'Azariah, we learn, who copied an Arabic book for the benefit of Obadiah Kamal el-Dawla Abdul Khaliq. The book, written a few decades previously by Sa'd ibn Mansur ibn Kammuna, is entitled *Tanqih al-Abhath f'il-Milal al-Thalath* (*Examination of the Enquiries into the Three Faiths*), and its main interest in the context of our present account resides in the fact that it was written by a Jewish oculist and philosopher who lived in Baghdad in the second half of the thirteenth century and who was a distinguished member of the Jewish community. Written in 1280, a decade or so before the first Mongol ruler was to embrace Islam, the book opens with an objective examination of religion in general, followed by chapters on the three monotheistic faiths. Two-thirds of the book are devoted to a discussion of Islam and its prophet.

Professor Moshe Perlmann, who edited the Arabic text and furnished a scholarly and painstaking English translation, sums it up in this way: 'The cumulative impression one gets [from the book] of Islam and Muhammed is hardly favourable. The general though subdued tenor is: *if* there is revelation, *the Jews'* claim to having preserved it is good.' There is an account, by a contemporary chronicler, ibn al-Fawti, of the way in which the Muslims of Baghdad reacted to the book; it is worth quoting in full since it seems to reveal more about the period than just ibn Kammuna's story.

> In this year [683 H: AD 1284] it became known in Baghdad that the Jew 'Izz al-Dawla ibn Kammuna had written a volume entitled *The Enquiries into the Three Faiths*, in which he displayed impudence in the discussion of the prophecies. God keep us from repeating what he said. The infuriated mob rioted, and massed to attack his house and to kill him. The amir Tamaskai, prefect of Iraq, Majd al-Din ibn al-Athir, and a group of high officials rode forth to the Mustansiriyya madrasa [school] and summoned the supreme judge and the [law] teachers to hold a hearing on the affair. They sought ibn Kammuna but he was in hiding. The day happened to be a Friday. The supreme judge set out for the prayer service but, as the mob blocked him, he returned to the Mustansiriyya. Ibn al-Athir stepped out to calm the crowds, but these showered abuse upon him and accused him of being on the side of ibn Kammuna and of defending him. Then, upon the prefect's order, it was heralded in Baghdad that, early the following morning, outside the city wall, ibn Kammuna would be burned. The mob subsided, and no further reference to ibn Kammuna was made. As for ibn Kammuna, he was put into a leather-covered box and carried to Hilla where his son was then serving as official. There he stayed for a time until he died.[1]

A few samples of ibn Kammuna's pronouncements about Islam and Muhammed would suffice to show where his 'crime' lay.

> Thus it becomes clear that there is no proof that Muhammed attained perfection or the ability to perfect others, as claimed . . . nor that [since Muhammed] the world turned from falsehood to truth, from lie to veracity, from darkness to light, and so on. Yet precisely this has been the subject of dispute. That is why, to this day, we never see anyone become a convert to Islam unless in terror, or in quest of power, or to avoid heavy taxation, or to escape humiliation, or if taken prisoner, or because of infatuation with a Muslim woman, or for some similar reason. Nor do we see a respected, wealthy, and pious non-Muslim well-versed in both his faith and that of Islam, going over to the Islamic faith without some of the aforementioned or similar motives. . . . A multitude of followers and the diffusion of a cause in many lands do not prove the truth of a claim. A student of history will observe many cases wherein an individual, even a slave, revolting single-handedly, will enjoy success, and attract thousands of followers. . . .[2]

It is clear from the little we know about ibn Kammuna that he was a distinguished member of the Jewish community, a teacher of philosophy, the author of several volumes mostly on philosophy, and with connections outside Baghdad. How did it come to pass, then, that a man with so much to lose could have taken such a perilous course, antagonizing the Muslim majority in so open a way and risking so horrible an end? Part of the explanation, as Professor Perlmann suggests,[3] is that the Mongol rulers were pagans or Buddhists, and that not until a decade after ibn Kammuna's death did one of them, the ilkhan Ghazan, embrace Islam. Although Islam was the majority faith in Baghdad, it was not the dominant faith. 'It had been reduced [since the Mongol conquest in 1258] to the status of one of the officially tolerated faiths – that is, to the status allotted to the Christians and Jews under Muslim domination.'[4] Indeed, as a rule religious discussions under the Mongol rulers during the thirteenth century were frequent and free, and it was largely a matter of coincidence, or hard luck, that ibn Kammuna's *Examination* should have appeared at a time of transition. There was also the consideration that Muslims generally resented non-Muslims dabbling in Islamic theological disputations. This was no doubt why, though most of the arguments ibn Kammuna adduced may occur in discussions by Muslim authors, 'the cumulative sting of their array was . . . resented by some people as malevolent and arrogant'.[5]

It seems that about this time the title of Exilarch disappeared, giving way to that of *nasi*. The descendants of 'Azariah ben Yahalalel, who himself was the son of a *nasi*, continued to bear the title, and their names are found in various genealogical lists and poems. Sassoon informs us that the list to be found in the Shemtob Bible supplies the name of Sar Shalom the *Nasi* ben Phinehas the *Nasi*, and that the poem dedicated to this *nasi* contains information about his many sons, all of whom were, to judge from their titles, high dignitaries and officers of the Crown. Malkitzedeq, for example, is called Khawaja Khalifa; Phinehas, Khawaja Badi' el-Zaman; and Hezekiah, Khawaja Bazur Jamhar. At the end of the fourteenth century, too, we find the name of another *nasi*, David ben Hodayah of Baghdad, probably a descendant of the old Baghdadian Exilarchs. 'From this time onward', writes Sassoon, 'till the middle of the sixteenth century all our sources keep silent about the existence and the fate of the Jews in Baghdad. This silence cannot be interpreted as evidence for the non-existence of the Jewish community in Baghdad.'[6]

But if there is little or no information about the Jews of Iraq during those confused and confusing years, we know fairly well what went on in that country's political fortunes. The reign of the White Sheep dynasty came to an end in 1508, and subsequently Iraq was ruled by the Safawis, a Shiite dynasty from Persia (1508–34); the Ottoman Turks (1534–1623); the Persians, who with the help of a traitor from the Ottoman ranks ruled the country for fifteen years; and finally the Ottomans again, who remained there until the end of World War I. By the time the Safawis managed to dislodge the Turkoman dynasty of the White Sheep, the Jews had begun to come back to Baghdad. According to one Christian source, Ismail Shah ibn Hayder al-Safawi, though a Shiite, on entering Baghdad spared the Jews of the city while ordering the slaughter of many Muslims and Christians. The Jews, it is reported by the same source, received the conqueror with great pomp and overwhelmed him with gifts.

The rule of the Safawis was ended on the last day of the year 1534 when the Ottoman Sultan, Sulaiman al-Qanuni (the Magnificent), entered Baghdad, accompanied by a number of Jewish scholars and physicians. He,too, is said to have been aided and warmly welcomed by the city's Jewish community, as the Persian rulers who succeeded Ismail Shah had adopted a distinctly anti-Jewish stance. One of the Jews who came with the Ottoman Sultan was Rabbi Moshe Hamon who, on being shown the manuscript of the Persian translation of the Pentateuch by Rabbi Jacob Josef Tawwas, took the work with him to Constantinople and had it printed in 1546, together with Saadia *Gaon*'s Arabic version and the standard Greek translation.

The Turks ruled Iraq through viceroys, known as pashas or walis. The first wali was Sulaiman Pasha, the former governor of Diyarbakr. Although the pashas were called viceroys 'of Baghdad', it is important to point out here that as a vilayet Baghdad signified much more than the city known by that name. It consisted of seven sanjaqs, which included practically all the parts of Iraq that the Turks could meaningfully control. These were the sanjaqs of Hilla, Zangabad, Jawazir, Rumahiyya, Janqulah, Qara Dagh and one other. Turkish rule in the towns at that time has been described as being 'tolerably conservative' though plainly unprogressive. Religious oppression in Iraq was less severe than anywhere in Turkey. 'If there was bullying and extortion,' writes Longrigg, 'it was not confined to Baghdad, to Turkey, or to that age. Jew and Christian paid a moderate poll-tax to the tax-farmer; Muslims their customs, their octrois, date-tax and sheep-tax, their bazaar-dues on weighing and vending. The pasha was no economist: the incidence of taxation obeyed no rule but that of maximum and immediate yield.'[7]

By the middle of the sixteenth century the Jewish community of

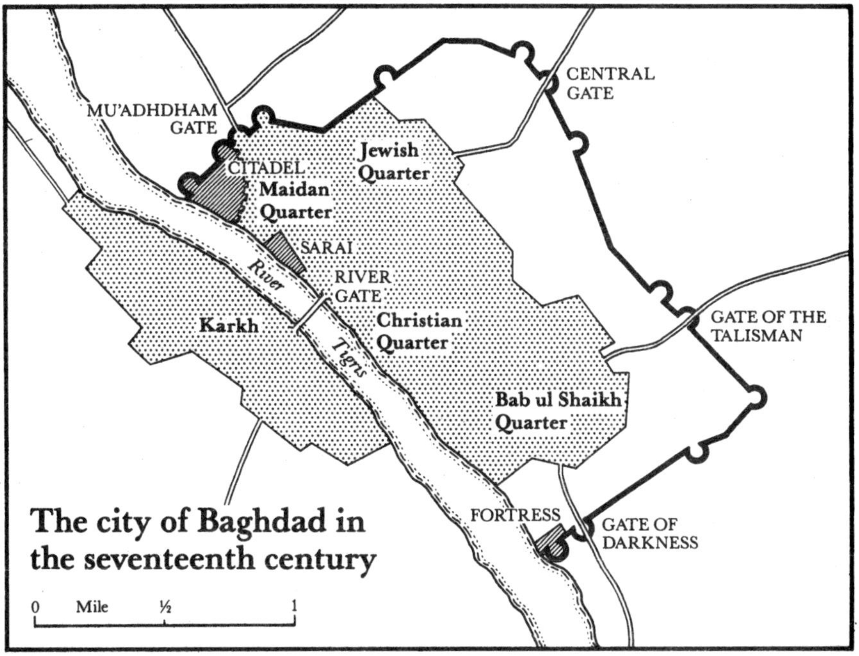

The city of Baghdad in the seventeenth century

Baghdad started to reassert its existence. We find a few details in a record left by the Yemenite traveller Zechariah al-Dhahiri, who visited Baghdad in the second half of the sixteenth century. Describing his experiences and what he observed of the conditions of the Jews there, he wrote:

> I travelled from Hormuz [in Persia] to Babylon, which is situated on the Tigris. I carried 500 musical instruments for sale in order to make joyful the weary and the exiled. After a forty days' journey on the sea I landed in Basra, whence I boarded a boat for twenty *sheqels* on the Tigris. Passing on the river I saw the grave of Ezra the Scribe and that of Ezekiel ben Buzi. After another forty days' journey I arrived in Baghdad, where all my trouble and sorrow ceased. I hired temporary lodging with board. This happened on a Friday. I went to bath to refresh myself. Then I went to the Great Synagogue, where I offered my prayers and read out of the Book of the Lord. I vowed twenty *gerah* for oil for the perpetual lamp, then I went with the community to fulfil the duty of visiting the sick.[8]

Early in the seventeenth century, when the Portuguese traveller Pedron Teixeira visited Baghdad, he found there 25,000 houses, some

250 of them inhabited by Jews. Twelve of the Jewish families he talked to told him they and their forefathers had lived in the city since the destruction of the first Temple. The Jews, we are told further, had many synagogues; they earned their livelihood by working in various crafts and by trade; they inhabited a certain part of the city where their synagogue – a reference no doubt to the Great Synagogue – was situated. Teixeira also had a few very flattering words to say about the city's delicate women and the excessive beauty of their eyes. He was not the only traveller to remark on these qualities of the women of Baghdad. Two others, both Jews, wrote in the same vein about the Jewish women of the city – Wolff Schur in a book called *The Oriental Jewel*, and Moritz Guttfarb in an article in *Ha-Tzefirah*.[9]

After a short interlude of Persian rule, the Turks reconquered Iraq in 1638, and stayed there until 1917. Despite the frequent and often arbitrary changes of viceroys (in the years 1638–1704 alone no less than thirty-seven pashas were named by the sultan in Istanbul), the position of the Jews remained fairly stable. Judging by the standards then prevailing in these matters, the Jewish community along with other minority communities lived under a fairly tolerant regime. Baghdad, as Longrigg rightly observes, was too cosmopolitan a place, and the Islamic sects themselves were too deeply divided, to cultivate or encourage fanaticism.

> These minorities, moreover, were well behaved . . . and familiar by long residence and unrestricted intercourse. It is likely enough that some minor distinctions against them were in force, as at Cairo and Damascus. They might not own white slaves or ride horses; negroes and asses were their portion. The greater humiliation of not riding at all, or of dismounting at sight of a Sayyid, was but little enforced.[10]

The year 1705 opened a new era for Iraq with the appointment of Hasan Pasha to the Baghdad *ayalat*. After a period in which the average was one pasha every two years, Hasan ruled for two decades without interruption, and although he spent much of his energy and resources on fighting the Persians, he left an indelible legacy of organized government. After his death in 1723, a succession of pashas ruled Iraq, now trying to pacify the unruly tribes in the south, now to stave off repeated Persian encroachment. During this period we hear little about the Jews, except that they willingly joined in the fight against the Persians, of whose rule in Iraq they had only unpleasant memories. In 1733 in Baghdad, and in 1775 in Basra, the Jews of these two large centres partook in the effort to foil Persian attempts at conquest and siege – and when the effort was successful, they declared the occasions 'days of miracle' commemorated in their prayer-books. It is related that during the siege of Basra, which lasted thirteen months, the Turkish governor's chief banker, a Jew by the name of Rabbi Jacob ben Aharon Gabbai, proved to be of great help to the Turks in their predicament – so much so that in 1780, in a gesture of gratitude, the governor obtained a special firman from Sultan Abdul Hamid bestowing on Gabbai certain state privileges. This in turn served to enhance the status of the Basra community, of which Gabbai was *nasi*. Apart from Basra there was a large Jewish community in the town of 'Ana, whose members were divided into 'western' and 'oriental' communities. The head of the oriental community was Rabbi David Thabit, who was *dayyan* (religious judge) and well versed in the Torah. 'Ana's Jews maintained relations with the communities of Baghdad, Palestine, Syria and other neighbouring countries.

Twelve pashas, Mamluks and Turks, ruled Iraq in the years 1750–1831. The attitude of these governors to the Jews was by no means uniform, and all in all only a few of them can be described as just rulers. The best of them, as far as the Jews were concerned, is said to have been Sulaiman the Great (1780–1802), and the worst was Daud Pasha (1817–31), the last of the Mamluk governors. During Daud's reign, the head of the Jewish community was Heskel ben Yosef ben Nissim Menahem Gabbai, who was extremely rich – the richest man in the vilayet – and very generous. He also furnished the Jewish 'connection' in the career of the notorious Daud Pasha. In ways which remain unclear and unaccounted for, this wealthy Jew is said to have 'aided' Sultan Mahmud II in his fight against the pasha, who had rebelled against his master in Istanbul. Thanks to his services and his rare abilities, he was called to Istanbul, where the sultan appointed him Chief Treasurer. He was, however, to meet a tragic end: officials in high places in Istanbul, consumed with envy, managed to turn the sultan against him, and he was put to death by order of the Porte.

In the first quarter of the nineteenth century the number of Jews in Baghdad was about 6,000. Some of them were very wealthy, the majority fairly well-off, and a small minority were poor. Most Jews were active in trade, in buying and selling and in forming business connections which sometimes extended to neighbouring countries like Turkey, Syria, Persia, Yemen and India. Some Jews were craftsmen – goldsmiths, dyers, etc. A few worked as government officials. The Jews lived in a separate neighbourhood which, though inhabited almost solely by Jews, was in no sense a ghetto of the kind into which their co-religionists in the West were forced to be segregated. In the year 1831 a plague caused thousands of deaths among the inhabitants of Baghdad. It was the third such calamity in the space of ninety years (the previous two struck in 1743 and 1773). Many Jews fled the city on such occasions, but the toll was great in all three, and there is no doubt that the loss of life incurred was one of the factors leading to the decline of the world of Jewish learning in Baghdad, a decline whose effects were to prove lasting.

We have already seen how the dignity of the Exilarch gave way to the office of *nasi* as leader of the community. Up to the year 1849, when the office of *Hakham Bashi* (Chief Rabbi) was created, a number of prominent *Nesi'im* occupied the office. These included Moshe bar Mordechai Shendukh, David ben Mordechai Cohen, Rabbi Isaac ben David Gabbai, who was known as Sheikh Isshaq Pasha and died in 1773, and Sassoon ben Salih bar David, the first of the famous Sassoons, who was *nasi* in the years 1781–1817. It was this Sassoon who fled Daud Pasha's tyrannical rule, went to Persia with his son David Sassoon, and from there sailed to India where the first Sassoon business empire was founded. Sassoon bar David was followed in turn by Ezra ben Yosef Gabbai, Isshaq Garih, Shaul Yosef Laniado, and Yosef bar Moshe ben David Benyamin, nicknamed Abu Farha. Benyamin was the last of the *Nesi'im*. After him the office of *Hakham Bashi* was created. By that time the Turkish governors of Baghdad came to be known as *walis* – and a decade or so later the famous Ottoman reforms were introduced.

PART THREE
A Century of Radical Change (1850–1951)

The Ottoman system was far from perfect. It was narrow and hidebound. It knew nothing of the richness, the flexibility and the opportunities existing in the Western tradition. But its conventions were well established and its modalities well understood. In due course, the habits perhaps would be capable of being fostered, 'that made old wrong/Melt down as it were wax in the sun's rays'. If reforms were needed or were practicable, there is nothing clearer than that they could succeed only if they proceeded from native traditions and were accomplished with native means. The pressure, the example and the inevitable influence of Europe put this out of the question. But even if European ways had not been alien and confusing, the fact that reforms were inextricably mixed with the interests of the Powers was enough to bedevil everything. . . .

Elie Kedourie[1]

CHAPTER 21

The Road to Equality

The state of near chaos which prevailed in Iraq in the seventeenth century was by no means peculiar to that part of the Ottoman Empire. As a matter of fact, the period of decline and stagnation started a few decades earlier and affected the whole imperial body politic, the administration and the society as a whole. Some historians have maintained that the process started in the year 1683, when the Ottoman armies were forced to abandon the siege of Vienna and the symptoms of decay appeared for all the world to see. Others believe that the beginnings of the decline are to be sought far earlier, in the golden days of Sulaiman the Magnificent himself, in the second half of the sixteenth century.

> For Sulaiman sat so securely on his throne that he forgot how his ancestors had won the throne: he ceased to be the Ghazi and became an Emperor. The Ottoman Empire was doomed from the moment that its leaders lost sight of their *raison d'être*. For a time they enjoyed the fruits of their ancestors' conquests and then suddenly they found themselves on the defensive. They had been betrayed by their contempt for the West, which was based partly on centuries of military superiority, partly on the Muslim tendency to see non-Muslims as 'abject-infidels' . . . necessarily inferior to the followers of the one true faith.[1]

The symptoms started to make themselves felt after the death of Selim II, Sulaiman's successor, in 1574. As frontiers in Europe were extended, the enemy increased in number and campaign costs became staggering. The booty obtained hardly met expenses and little was left for palace extravagances. 'Without loot from beyond the frontiers coming into Istanbul it was difficult to maintain the magnificence to which all had grown accustomed. To make up for this loss of revenue officials were obliged to give liberal sums to the sultan upon promotions. With the reign of Murad III (1574–95) the sultan obtained bribes for appointments, and by the time of Sultan Ibrahim (1640–48) there was open trafficking in offices at the Porte. Such corruption quickly filtered down to the lowliest official.'[2] The doubling of the empire's size as a result of earlier conquests, too, made administrative problems increasingly difficult and complex. 'As the paper work increased to irksome and unbearable proportions, the sultan left more affairs of state to the grand vizir. . . . Later sultans were unwilling to perform any onerous duties as heads of the state and gave themselves up to a life of total voluptuousness and frivolity. Meanwhile, vizirs, beylerbeys, and leading officers drew unprecedented power into their hands. . . .[3]

The lot of the Jews, in Iraq as well as in other parts of the empire, went from bad to worse, although – depending on the whims and predilections of the numerous pashas who governed the land uncontested and unchecked – there were ups and downs. Among many other factors leading to the almost total ebb of Babylonian Jewry, one had started rather early: the policies of the Mongol khans, which by and large were tolerant towards the Jews and even opened up administrative and state posts to them, led to a movement of migration from Baghdad to Tabriz, the city in north-east Persia which the Mongols chose for their seat of power. This trend, which had in fact antedated the coming of the Mongols, served only to accelerate the process of decline and decay which had started with the death of Hai *Gaon* and – later – the retreat and eventual fall of the Exilarchate. The other leading factor in this process was even deadlier, namely the plagues of fearful dimensions which periodically struck the country, coming from the Far East via India and Persia and causing scores of thousands of deaths. These plagues, especially those of 1743, 1773 and 1831, claimed a very high toll of dead among the Jews of Baghdad and left the community debilitated, the schools and *yeshivot* half-empty, and the rabbinate virtually crippled. Those of the Jews who managed to survive – usually the well-to-do – did this through emigration to other places in and outside Iraq; their places were eventually taken by Jews hailing from Kurdistan, Persia and Syria. The 1831 plague, accompanied by a ferocious flood caused by the waters of the river Tigris, resulted in the destruction of the population of Baghdad, and it took the city years to regain some of its past glory. It was only by the middle of the nineteenth century that effective means were devised to avert the spread of plagues.

It is important to point out here that the movement of populations caused by the plagues – as well as by political and economic factors – had the effect of weakening the community not only numerically but socially and intellectually as well, and in the end it inevitably deprived the Babylonian community of its uniqueness and position. One of the principal reasons for this was that the newcomers brought with them not only their languages, their customs and mores, and their distinctive approaches and traditions in matters of religious observance, but also their habit of turning to their own rabbis and scholars in matters of tradition and religious behaviour seeking their decisions on disputed issues. In fact, as early as the beginning of the seventeenth century the Jews of Baghdad used to seek such decisions – even on matters which seem of rather minor importance – from the rabbis of Aleppo on one side and those of Safed on the other. At about this time, too, the custom spread among the Jews of Baghdad to adopt family names. This custom, until then unknown among these Jews, was a means of identifying the place of origin (e.g. Shirazi, Karkukli, Hillawi, Mandelawi), the profession (e.g. Haddad, Shohet, Baqqal, Sa'atchi) or pedigree (e.g. Cohen, Nasi, Hakham, Lawi, Siddiq) of a person.

It was no doubt owing to its visible decline and the weakening of its intellectual and religious standing that Babylonian Jewry eventually accepted the adaptation of its prayer-book to the so-called Sephardic Version, which was acceptable to the rabbis of Safed who enjoyed a great measure of popularity among the Jews of Baghdad and who had incorporated in it various cabbalistic innovations and additions. Babylonian Jewry also accepted without reservations Rabbi Joseph Karo's *Shulhan 'Arukh* (a compendium of Jewish law). Karo, a codifier and cabbalist born in Spain but eventually settled in Safed, composed his 'Prepared Table' on the basis of Sephardic tradition of the *Halakhah*, and by adopting this code the Jews of Iraq joined with Sephardic Jewry in matters of both *Halakhah* and liturgy.

Other factors helping in the absorption into the community of newcomers from various parts of the empire were the many socio-economic conditions they shared as subjects of the Muslim sultan and their mutual need for the variety of communal services Jews usually share. The common practice of visiting the tombs of holy men – especially those of Ezra the Scribe and the Prophet Ezekiel – also contributed to the meeting of Jews from various communities and backgrounds. Both Benjamin of Tudela and Pethahiah of Ratisbon tell of the custom common among the Jews of Baghdad to visit and prostrate themselves at the Tomb of Ezekiel during the ten Days of Repentance preceding Rosh Hashanah (the Jewish New Year) and the Tomb of Ezra the Scribe during Shabuoth, the Pentecost.

The net result of all this was that the Babylonian community all but lost its distinctiveness. Although we have no exact statistics about the Jews of Baghdad at any given period, we know that their number dwindled beginning with the seventeenth, and probably as early as the fifteenth, century. Muslim historians and chroniclers spoke of the Jews of Baghdad during the days of Sa'd el-Dawla in the thirteenth century as being something in the region of 100,000. There was a great deal of exaggeration in this, owing to the hostility harboured by these chroniclers at a time when the Jews were thought to wield great power and influence, and also to the general tendency to exaggerate and to the lack of adequate statistics. No matter how gross the exaggeration was, however, the number of Jews in Baghdad must have undergone little change in the course of the following five centuries; in the year 1890–91, the total number of Jews who paid military tax, as given in Daftar Tawzi' Badalat el-'Askariyya, came to 2,483. If as many Jews as that paid *badal* tax to obtain exemption from compulsory military service in one year, the total number of Jews in Baghdad in that year must have exceeded 80,000.

Apart from Baghdad the only other sizeable Jewish community lived in the north of Iraq. But the Jews of Kurdistan, though less detrimentally affected by the Mongol invasion, sustained a severe set-back five centuries later when, in 1832, their main intellectual and economic centre, the city of Mosul, was sacked and destroyed by the governor of a neighbouring province who had rebelled against the sultan. This event marked the end of a process of decline from which the Kurdish community did not manage to recover until the twentieth century.

In southern Iraq the situation differed in that this part of the country was almost without any Jewish settlements, with the exception of small communities in Basra, Hilla and 'Ana, since the thirteenth century. The reasons for this were largely economic and pertained to matters of geography and administration. In the first place, southern Iraq did not have many urban centres owing to the difficulty of the terrain, it being strewn with marshes which caused disease and made life all but impossible. Secondly, with the single exception of Basra, there was no central government in the south – a state of affairs which made life insecure and the rule of law almost unknown. The third reason was the lack of economic and commercial activities. The fourth and last factor which deterred Jews from settling in southern Iraq was that the area was populated largely by Shiite Muslims, who observed extremely strict rules in their relations with non-Muslims, making contact with them rather difficult. It was not until the beginning of the eighteenth century that some measure of progress was made, both in respect of numbers and the socio-economic status of the Jews.

The fact that this improvement started at roughly the same time as the first Ottoman reforms were announced was, of course, no coincidence. Following two centuries of social, administrative and moral decline, Mahmud II ascended the throne in Istanbul in the year 1808. It was during the reign of this sultan that the first reforms were contemplated. On his accession the new sultan realized that he had to put an end to the growing power of the janissaries; these were troops who originated in the Christian children captured by the Turks in the course of their various conquests in the West. He had to wait some eighteen years to accomplish this task (by blowing the whole lot up in their barracks). He also set out on a course of modernization by opening a school of medicine and a military academy, as well as a number of secondary schools, and he ordered 150 students to be sent to Europe for higher studies. Primary education was made compulsory, a postal service was established, and the foundations were laid for a nation-wide police system. The time-honoured practice of replenishing the treasury by confiscating the property of officials and private citizens was abolished.

One of the innovations which Mahmud II introduced, and which had a bearing on the Porte's attitude to minorities and to his non-Muslim subjects generally, was the ordinance that the various types of male head-dress used at the time were to be replaced by one uniform headgear, the fez. The move, besides arousing great resentment among the Muslims – although in practice it was only enforced largely in the case of soldiers and officials – was significant in that it stressed the sultan's desire that his subjects of various faiths should no longer be distinguishable by their attire. As one historian of modern Turkey has put it:

> The traditional Muslim tolerance, based . . . on contempt for the benighted adherents of other creeds, was to be replaced by a true equality of religions. Mahmud is reported to have said, 'Henceforth I recognize Muslims only in the mosque, Christians only in the church, Jews only in the synagogue. Outside these places of worship I desire every individual to enjoy the same political rights and my fatherly protection.'[4]

This and other changes which Mahmud II introduced did not pass without some fierce opposition, especially on the part of the Muslim religious leaders, the *'ulema*. Accordingly the sultan silenced the more vocal among them, and after ordaining the introduction of the fez he went on to order adoption of the frock-coat – and within a few years the fez and the frock-coat became the standard dress in urban centres in many parts of the empire. In his zeal for these measures, which were intended to enhance a sense of equality between the various religions and cultures, Mahmud went so far as to remove the highest Muslim dignitary of the empire, the Sheikh al-Islam, when he publicly objected to these innovations.

It was during Mahmud II's reign that the Turks subdued Iraq again after eighty years of Mamluk supremacy and misrule. In other parts of the empire, local lords and semi-independent governors and pashas began to feel and respect the Sultan's authority, and a deeper sense of security was felt by people throughout the empire when the sultan further curbed the power of local rulers by forbidding governors to execute anyone without referring the case to Istanbul. Although many of these changes and reforms were only partly successful and others were observed only in parts of the empire, a return to the old order was now virtually impossible, and a reform movement of liberalization was to continue after Mahmud II's death in 1831.

CHAPTER 22

Exilarch to *Nasi* to *Hakham Bashi*

During the first few decades of the nineteenth century, the fortunes of the Jews of Iraq began to improve noticeably, and on all fronts. The number of Jews in the two main urban centres, Baghdad and Basra, increased. Whereas according to the missionary Joseph Wolff, who visited Baghdad in 1824, the number of Jewish families living in Baghdad was 1,500; the Jewish traveller Benjamin ben Joseph, who visited the city twenty-four years later, speaks of 3,000 families; and according to Yehiel Fischel Kastelman (1860) the Jews there numbered 20,000. In Basra, too, the Jews increased in number: in 1826, David d'Beth Hillel found about 300 families there, among them merchants and men serving in important posts with the district governor. In the north, Mosul, too, had a considerable Jewish community – and, indeed, in the middle of the nineteenth century, following a plague which struck Basra and caused thousands of deaths, Mosul became the second largest Jewish centre in Iraq, followed by Basra and Hilla in the south.

Improvement in the economic conditions of the Jews, especially those of Basra, came with the decision of the British to use a new route for the transportation of their goods to India and the Far East via Egypt, the Red Sea, Basra and the Indian subcontinent. This affected the Jews in Iraq in two ways: firstly those Baghdadi Jews with initiative moved to the port of Basra in search of greater business and financial opportunities, and, as a result of this, the lot of those Jews who lived in Basra and its surrounding areas began to improve. In the second half of the nineteenth century, two Basra financiers, Khoja Ya'qub and Adon Abdallah, acted as chief bankers and advisers to the governors of the district.

Earlier in the century, in Baghdad, the Jews resumed their old activity as chief bankers and financial advisers after a few centuries of decline, and the names of three well-to-do Baghdadi Jews became prominent: Sheikh Sassoon ben Salih, head of the famous Sassoon family; Isaac the Banker; and the money-changer Menahem 'Ini. With these signs of economic and social recovery came a resurgence of Torah study and rabbinic scholarship, and these two developments combined led to a renewal of ties with the Jewish world. Following centuries of slumber, a number of scholars and rabbis emerged in Baghdad who managed to attract considerable attention from Jewish communities in the empire and in Asia – Kurdistan, Persia, India and Aden. Among these were Rabbi Sassoon Mordechai (d. 1830), Rabbi Moshe Hayyim (d. 1837), Rabbi Jacob ben Rabbi Joseph the Physician (d. 1851) and Rabbi Abdallah Somekh (d. 1889). Some of these and other rabbis attained fame either for their work in theological and *Halakhah* studies or for the religious verses they composed, and gradually Baghdad began to regain the central position it used to hold in the old days – at least where significant parts of the East were concerned. Enquiries and questions started coming in again, asking for guidance and advice on interpretation and application of Talmudic laws and regulations.[1]

But it is in the sphere of education that the changes proved both more consequential and more lasting. Since the end of the *Gaonate*, and with it the academies and the *yeshivot*, late in the thirteenth or early in the fourteenth century, all the education a Jewish male child in Baghdad received was from a few years spent in *el-istadh*, the Iraqi equivalent of the well-known East European Jewish institution called the *cheder*. Here a single *istadh* (teacher) spent the morning hours with a group of children teaching them the rudiments of Hebrew and some Torah, which usually never passed the limits of the Pentateuch at best. It was only in 1832 that a large Talmud Torah school was opened in Baghdad, and from the graduates of this school came the first students of the first *yeshivah* which Baghdad was to accommodate after a gap of five centuries. At the head of this *yeshivah*, which was opened in 1840, was Rabbi Abdallah Somekh; and by the year 1848 about sixty young men were attending the new institution, according to Benjamin the Second.

Politically, too, the period saw a change for the better in the Jewish situation. A few months after the death of Sultan Mahmud II his successor, Abdul Majid, inaugurated the famous programme of reform known as *Tanzimat* (Regulation). Its architect, Mustafa Rashid Pasha, was a far-sighted statesman who had served as ambassador in Paris and was anxious to save his country from a fate similar to that suffered by the French monarchy. The Khatt-i Sherif (Noble Words) of the Gulkhane (decree), which incorporated the reforms, was proclaimed at the Gulkhane Court on 3 November 1839 in a most solemn ceremony, ushering in a new political era in the Middle East. The decree abolished capital punishment without a trial; guaranteed justice to all with respect to life, honour and property; ordered the promulgation of a new penal code against which no infringement would be tolerated because of personal rank or influence; ended the system of tax-farming and instituted the collection of taxes by government officials; and, most important of all in our context, stipulated that the provisions of the decree applied to all the sultan's subjects irrespective of religion or sect. A little over sixteen years later, on 18 February 1856, the same sultan issued a second decree, Khatt-i Humayun (Imperial Words), which was more specific in its details and more extensive in scope, although in the main it reiterated the same principles contained in the previous decree and sought merely to strengthen them.

The impact of these decrees on the Jews of Iraq was visible and, on the whole, laudable, although the complete equality they stipulated was not always granted in practice, since the situation varied from district governor to district governor and to the extent of influence Istanbul exercised on them. Having ceased to be protected subjects without rights, however, the Jews were now exempted from the poll-tax (*jizya*). But the order which abolished the tax, and which was issued in 1855, imposed in effect a new tax on them. Whereas the *jizya* had in the past entitled them to the protection of the authorities – in accordance with Muslim law – it was now another tax, called *badal el-'askar* (in lieu of military service), which granted them that protection. The rationale of the new tax was that since Jews were not recruited into the army, they were obliged to pay a collective tax, ostensibly representing the cost of their protection by the non-Jewish soldiery. It should be noted, however, that the Jews were not prevented by law from joining the army; whoever did wish to do military service was able to do so – and, indeed, a number of cases are known of Jews serving in the Ottoman army at this period, mainly as officers in the medical corps. The decision to impose the *badal el-'askar* tax on the community was based on the assumption that Jews would not want to serve in the army. (Six decades later, in 1909, the *badal el-'askar* was itself abolished, and Jews were required to serve in the army alongside all others.)

Although the origins of the office of *Hakham Bashi* remain obscure, it is certain that the post was created either shortly before or shortly after the Khatti-i Humayun was proclaimed in 1856. The *Hakham Bashi* of Baghdad – there was one in every large Jewish centre throughout the empire – received his appointment from the sultan, but he was, in fact, chosen by members of the community themselves. As far as the Baghdad Chief Rabbinate was concerned, there were almost from the outset unceasing disputes and rifts associated with the holders of the office, with the community usually divided in its allegiances. The cause of the strife usually had to do with the dependence of the *Hakham Bashi* on the lay authorities. We know of two such public quarrels concerning two Chief Rabbis serving in the 1850s: Raphael Qatzin and 'Obadia ben Abraham ha-Levy, the former being a native of Aleppo who had come to Baghdad as an emissary of the Jewish community of Safed. A third *Hakham Bashi*, Sassoon ben Elijah Smooha, officiated for thirty-five years as rabbi and was then appointed to the high office in the mid-1870s. In 1879, however, the whole Jewish community turned against him and sent a petition to the pasha of Baghdad to remove him. The charges levelled against him included bribery and embezzlement of the *badal el-ʿaskar* tax. The pasha at first favoured the *Hakham Bashi*, who is said to have rendered important services to the authorities. In the end, however, he bowed to the wishes of the community and consented to the removal of Rabbi Smooha from his office.[2]

The rest of Smooha's story may not be too interesting in itself, but the way it developed and the measures taken present something of a case-study from which we learn a good deal about the community and how its affairs were run and the extent to which it was autonomous in running them. We learn, for instance, that while the legal battle was going on the affairs of the rabbinate were entrusted to a three-man court, and non-religious community affairs were put in the hands of a board of representatives consisting of ten members. Following his removal by the pasha, Smooha did not give in, and he seems to have left no stone unturned. Finally, in 1881, thanks to the intervention of the *Hakham Bashi* of Istanbul and to other wire-pulling devices, the district Majlis in Baghdad ordered the reinstatement of Smooha. The reason submitted for his rehabilitation is highly interesting. It was argued that, simply by his removal from office, his farman (the royal order affirming his appointment) and the various privileges bestowed on him by the sultan for his services had not been invalidated. On the strength of these he was reinstated.

On resuming office, the *Hakham Bashi* promptly dismissed the three-man court, which had been formed after his removal, and assumed the power of arbitration in legal and religious matters and disputes. This action, which the community considered rather high-handed, became the cause of another outcry against Smooha. Lay as well as religious leaders gathered together in protest, and offered the problematic *Hakham Bashi* a modest monthly salary (2,500 *qirsh*) should he agree to retire of his own will. The offer was rejected, and it was only after a fierce and bitter struggle that Istanbul finally agreed to Smooha's removal from his office. His successor as *Hakham Bashi* of Baghdad was Rabbi Elisha ben Nissim Dangoor.

Another change for the better in the fortunes of the Jews of post-Tanzimat Iraq took place in 1876, when the first parliament was convened in Istanbul. The Jews of Baghdad were represented in parliament by one deputy, a practice which was resumed in 1908, when parliamentary life was reintroduced in Turkey. Jews were also appointed to government courts and to district and municipal councils; they also entered the civil service in small numbers. However, many Jewish young men were not able to enrol in the officers' academies, though some of them were accepted, and we have a letter written by the Chief Rabbi of Baghdad in 1912 protesting against the small number accepted.[3]

By this time a small number of Jews started to come to Baghdad from some of the countries of Central Europe, and especially Austria, either directly or after a brief stay in Turkey. These Jews, who had heard about the opportunities open to their co-religionists in the Ottoman Empire, saw Iraq as a place where they could escape the discriminatory practices to which they were subjected in their own countries. They not only brought with them their skills and know-how but also their many connections made in the European continent. In 1850, two such Jews came to Baghdad – Isaac Lorion, a clockmaker, and Hermann Rosenfeld, a tailor. They settled in the city, and apparently became active in the community's affairs. In 1860, when they heard through their European connections that the *Alliance Israélite Universelle* had been founded in Paris, they urged the Jewish community to ask the new organization to open a school in Baghdad. In due course, a letter dated 19 January 1864 was sent by the community to the headquarters of the new society asking that an *Alliance* school be opened in Baghdad. The reply came promptly, and on 10 December the same year the first modern elementary school was opened in the city – to be followed five years later by the first elementary school for Muslims, opened by Midhat Pasha.

The 1870s witnessed two other developments which likewise affected the life and position of Iraqi Jewry. In 1869, the Suez Canal was opened, and in the same year Midhat Pasha was appointed *wali* of Baghdad. It was Midhat who first introduced modern elementary education in Iraq, as well as a number of important administrative reforms aimed at putting an end to the corruption, nepotism and general mismanagement which had prevailed in Iraq and the empire as a whole for some centuries. He also became famous for the reforms he initiated for a constitutional administration directly after returning to Istanbul. Midhat's reforms and innovations, coupled with outside developments like the opening of the Suez Canal and the proclamation of the Constitution in Istanbul towards the end of 1876 brought in their wake a series of radical changes throughout Iraq, which were deeply to affect the Jews politically, economically and culturally.

During the first few decades of the nineteenth century, a number of enterprising Jews began leaving their native land in search of better opportunities abroad. At first their destination was almost invariably India, to which a number of Jewish families had left as early as the eighteenth century. It is not possible in the confines of this short history to go into this subject in any detail but the activities and fortunes of one particular Baghdadi family were, perhaps, typical. This family, which was to attain wealth and influence and was to contribute towards the well-being of the community long after their forefathers left Iraq, is of great interest in the context of any account of Iraqi Jewry. This was the Sassoon family whose head, Sheikh Sassoon ben Salih (1750–1830), was the *nasi* of the Jewish community in Baghdad for almost forty years as well as being chief treasurer of the Ottoman pashas who governed the city during his tenure of office. In 1828, during the tyrannical rule of Daud Pasha, Sassoon's son David S. Sassoon, then thirty-six years old, fled to Bushire on the Persian Gulf, where he was joined by his aging father, who eventually died there. In 1832, David with his large family sailed to Bombay, where he established a business which was to achieve international fame.

David Sassoon was not the first Iraqi Jewish businessman to settle in India. Apart from the numerous traders who came to India and resided there for short periods for purposes of business, the first settler was one Shalom ben Aharon ben Obadiah Ha-Cohen, who was originally from Aleppo. He had arrived in Bombay from Baghdad in 1770. Seven years later, Ha-Cohen had built up a prosperous business, and he was joined early in the nineteenth century by others who came from Baghdad and Basra.

The first leader of the Iraqi Jews of Bombay – generally known as 'the Baghdadis' – was Soliman ben Jacob Soliman; but it was only after the arrival of David Sassoon that the Baghdadi community established itself in the city on firm foundations. At first, these Jews worked in the export–import trade around the Persian Gulf, some of them participating in the opium trade with China. But soon afterwards the Sassoons entered the field of real estate, where they made a fortune.

Benjamin Israel, the author of a short history of the Jews of India, speaks with great awe about the Baghdadis, and especially about the Sassoons.

> [The Baghdadis] had an uncanny appreciation of the directions in which the cities of Calcutta and Bombay would grow; the Sassoons in Bombay and the Ezras in Calcutta bought up at rock-bottom prices extensive real estate which, within a short time, became ripe for development and provided enormous capital gains at a time when the State did not take away in tax the bulk of the unearned income. Again, in Bombay, it was the Sassoons who foresaw the growth of shipping and constructed the first dock in Bombay, still known as the Sassoon Dock, as a pointer to future development of port facilities. . . .[4]

We have no way of knowing what proportion of this vast fortune was allotted by the Sassoons to philanthropic pursuits. What we do know is that their activities in this field were extremely varied and extensive. According to Israel – who does not seem to be overly enthusiastic about the Baghdadis – the Sassoons right from the start made arrangements in Bombay 'for the free education of Baghdadi children in the David Sassoon School, of which the first three or four headmasters happened to be Bene Israel. The school took the children only to the middle school level; but later Sir Jacob Sassoon endowed a High School in which Baghdadi children got an excellent education in English up to the Senior Cambridge level. . . . Many completed their education in Great Britain.'[5]

In 1861, David Sassoon built the Magen David Synagogue in Bombay, Byculla, and some of the most cultural and civic institutions in the city, including hospitals, orphanages, libraries, museums and schools; and many charitable organizations owe their existence to the generosity of David Sassoon and his eight sons. David Sassoon was also instrumental in the publication of the Bombay paper *Doresh Tob le-'Ammo*. This was printed in Hebrew characters in the Judeo-Arabic dialect of Baghdad and appeared during the years 1855–66. Sassoon also supported scholars and scholarly publications. Albert (Abdalla) Sassoon, David's eldest son, established one of the first large-scale textile mills in Bombay, and later took the initiative in establishing Bombay as a modern port city. He also maintained a Jewish school, the David Sassoon Benevolent Institution, contributed a new building to the Elphinstone High School, and set up a fund for university scholarships. In the mid-1870s he settled in London to run his family's growing business interests; and he was made a baronet in 1890 in recognition of his role in the industrialization of India. He was also on terms of personal friendship with the Prince of Wales, later King Edward VII.[6]

Another of the eight sons was Solomon Sassoon (d. 1894) whose wife Flora, a great-granddaughter of the original David Sassoon, achieved renown as a Hebrew scholar and was often consulted on questions of Jewish law. She survived her husband by forty-two years, having settled in England in 1901. In 1924, at Jews' College in London, she delivered a learned discourse on the Talmud; and in 1930 she published an essay on Rashi in *The Jewish Forum*. She was strictly observant, and included in her entourage a ritual slaughterer and a *minyan* (a quorum of ten needed by law to hold proper prayer) when travelling. Her son David Solomon Sassoon (1880–1942) became an outstanding Hebraist and bibliophile, whose private collection contained over 1,000 rare Hebrew and Samaritan manuscripts, which he catalogued in two scholarly volumes, *Ohel Dawid*. His books include a pioneer edition of the *Diwan* of Samuel ha-Naguid from a manuscript in his own collection; *A History of the Jews in Baghdad*, published by his son Solomon in 1949; and *Massa' Babel* (*Iraq Journey*), a description of the author's travels in Iraq in 1910, edited by Meir Benayahu and published in Jerusalem in 1955. He also contributed to scholarly Jewish journals, including a very substantial article on 'The History of the Jews in Basra' published in 1927 by the *Jewish Quarterly Journal* and scores of shorter pieces and notices. David's son Solomon, who was ordained as a rabbi in 1936, settled in Jerusalem in 1970, retaining his father's valuable collection and increasing it to some 1,350 items.

The other centre of Iraqi Jewish settlement in India was Calcutta, where the Ezra family was the first to arrive, in 1821. A number of Judeo–Arabic periodicals appeared there, the first being *Ha-Mebasser*, a weekly started in 1873, followed by *Perah*, *Meguid Meisharim* and *Shoshana*. Emissaries from Palestine and from Baghdad carried out missions in India; those coming from Baghdad included Rabbi Ezra Dangoor (1894) and Rabbi Menashe Shahrabani (1924).

In the late 1930s travellers estimated the number of Jews of Iraqi origin living in India at 6,000. As the position of the Jewish community in Iraq improved, and with the death of the first- and second-generation emigrants, the links between the 'Baghdadis' of India and the mother community started to weaken somewhat. Nevertheless, many Iraqi Jews sought refuge in India during and after the mass emigration of the Jews in the early 1950s.

CHAPTER 23

The Impact of Modern Education

Throughout these decades of radical change the Jews of Baghdad displayed a remarkable knack for adaptation and a willingness to accept change seldom encountered in Jewish communities elsewhere. But the far-reaching shift from traditional to modern methods of education, such as that represented by the establishment of the first *Alliance* elementary school towards the end of 1864, did not pass totally without opposition. The religious hierarchy opposed the move bitterly, and the traditional teachers of Torah in the various *istadhs* – partly, no doubt, out of fear for the sources of their livelihood – called the new schoolteachers 'heretics'. Indeed, the school and its staff were excommunicated and the Jewish population forbidden contact with them. Other difficulties facing the new enterprise were the climate, which proved too much for the Paris-born school principal to bear; the high rate of absenteeism among the pupils, some of whom were married; and the general resistance to new and rather novel ideas such as those the teachers taught regarding the shape of the earth and its alleged orbit around the sun. The result was that the school closed and the principal left the country. But this was only for a short while. Another appeal was sent to the headquarters of the *Alliance Israélite Universelle* in Paris, a new principal arrived, an imposing building was completed to house the new school – donated by Albert David Sassoon, grandson of the famous Sheikh Sassoon ben Salih – and the school was reopened in 1872. It is interesting to note here – as a testimony to the flexibility and comparative liberality of attitude of the Jewish leadership in Baghdad – that the man who was instrumental in the rehabilitation of the *Alliance* school was none other than Chief Rabbi Abdallah Somekh, who went so far as to send his own son to the new school, ignoring the protestations of leading religious personages at home and in other parts of the empire, such as Rabbi Akiba Joseph Shlesinger of Jerusalem who addressed a personal appeal to the Baghdad rabbinate to boycott the institution. (Later, in 1876, one of

Rabbi Somekh's grandsons enrolled in the *Alliance*'s teachers' seminary in Paris, during his grandfather's lifetime.)

In the first two decades of the *Alliance* elementary school, no more than 200 pupils ever attended the school in any given school year; and the 150 who completed all its four classes were all boys. Towards the end of the 1880s, however, the situation began to change radically, not only in Baghdad but in other parts of the country as well. In 1890, the *Alliance* opened a vocational school for girls, and three years later the first elementary school for girls – the Laura Kadoori School – was opened in Baghdad. In the same year, an *Alliance* school was established in Basra, to be followed a few years later by a school for girls; and at the beginning of the twentieth century *Alliance* schools were opened in Mosul, Hilla, 'Amara and Kirkuk. Shortly afterwards, the Jewish communities of Baghdad and other Jewish centres in Iraq started building their own modern schools, and the role of the *Alliance* schools became gradually less crucial in the education of Iraqi Jewish children, most of whom attended the schools founded and administered by the local Jewish communities.[1]

The changes introduced in the educational sphere in these Jewish communities within this comparatively short span of time were as far-reaching as they were fast. Apart from an increase in literacy, there was a marked increase in the number of children attending modern elementary schools accompanied by a decrease in traditional education; a growing number of girls attended kindergarten and school; and the number of years spent in these schools also increased progressively. It is interesting to note here that as far as kindergartens were concerned, far more girls attended them than boys, most probably because parents preferred to send their sons to *istadhs* to learn the rudiments of Hebrew and some Torah before they reached the age for elementary schooling. Most of these kindergartens were attached to existing schools and virtually formed part of them, so that children attending them automatically moved to the mother schools. In many of them, the children learned two languages, taught by schoolteachers who usually had no training in dealing with small children of pre-school age. In these kindergartens, too, games and songs were comparatively rare. In those attached to the five Jewish community schools in Baghdad, an average of nineteen hours a week were devoted to Hebrew, thirteen to Arabic, and only five to handicrafts and drawing.

Another important change in the educational sphere was in the curriculum. In the last three decades of the nineteenth century, Jewish children attending mainly *Alliance* elementary schools had to learn, within four years, five languages: Hebrew, Arabic, French, Turkish, and English – in roughly that order of importance. In the first two years they were taught Hebrew, French and Arabic, while in the remaining two years Turkish, and sometimes English, were added. This, of course, was in addition to the regular subjects – arithmetic, geography, history and others. Considering the size of the curriculum, it is not surprising that the level of attainment was not high, and comparatively few children dared to enrol in the school or – having enrolled – managed to finish their studies successfully. When those in the Jewish community who were responsible for education asked the *Alliance* Central Committee for its opinion on the situation, the reply they received was that in the East many languages were required, and that the pupils learnt them quickly anyway. In the annual report for 1909 from the headmaster of the *Alliance* school in Baghdad, we find a passage about the study of Turkish: 'The study of Turkish was neglected in the past by the Jews of Baghdad. They did not use it in business, and they did not aspire to governmental posts. But now, since the coming of the liberal regime [in Istanbul], they are zealous in the study of this hitherto neglected language.'[2]

It was only after the British occupation of the country in 1917 that the number of languages taught at Jewish schools was reduced to four, as there was no more need for Turkish, to which, in any case, only a few hours were devoted even after the consolidation of the Young Turk regime and the onset of what the *Alliance* school headmaster called the 'liberal' era. Nor did Arabic fare much better, and even Hebrew got second or third place despite the community's suggestions to the *Alliance* executive in Paris that it be taught as a first language. The result, paradoxically, was that those who finished the *Alliance* school successfully knew mainly French and a good deal of English, with only some working knowledge of Hebrew and Arabic, depending in the case of the former on the amount of Hebrew they had learned before joining the school. Nevertheless, the spread of knowledge of European languages through the *Alliance* schools was of historic importance in the growth and progress of the community. *Alliance* graduates became a highly needed class of employees, and were appointed as clerks, accountants and correspondence clerks in banks and commercial companies; they also proved very handy when the British came to Iraq, many of them serving in the new administration.

A word must be added here about religious education among the Jews of Iraq. We have mentioned in Chapter 22 that up to the 1830s the *istadh* was virtually the only educational institution available to the Iraqi Jewish child. It is remarkable that the *istadh* continued to exist for some years after the end of World War I, when it functioned only as a pre-school morning institution for the teaching of Hebrew. In the days of its prime, however, the *istadh* played a leading role in the education of these children. The *istadhs* were essentially neighbourhood affairs and many of them had to be there to cater for a growing number of children. They were also one-man enterprises. The teacher (*el-istadh*) usually put aside a room in the house in which he and his family lived to accommodate anything up to fifty or more children ranging in age between four and twelve. (In the hot summer months the inner courtyard of the house was used.)

The method of instruction was as primitive as the surroundings. In the bare room allotted to them, the pupils sat on mats and sometimes on simple benches without backrests. No blackboard was in evidence, and no furniture except what the teacher's family might have stowed away in a corner of the room. Punishment was wielded by the master's cane, with which he usually struck the children on the palms of their hands but, when the felony was considered sufficiently enormous, across their fingers. Having settled them each in his specified place, the teacher would then call his pupils one by one in turn and teach each a character of the Hebrew alphabet, or a word, or even a sentence – depending on the child's level of knowledge. In cases where the children reached the stage of writing, the teacher would write characters or words or sentences in their copy-books, which they then had to copy for the teacher to inspect afterwards. Because of the large number of children seeking knowledge in these rather uninspiring circumstances, the teacher often had enough time to call each of them only once throughout the morning. The result, of course, was that while the teacher was busy with one child the others were left to their own devices, and near chaos would reign. Even in cases where there was an 'assistant' to help the teacher in precisely this kind of emergency, the helper, too, was rendered helpless by the collective mischief.

Incredible though it may sound, many of the children who attended *istadh* managed to learn Hebrew no matter how hard the way was. They first learnt the alphabet, then words, then sentences, the same process being then repeated in writing – and finally they were able to read from the Scripture, with different tunes for the different Books. In some of these educational institutions, depending on the ability and keenness of the teacher, children passed on to more advanced stages, where they learnt to translate certain passages from the Bible into the Judeo–

Arabic (spoken Arabic written in Hebrew characters) as spoken and written by the Jews of Baghdad; and sometimes the elements of arithmetic and book-keeping were also taught. Older children were shown how to write commercial letters, again in Judeo–Arabic. None was taught Hebrew as a spoken language, and no Talmud or religious law was taught. What made the *istadh* even less effective than it could have been was that many of the children had to leave it at a rather early age, mostly to help their parents in earning a living. Others left to join one of the few crafts and skills open to them, to get married and raise families, or all of these pursuits combined.

This state of affairs prevailed for what must have been close on five centuries, during which we do not even know where aspiring Jews learnt to become rabbis and who ordained them, or where – if anywhere – the Talmud was taught, and under what circumstances the *dayyanim* were selected and appointed. Be that as it may, it was only in 1832 that the first Talmud Torah (religious instruction) school was founded – to be followed by a second as late as 1907. These new institutions were, strictly speaking, only enlarged and better organized versions of the *istadh*. They were divided into classes according to the children's level of knowledge, with a teacher for each class. They were not privately owned and run like the *istadhs* but directed by a public committee acting for the community as a whole; they were, in effect, elementary schools in the last four years of study. The Talmud Torah admitted children from the age of four, but only a few remained there until the age of thirteen. In 1880, almost fifty years after its founding, there were about 1,000 pupils in the Baghdad Talmud Torah. In later years, even though the number of pupils increased considerably (the two Talmud Torahs had 2,300 pupils), these institutions underwent a sharp decline, mainly because of the refusal of the religious hierarchy to modernize them and introduce secular subjects in order to prepare the young people for the new conditions prevailing outside the walls of the institutions. Thus many parents, judging otherwise, gradually stopped sending their children to the Talmud Torah, although at one stage, in an attempt to counter the clamour for secular education and attract more pupils, the rabbis decided to abolish attendance fees.

Eight years after the founding of the first Talmud Torah, the first Beth Midrash (*yeshivah*) was opened, and pupils who had completed their study at the Talmud Torah successfully were eligible for admittance. This Talmudic school, which was opened in 1840 and was called the Zilkha Yeshivah, had about sixty students in 1848, thirty in 1863, and twenty in 1879 – a gradual decline which no doubt reflected the Jews' growing interest in worldly occupations on the one hand and increased attendance of the new modern schools on the other. However, despite this decline a second *yeshivah* was opened in 1908, named after Meir Eliahu. From these two institutions graduated the rabbis, ritual slaughterers, religious court judges and Talmud scholars whom the community needed. Some of these graduates found their way to other Jewish centres in Iraq, where they filled the same positions, and a few emigrated to the countries of South-East Asia and the Far East to undertake similar work with the Jewish communities there.[3]

Religious education and rabbinical training in the rest of Iraq existed only in a few Jewish centres. There was a *yeshivah* in Arbil, in the north, which trained rabbis, beadles, cantors and ritual slaughterers for work in Kurdish villages in the vicinity. But this was not a full-time *yeshivah*; it was open only in the evenings and on Sabbaths and holidays. In other parts of the country, however, Talmud study was confined to groups using the synagogues as meeting-places.

In the sphere of modern education, the Baghdad community and a few others outside the capital founded schools of their own, although the main activity remained in the hands of the *Alliance* group of schools. The chief *Alliance* school in Baghdad, now known as the Albert Sassoon College, grew into a fully-fledged secondary school in addition to its elementary classes, and in 1908 was recognized as such by the Ottoman authorities. The number of its pupils increased accordingly – from forty-three in January 1865 to 731 in 1913. Also, in the year 1893, Sir Eliezer Kadoori of Hong Kong and Shanghai donated funds with which the *Alliance Israélite Universelle* founded a school for girls bearing the name of the donor's wife, Laura Kadoori. The curriculum was the same as that of the *Alliance* school for boys, and according to one source 1,177 girls received tuition there in its first few years. This was the first school for girls ever to be established in Iraq; the first government girls' school was to open in 1898. It is interesting to note that the number of girls enrolled in the Laura Kadoori School in 1913 was 788, nearly sixty more than the male pupils attending the Albert Sassoon College in the same year. This was not because more Jewish girls than boys went to school in Baghdad that year but because by then boys had a number of other schools to choose from.

In other Jewish centres *Alliance* schools were founded in the first years of the twentieth century – in Basra in 1903 for boys and in 1913 for girls; in Mosul, in 1906 and 1912 respectively; in Hilla, in 1907 for boys and in 1911 for girls; in 'Amara, a school for boys was opened in 1910; in Kirkuk in 1913; and in Khanaqin a mixed school was founded in

1911. In all these schools a total of 2,800 pupils received their education in the year 1913. In the few years preceding World War I, in Baghdad, the community initiated schools of its own – the Nuriel School for boys; the No'am Tobah School for girls; the Ta'awun School for boys; and the Gan Menahem Daniel School for girls. In addition to these schools, Jewish boys enrolled in government schools, either because of their proximity to their places of residence or because they charged no fees.[4]

CHAPTER 24

World War I

In 1889 a group of students at the Army School of Medicine in Istanbul formed a secret organization which they called The Ottoman Society for Union and Progress. When the organizers distributed pamphlets attacking the sultan's arbitrary rule, some of them were exiled, others summarily executed. This, however, failed to stem the tide, and by 1908 the underground movement spread so widely in the ranks of the army that Sultan Abdul Hamid was terrified into accepting the society's demands and the Constitution was proclaimed on 23 July the same year. It is to be noted that this was the same Constitution that had been drafted and proclaimed in 1876, and which granted equal rights of citizenship to the non-Muslim subjects of the empire.

While granting non-Muslims civic rights, however, the Constitution also imposed on them certain duties – such as compulsory military service. This made the reception accorded by the Jewish community to the introduction of *hurriyat* (freedom) rather ambiguous. The headmaster of the *Alliance* school in Baghdad, in his annual report for the year 1909, made an assertion which is not borne out by impressions obtained from contemporary eye-witness accounts:

> The Jews [he wrote] were of the most enthusiastic over the triumph of liberty in this country. Well understanding the importance of the new duties which they now have to shoulder, desirous of preparing themselves for the tasks of citizenship, wishing to have a share in the economic revival which is taking place in the empire, their first thoughts turned, as they should, to the active promotion of the official language in their schools. The study of Turkish was neglected in the past by the Jews of Baghdad. . . .[1]

Turning to the more specific subject of conscription, the headmaster displayed a rare degree of enthusiasm:

> Military service will help the bodily regeneration of this enfeebled race. It will also have other notable results. The rough life of the soldier will not only season their weakened bodies, it will also fortify

> their courage and give them a heightened conscience of their dignity as men and citizens. Life in common under the tent or in the dormitory, the fact of undergoing the same trials and privations . . . will create links of solidarity and of mutual respect and esteem between the members of different races.

And so on and on. As Elie Kedourie, who quotes this passage, puts it, 'All the prestige of Europe lay behind these plausible sentiments.'[2]

The Young Turks, with their declared attachment to such novel concepts as equality, liberty and fraternity, were welcomed with general enthusiasm at first, especially by the non-Muslim inhabitants of the empire. The Jews of Baghdad did not hide their pleasure; but their demonstration of support was not received well by their Muslim neighbours, and on 15 October 1908 a group of Muslims attacked the Jews of the city. The disturbance lasted a few hours, and an end was put to it only after some Muslim notables intervened.

To the new parliament in Istanbul in 1908 a Jewish notable, Sassoon Heskel, was appointed as deputy to represent the Jews of the vilayet. He was a graduate of the *Alliance* school and of institutions of higher learning in Vienna, Paris and London, and in 1909 was appointed Turkey's representative at the talks aimed at concluding a treaty of friendship with Great Britain. Sassoon Heskel – 'Sassoon Afandi', later Sir Sassoon – was appointed Minister of the Treasury in the first government to be formed under the British Mandate, a post which he kept throughout the first five Iraqi cabinets.

Liberty, however, had its drawbacks. Contrary to the opinion expressed by the *Alliance* school headmaster, the Jewish community was far from happy about compulsory military service for its sons; and in 1909 the annual collective tax which the previous regime had imposed on non-Muslim communities in exchange for exemption from army service was reintroduced. The task of collecting the new tax continued to be entrusted to the *Hakham Bashi*, who appointed a special committee whose task it was to estimate the share of the burden to be borne by those involved, each according to his ability. Notwithstanding this, however, a number of young Jews began to appear in military uniforms, some of them as officers.[3]

For many decades prior to World War I Iraq had remained virtually closed to the outside world, and our information about the Jewish community there in those years is very scant indeed. However, thanks to the work of a local Jewish employee of the British Consulate-General in Baghdad, we have a document which contains some first-hand information about the Jews of that city and their conditions towards the end of the first decade of this century. The document was entitled 'An Account of the Jewish Community at Baghdad' and was enclosed with the Consul-General's despatch to the Foreign Office of 27 February 1910. It was signed H.D.S. According to Kedourie, who was the first to publish the document, the initials seem to refer to Haron Daud Shohet, then employed as a dragoman (interpreter) at the consulate. The 'Account', Kedourie believes, 'has a claim to our attention because it comes to us under the auspices of the learned J.G. Lorimer (author of the *Persian Gulf Gazetteer*), because it brings together details which are not easily, if at all, available in any other source, and because it constitutes an inside view, intelligent and well-informed, of this community at that point in its history.' The report is also annotated by Lorimer, the Consul-General, and his notes and explanations are themselves of some interest.[4]

Of the general situation of the Jews of Baghdad shortly after the Young Turks revolt the writer of the report is rather optimistic. 'These Jews', he writes, 'are no longer persecuted and despised. They are now placed on the same footing as the Muhammedans and the Christians.' The community, moreover, 'is full of initiative, especially the younger generation'. He continues:

> The Jews on the whole are practical people; their ideal is to work hard and make money. They are awaiting with breathless impatience the result of Sir William Willcocks' inspection, because they hope that Baghdad will soon acquire increased importance from the irrigation works and the projected railway line across the Syrian desert. They think that Baghdad will soon be a very important centre of commerce and residence, and that they will then be able to throw themselves into a stream of speculations. . . .
>
> The Turkish government fully realize that the Jews are one of the chief elements in the progress of the country. The Turks have all along regarded the Jews as very faithful subjects of the Sultan and have placed confidence in them. On the other hand the Jews of Baghdad have borne feelings of gratitude towards the Turkish government ever since the immigration of their co-religionists from Spain into Asia Minor some hundreds of years ago. The community is anxious to co-operate with the government for the improvement of the country, if only the government gain their confidence. It may be said that some of the Jews are sceptical about the future and do not believe much in the so-called 'convalescence' of the 'Sick Man'.

It is worth noting the footnote which Lorimer here adds to the reference made to the immigration of Jews from Spain into Turkey. 'I am informed', he writes, 'that the greater number of the Jews of Baghdad are supposed to be descended from those of the Captivity; but there has also been considerable immigration of Jews from Persia, and the Arabic spoken by the Jews here contains a number of Persian words. Baghdad was Persian in the seventeenth century. There has also been some immigration of Jews from Syria.'

The 'Account' itself opens with an estimate of the number of Jews living in Baghdad at that time. The writer asserts that the Jewish community in that city 'is, after that of Salonica, the most numerous, important, and prosperous in Turkey'. He then cites 'a revised census made by the authorities about two years ago', according to which the Jews of Baghdad number about 25,000. He adds, however, that 'in well-informed circles the belief is held that they are as many as 50,000'. He also cites the latest reports of the *Alliance Israélite Universelle* in Paris and of the Anglo-Jewish Association in London, both of which estimated the total at 45,000. These last two figures seem to tally with the French Vice-Consul's estimate of January 1904, namely that the Jews at Baghdad numbered 40,000, out of a total 60,000 in the whole vilayet. (The French diplomat noted further that these Jews constituted the most numerous, the most well-to-do and the most industrious community in the city.)

The writer of the report divides the Jews of Baghdad into four classes. The first, comprising five per cent of the total, is a rich and well-off class consisting almost entirely of merchants and bankers. The second, a middle class, consists of 'petty traders, retail dealers, employees, etc.' and comprises thirty per cent. The third, comprising sixty per cent, is 'a poor class'. And the fourth consists of 'beggars' and comprises as much as five per cent of the total. Most of the 'professional beggars', we are told, come from Kirkuk, Mosul and their environs which are 'in a very miserable condition'.

One of the more interesting parts of the report is the one which deals with the office of the Chief Rabbinate.

> The community is headed by the Chief Rabbi who is, as a rule, provided with a Farman from the Sultan. He can be removed by the Jewish community at Baghdad through the Chief Rabbinate at Constantinople, as he draws his salary from the Treasury of the Baghdad community. He is not under the orders of the Chief Rabbi at Constantinople; but, in special cases, he applies to him for help.

He attests documents and keeps an eye on Hebrew education. He is the medium of correspondence between the Turkish authorities and the community. This is merely a matter of form: the Chief Rabbi is simply a mouthpiece. He exercises no real influence over either the Turkish authorities or the members of his own community.

Going on to analyse the reasons for this visible decline in the authority of this high office, the writer states: 'In contradistinction to past days, the clergy enjoy no influence over their co-religionists, and this may confidently be ascribed to the effect of education diffused among the classes of the community.' Even religious jurisdiction falls outside the prerogative of the Chief Rabbinate: 'There is an Ecclesiastical or Religious council, composed of three rabbis, to settle purely religious disputes. Some other rabbis teach Hebrew literature and are paid by the community. The council and the educational rabbis are not connected with the Chief Rabbinate: but, in special cases where authoritative help is required, they apply to it for assistance.' The writer gives a list of the names of 'the chief and really influential personages of the community', those of Meir Elias and Menahem Daniel, who he asserts are the ones 'who discuss measures together in cases of emergency, and who form deputations in important questions, to the *wali* and other high officials'. The Chief Rabbi himself 'is under the influence of these persons, and is, so to speak, a mere puppet in their hands . . .'. Elias and Daniel are singled out as 'liberal in money matters', but all the persons on the list are described as 'intelligent, tactful, and energetic'.

The writer's remarks about the impact of modern education on the Jews of Baghdad occupy a central part of his report. He writes:

It is a well-known fact that the emancipation of the Jews in Baghdad, their prosperity, and the development of their trade are mainly due to the very generous work done in this city by the *Alliance Israélite Universelle* during the last forty-five years. The *Alliance* has three flourishing schools for boys and a fourth for girls. . . . The schools have always been managed by capable and energetic representatives. They are admitted to be the best schools in Baghdad. The community owns and supports a large Hebrew school [or Midrash] containing about 2,000 pupils, all poor.

Since the declaration of the constitution, the Jews have not failed to give signal proofs of their tendency towards education and progress. Mr Daniel some time ago moved the *Alliance* to open an Infant School, offering at the same time to provide a building and

> contribute the fixed sum of 100 Lires per annum. This school has been open five months and is in excellent condition. Mr Elias . . . is making a fine hospital at the north gate for poor Jews, to which Christians and Muhammadans will also be admitted. The cost will not be less than 5,000 Turkish Lires. . . . Six or seven small houses at the east gate have lately been purchased by some of the rich Jews, which are to be reconstructed as a Hebrew school for the poor. Meir Elias . . . is going to build this school at his own expense. The total cost will be 3,000 Lires at least.

The writer also reports about a new educational venture. This concerns 'seven Jews of the rising generation' who had lately formed a committee and started a school for Turkish instruction. The subjects were to be the same as in the government military schools. 'The idea is (1) to diffuse Turkish among the young, and (2) to qualify them for superior military service, thus enabling them to obtain positions as officers and not merely to serve as rank and file. This "Mutual Help School" is partly supported by the community and partly by voluntary contributions, and it is managed by the said committee. It has been open for a month and promises very well.'

The source of the Jews' livelihood was trade – at least where the higher and middle classes were concerned. The Jews of Baghdad, we are told, 'have literally monopolized the local trade, and neither Muhammedans nor Christians can compete with them. Even the few leading Muhammedan merchants owe their prosperity to the capable and industrious Jews whom they have for years employed as clerks. The Jewish clerks are practically the managers of their firms.' The chief item of Jewish trade was Manchester piece-goods and the local merchants 'have amassed riches by importing these goods from Manchester and exporting them to Persia'. The writer reports that in Manchester and London 'there are over twenty Jewish firms belonging to Baghdad, and there are a similar number in Kirmanshah and Hamadan in Persia'.

Beside piece-goods, the Jews also traded in groceries, drugs, iron, coffee, tin, loaf sugar, soft sugar, copper and the like. 'A trade by the Jews in haberdashery, with Germany and Austria, is gradually increasing.' Here Lorimer adds a footnote to the effect that the principal dealers in precious stones and jewellery and the leading goldsmiths and silversmiths are Jews. The report also speaks of a large export trade in wool, skins, gums and carpets. As to speculation in land, the writer says that 'the Jews as a body' refrain from this owing to 'the aggressive nature of the Arab tribes, to lack of protection on the part of the government, and to various other reasons'. The only real land holders were Menahem Daniel and other members of his family, whose total holdings were said to be worth about 400,000 Lires.

As to how the affairs of the community were run, apart from the religious council – *al-Majlis al-Ruhani* – there was a council known as the *Majlis al-Jismani*. This *majlis* was composed of ten unpaid members with a paid secretary, the members having been elected for a period of three years. 'The Communal Council levies taxes and directs the expenditure of the proceeds of same.' A large tax on meat had *ab antiquo* been enforced. The tax had been recognized a few years before by the Turkish authorities at Constantinople and was known as the Gabelle. This tax came from the sheep that, after being slaughtered, had to be examined by trained persons (*shohets*) who had been provided with a certificate from the religious authorities. The *shohets* were paid by the community. The Gabelle tax constituted about sixty-five per cent of all the taxes collected, the rest being supplied by taxes on intestines, fees for the verification of signatures, and marriage fees. The total income of the community from taxes amounted to 3,730 Lires for the year mentioned by the writer, a little over half of which went to salaries for the Chief Rabbi and other rabbis, slaughterers and other employees of the community. The community paid a yearly contribution to the *Alliance* school to the amount of 366 Lires, while the 'dispensary for poor Jews' amounted to 380 Lires and 'help to other communities' to 185 Lires.

In a kind of tribute to the community towards the end of his report, the writer states:

> The Jews are very ambitious, hard-working, capable, and economical. They are also very cunning, timid, and tactful. They are becoming richer day by day; and, as a result of education, a great many of them now understand that happiness in life does not only consist in massing money, but also in living well in the meantime. They have taken a fancy to the Christian quarter of the city because it is comparatively clean and airy. They are enormously increasing the rents in that quarter and are literally turning out old Christian tenants, who cannot cope with them from a financial standpoint. . . .

It will be seen from the above account that a process of radical change in the conditions and status of the Jews of Iraq was almost at its peak just before the outbreak of World War I. It is important to point out, however, that this change affected only a small proportion of the community, probably the five per cent comprising the 'rich and well-off class' which the British Consul-General's report mentions and just a small part of the 'middle class'. Be that as it may, it can be said with certainty that World War I and the British occupation found the Jews of Iraq well and adequately prepared. Basra was occupied in November 1914, and a few months later the whole of southern Iraq was in British hands. Baghdad, however, fell only in March 1917, to be followed a year afterwards by Arbil, Kirkuk, Mosul and the rest of northern Iraq. For the Jews of Baghdad, this meant a great deal of suffering and tribulation. The defeats suffered by their armies, the lack of organization, endemic corruption and habitual tyrannical methods of government – all these made the Turkish authorities panicky and even more arbitrary in their ways than they usually were. All able-bodied Jewish males were mobilized, most of them untrained and unequipped, to be sent in great haste to the front which few of them reached alive; the rich were dispossessed, their gold money taken in exchange for worthless banknotes; and a number of Jews – together with Muslims and Christians – were executed either because they deserted the army or because they were not able to produce the gold they were asked to contribute. Some of the Jews in Baghdad, hearing about the affluence and the freedom the British occupation had brought with it, managed to make their way to Basra and the southern parts of the country already in British hands – and when finally Baghdad was occupied the Jewish community declared the day 'a day of miracle' and for years to come the Jews commemorated it in their prayers. The same was the case with the Jewish communities of Mosul and Kirkuk.

CHAPTER 25

Rumours of a Brave New World

In the archives of the *Alliance Israélite Universelle* in Paris there is a file bearing the legend 'Zionist Activity in Iraq, 1899'. This file contains a body of circumstantial evidence, including a letter written by the protagonist himself, to show that the first Iraqi Jew to be attracted by the new ideology of political Zionism was a schoolteacher by the name of Aharon Sassoon ben Eliahu Nahum, nicknamed *Ha-Moreh* (The Teacher). It would appear from a number of letters written by this precursor of modern Zionism in Baghdad that the Zionist activity referred to in the *Alliance* archives amounted to little more than the reading, in groups, of Hebrew newspapers and periodicals reaching Baghdad from Europe, Palestine, Britain and the United States as early as the 1860s. These included *Ha-Lebanon, Ha-Meguid, Havatzelet, Ha-'Olam* and others, to some of which a number of Iraqi Jews actually contributed articles and reports on the situation of the Jews in Iraq. It was from these and other Hebrew publications that *Ha-Moreh* and his associates learned about the rise of the Zionist movement in Europe. In an interview given in 1942, Aharon Sassoon recalled that in those far-off days,

> I was always interested in Hebrew papers. One of these, which came from America and was called, I believe, *Matzpeh*, used to print reports about Jews who were active in promoting the Jewish cause. I was especially heartened by a speech delivered in Cologne by Tzvi Hermann Shapira and in which he spoke with great emotion beseeching the Jews not to assimilate. . . . Since then I became strongly oriented toward Eretz Yisrael and toward all those who are at the helm of the Zionist Movement. It was thus that I started on my Zionist activity.[1]

It is important to emphasize here that the beginnings of Zionist activity in Iraq did not mark the beginning of the ties between Iraqi

Jewry and the Holy Land. These ties had always been very strong, and had continued uninterruptedly since time immemorial. During the centuries of decline, following the fall of the *Gaonate* and the closure of the academies, these ties were most probably confined to prayers and supplications for the coming of the Messiah and the final deliverance. These primarily religious sentiments were no doubt also responsible for the few Iraqi Jewish families which emigrated to Palestine during the nineteenth century and perhaps before. Some Iraqi Jews used also to purchase burial plots in Eretz Yisrael through the many emissaries who came to Iraq fairly regularly. These purchases used to be made in the form of certificates which the emissaries issued against certain sums of money, and the Jews who purchased them thought that, even should they not have the privilege of actually being buried in the Holy Land, the mere fact that the certificates they had acquired would be buried with their remains in exile earned them the right to reach Jerusalem after their demise.

The Eretz Yisrael emissaries, besides selling these burial certificates, collected alms and donations for charity organizations in the four holy cities of Jerusalem, Hebron, Tiberias and Safed. Because they hailed from the Holy Land, they appear to have been received with great honour, and many emissaries continued to come to Iraq and visit various Jewish centres there up to the 1920s and beyond. There is on record the name of at least one Iraqi Jew who donated the whole of his estate to the Jews of Eretz Yisrael – Ya'qub Tzemah who died in Baghdad early in the 1840s.

Apart from individuals and families who emigrated to Palestine in those days, we know of one organized group of Iraqi Jews, consisting of *yeshivah* students and their families, who packed their belongings and emigrated to Palestine, driven by the belief that settlement in the Holy Land helps hasten the coming of the Messiah. They came to Palestine in 1854 and settled mostly in Hebron and Jerusalem. The children and grandchildren of some of these families – Mani, Yehuda, Aghababa and a few others – became prominent as rabbis, judges, academicians and businessmen. However, neither the purchasing of burial plots nor contributions to charity organizations, nor still the emigration of *yeshivah* students and their families, could be described as constituting Zionist activity in any acceptable sense of the term.[2]

We have already seen that Zionist activity of some sort did exist in Baghdad as early as the 1890s. This activity increased somewhat during the stay in the city of Yom-Tob Semah, headmaster of the *Alliance* school, in the years 1901–4. But this activity, too, did not exceed reading Hebrew periodicals and early Zionist literature. In an interview held decades later with one of the activists, Benjamin Sassoon, who later headed the Zionist Association in Baghdad, told Hayyim Cohen that when Semah was in Baghdad he used to gather a group of young Jews and read together with them from these periodicals, such as *Ha-Sefirah*, and tell them about Dr Herzl, whom he knew personally and was highly influenced by. Out of this small circle two persons emerged who were to continue to be at the helm of Zionist activity in Iraq until after World War I – Aharon Sassoon and Benjamin Sassoon. Although this activity did not include such obvious Zionist concerns as collecting money for the Jewish National Fund, the sale of shekels, or representation in Zionist Congresses, it, nevertheless, indicated some links with the world Zionist movement.

In 1914, three young Baghdadi Jews wrote a letter in which they said that as soon as they heard of the establishment of an Ottoman Zionist Association in Istanbul they hastened to form a group with the aim of establishing relations with the World Zionist Federation on an organizational basis, expressing the hope that their group would be able to set up a Zionist Association in Baghdad. In the same letter the three – Rafael Horesh, Maurice Fattal and Menashe Hakim – asked Berlin to send them information about the activities of the Jewish National Fund, newspapers and periodicals, books about the Zionist movement and stamps to be sold in Baghdad. 'And to appraise you of our fervent wish we enclose herewith the sum of 18.75 Francs which we three are donating; please send a receipt to each of us by return of mail. . . .' What they asked for from Berlin was duly supplied; but they were also told not to go ahead with their project for a Zionist Association until the fate of the Istanbul project was settled. Hakim, who signed the letter, was promised that he would be kept informed when the formalities connected with the Istanbul association were completed.[3]

In Basra, too, a number of individuals with initiative engaged in certain Zionist activities, such as establishing contact with the headquarters in Berlin, spreading the teaching of modern Hebrew, and preparing the way for setting up a Zionist Association. Like some Baghdadi Jews, a number of Jews in Basra also purchased plots of land in Palestine through emissaries from the Holy Land. As a matter of fact, this activity preceded by a year or two the emergence of similar signs in Baghdad. An exchange of letters remarkably similar to that quoted above took place between Basra and Berlin, bearing the dates 13 June and 6 September 1913 respectively. The correspondence was carried on in French, with the exception of the letter sent from Basra, which was in English.[4]

Summing up this period of Zionist activity, Hayyim Cohen concludes that though rather limited in scope, this activity in Iraq was started on the initiative of local Jews and was not induced from the outside, and that the reason why it was on such a small scale was twofold – the hostile attitude of the authorities on the one hand and the lack of potential Zionist leaders on the other. Another factor mentioned by Cohen is that, unlike certain other Arab countries, Iraq did not at that early phase witness the rise of an Arab nationalist movement, a state of affairs which he believes delayed the rise of a parallel movement amongst the Jews. It is interesting to note, however, that Cohen himself points out, in the very next paragraph, that the Zionist movement was not strong in countries like Syria, Lebanon and Egypt, where Arab nationalist movements did emerge.

Partly because postal and other links with Europe were disrupted and partly because the Jews of Baghdad and Basra were busy with other concerns, Zionist activity in Iraq during the war years decreased to a minimum, and it is only in 1919 that we hear of renewed activity. Even the publication of the Balfour Declaration does not seem to have been celebrated, and we have no evidence of its first anniversary in November 1918 being marked either. A more interesting question, however, is how Zionism was perceived by the Jews of Iraq in those days. Nothing like an answer to this question can be gleaned from the letters and the other written literature of the period. Apart from what some students of the subject have called 'Messianic Zionism', which Jews everywhere bore in their hearts throughout the ages, and which in one sense also included the idea of actually settling in Eretz Yisrael, we have no evidence as to whether Iraqi Jews in any significant sense, or numbers, were at this point in their history really aware of the political–national objectives of the movement with which they so readily sympathized. Nor, for that matter, do we know anything about the extent to which the new movement, in whatever sense it was perceived, actually entered the consciousness of these Jews.

It was Aharon Sassoon who again made an appearance in 1919, more than twenty years after he had first made the acquaintance of the new Zionist movement. In that year, following a short trip to Palestine, he wrote a letter to the chairman of the Council of Deputies in Jaffa. In this letter, he asserts that 'the national idea' had become 'deeply rooted in the hearts of all members of our community'. However, the letter also reveals that, up till then, he and his friends did not quite know what the

Zionist movement wanted from its adherents; that no Zionist association had by then been set up in Iraq; and that the aims of his group were to spread the knowledge of Hebrew, help those wishing to emigrate to Palestine, and establish a Zionist Association. We also learn from this letter that no donations had as yet been collected for the national institutions, and that this was not even included in the objectives of the association the group hoped to found. It was only in the autumn of 1919 that any money was collected for the Jewish National Fund, and it took Sassoon about half a year to verify the address to which the money was to be sent, namely the headquarters of the JNF in The Hague. In February 1920, Sassoon became the distributor of the Zionist weekly *Ha-'Olam* which was then published in London. The circulation rose from twenty issues to fifty in June of that year; of these, thirty-two were distributed to subscribers and the rest sold individually. In March 1920, Sassoon received 1,000 shekels for sale in Iraq, and it was thereby that funds started to be collected for Keren Hayesod (Foundation Fund). The year 1920 witnessed two additional important developments in this respect: Iraqi Jews in increasing numbers started purchasing land in Palestine, and the first Zionist association was founded, albeit in the guise of a literary society. The society, under the name 'Jewish Literary Society' (*Jam'iyya Isra'iliyya Adabiyya*), was founded on 15 July, and a club was opened as a meeting-place. Ostensibly, the group aimed at establishing better links with the Muslim population at a time of general unrest against the British Mandate. Contemporary and later evidence shows that its founders sincerely adopted this cause and believed that the new group would help attain more understanding with the Muslims. It is, therefore, somewhat strange to note that a society with the aim of increasing co-operation with the Muslim Arabs of Iraq should declare its objectives to be 'the study of the Hebrew language and of Jewish literature, and to extend help to groups and associations whose aims are identical with its own [a clear reference to Zionist groups]'. In order to promote its aims, the society 'will open a Hebrew club for its members, publish a literary weekly, found a library, and hold literary lectures'. The new society's first steps were successful enough. In a circular letter in English dated 8 September 1920 and signed 'With Zion's Greetings', by 'the Secretary, The Jewish Literary Society', it announced that a club had already been opened, and that plans were afoot for the opening of a library and the publication of a weekly paper. 'Our intention', the writer asserts, 'is to work for the moral and intellectual promotion of our co-religionists, here. . . . We shall be glad to maintain close relations with similar Jewish Societies, in rendering a mutual help with the view to pave the way for acquiring our position among the other nations of the world and re-establish the ancient glory of Israel.'[5]

In the real world, too, the society achieved a good deal of its declared aims. A library was opened dealing mostly in Hebrew books, many of which came from the private collection of Chief Rabbi Yeruham el-Yashar. By November 1920 twelve lectures had been given at the society's club; membership had leaped to more than 700, according to society figures; and a weekly, *Yeshurun*, was produced, half in Hebrew and half in Judeo–Arabic. In its first issue the weekly announced the opening, 'shortly', of evening classes for the teaching of Hebrew. After only five issues, however, the paper stopped publication owing to what was described as technical difficulties.

Far from being content with these cultural and educational activities, however, leading members of the Jewish Literary Society started 'playing politics' in earnest, setting for themselves the difficult task of infiltrating and subverting the governing body of the Jewish community. This, of course, led to a great deal of controversy and a lot of mutual recriminations, with the society's spokesmen accusing members of the Jewish establishment of spying and informing on its activities. In the end only the society's chairman, Salman (Shlomo) Hayya, managed to get elected to the Community Council in November 1920. A month or so later, on 24 December, Hayya (who was an officer in the secret police) was assassinated by the relatives of a criminal whom he had identified and arrested. After his death, sharp differences of opinion developed between the members as to the nature of the tasks ahead, and what seems certain is that the faction which advocated a more active and open Zionist line won the day. Early in 1921, the activists elected an executive committee for a new association which they had set up, and on 22 February they applied to the British High Commissioner for a licence, which they were granted less than two weeks later. The first openly Zionist organization ever to be allowed to function in Iraq was thus born – the Zionist Association of Baghdad. A circular was sent forth by the new group in which the name of its chairman was given, Aharon Sassoon, together with the names of a vice-chairman, a secretary, a 'representative' and an accountant.

The new association did not last long. Apart from some personal intrigues and gossip about its chairman, there was also a certain lack of interest on the part of the Jewish public. But the real reason for its suspension lay elsewhere. In July 1922, the Iraqi Law of Associations was published, requiring all such groups, including those already in existence, to register with the Ministry of Internal Affairs. The Zionist Association duly applied, and the chairman was asked to have a talk with the minister himself, Abdul Muhsin al-Sa'dun. From the account given by Aharon Sassoon of the meeting, in a letter addressed to Dr Chaim Weizmann, it appears that the minister spent a full hour with the Zionist leader in which he tried to convince him of the following: a) that he, the minister, liked the Jews and sought what was good for them; b) that he sympathized with the aims of the Zionists, since it would be wrong to think that only the Arabs were right, it being evident that the Jews suffered more and had no homeland of their own; c) that it would have been better for the Arabs to co-operate with the Jews and to seek an alliance with them, as this would help them more than all the world's rulers put together; and d) that few Arabs adhered to his point of view on this subject, and that this being the case a hostile attitude had developed *vis-à-vis* the Zionist cause, and that he, therefore, could see no place for the Zionist Association in such a hostile atmosphere. To Sassoon's plea that his association had thus far caused no trouble and that it was formally licensed by the High Commissioner himself, al-Sa'dun is said to have answered that the group could go on functioning, only that no new licence would be issued. The efforts made in London by the World Zionist Federation as a result of Sassoon's letter to Weizmann produced only a promise identical to that given by the minister, namely that the new law would not be enacted against the association provided that it refrained from pressing for official recognition. And, indeed, the group continued to work, in one form or other, throughout the 1920s. During this period of time Jews who sought to emigrate to Palestine were given permission to do so only on the recommendation of the association, which acted as a representative of the Immigration Department of the Jewish Agency.[6]

The wish expressed by the Iraqi authorities that the Zionists maintain a low profile was shared by the office of the British High Commissioner in Baghdad – a fact which antedated the publication of the Law of Associations. In April 1922, the representative of Keren Hayesod in the East, Dr Ariel Bension, wrote to his London office about a meeting he had had in Baghdad with the British High Commissioner, in which he was advised not to act in a way that would harm the relations between the Jews and their Gentile neighbours. The leadership of the Jewish community in Baghdad, too, was rather uneasy about the effect Zionist activity was likely to have on the position of the Jews. This uneasiness is best described by Menahem

Salih Daniel, a prominent member of the community, in a letter he addressed to the Secretary of the Zionist Organization in London on 8 September 1922. In this letter, written in reply to a request for aid from the Organization, Daniel propounds what must be the first and most articulate case against what he perceived as the disruptive effects on his community of growing Zionist activity. Declaring at the outset that he appreciates and admires 'your noble ideal', and that he 'would have been glad to be able to contribute towards its realization', he writes: 'But in this country the Zionist Movement is not an entirely idealistic subject. To the Jews, perhaps to a greater extent than to other elements, it represents a problem the various aspects of which need to be very carefully considered. Very peculiar considerations, with which none of the European Jewish Communities are confronted, force themselves upon us in this connection.'[7]

Daniel's analysis of the general Arab attitude to Zionism and to the Palestine problem is all the more remarkable for having been submitted so early in the day. Even though no active resistance to Zionism had thus far been in evidence, he writes, 'it is none the less the feeling of every Arab that it is a violation of his legitimate rights, which it is his duty to denounce and fight to the best of his ability'. Iraq having always been an active centre of Arab culture and activity, 'the public mind here is thoroughly stirred up as regards Palestine'. To an Arab, 'any sympathy with the Zionist Movement is nothing short of a betrayal of the Arab cause'.

The danger posed by this state of affairs on the position of the Jews of Iraq is also shrewdly and sensibly elucidated. As it is, Daniel writes, 'the Jews in this country hold, indeed, a conspicuous position'. This was quite true as the Jews formed one third of the population of the capital, Baghdad, had the larger part of commerce in their hands, and enjoyed a higher standard of literacy than their Muslim neighbours. He explains:

> In Baghdad the situation of the Jew is nearly an outstanding feature of the town, and though he has not yet learnt to take full advantage of his position, he is, nevertheless, being regarded by the waking-up Muslim as a very lucky person, from whom the country should expect full return for its lavish favours. He is, moreover, beginning to give the Muslim an unpleasant experience of a successful competition in government functions, which having regard to the large number of unemployed former officials, may well risk to embitter feeling against him.

It was clear that in this delicate situation 'the Jew cannot maintain himself unless he gives proof of an unimpeachable loyalty to his country, and avoids with care any action which may be misconstrued'. Iraq, Daniel continues, 'is now trying to build up a future of its own, in which the Jew is expected to play a prominent part. The task will be of extreme difficulty and will need a strained effort on the part of every inhabitant. Any failing on the part of the Jew will be most detrimental to his future.'

Daniel does not hesitate to acknowledge the great popularity which Zionist ideas had come to enjoy among the Jews of Iraq, the large majority of whom seemed to him unable to understand 'that all they can reasonably do for Zionism is to offer it a discreet financial help'. He laments the seeming lack of discretion on the part of Dr Ariel Bension, then in Baghdad. Since Bension's arrival, he writes, 'we have had a sad experience of the regrettable effects which an influx of Zionist ideas here may have'. For some time now, he adds, there was 'a wild outburst of popular feeling towards Zionism, which expressed itself by noisy manifestations of sympathy, crowded gatherings and a general and vague impression among the lower class that Zionism was going to end the worries of life, and that no restraint was any longer necessary in the way of expressing opinions or showing scorn to the Arabs'. Needless to say, 'this feeling . . . is altogether unenlightened. It was more Messianic than Zionistic. To an observer it was merely the reaction of a subdued race, which for a moment thought that by magic the tables were turned and that it were to become an overlord.' Daniel's minor critique of Zionist theory and practice is summed up in the following words:

> Very few stopped to think whether the Promised Land was already conquered, and if so how long it would take till all the Jews of Mesopotamia repaired to it, and whether any reasonable policy was in the meanwhile desirable. In this state of raving the Jews could not fail to occasion a friction with the Muslims, especially as the latter were then high up in nationalist effervescence, and a feeling of surprise and dissatisfaction ensued, which caused a prominent member of the Cabinet to remark to me reproachfully that after so many centuries of good understanding the Muslims were not at all suspecting that they had inspired the Jews with so little esteem for them. During my first interview with Dr Bension . . . I explained to him my anxiety as to the effect of the rather sonorous success of his mission on the political difficulty of the Jews at that juncture and requested him to postpone his mission, if possible till the political

outlook should be more reassuring. I am not aware that he actually took any steps in that direction but the enthusiasm of the Jewish population has never abated since then.

Towards the end of his letter Daniel informs the Secretary of the Zionist Organization that, in view of the circumstances explained above, 'I cannot help considering the establishment of a recognized Zionist Bureau in Baghdad as deleteriously affecting the good relations of the Mesopotamian Jew with his fellow citizens.' He adds:

> The Jews are already acting with culpable indifference about public and political affairs, and if they espouse so publicly and tactlessly, as they have done lately, a cause which is regarded by the Arabs not only as foreign but as actually hostile, I have no doubt that they will succeed in making of themselves a totally alien element in this country and as such they will have great difficulty in defending a position which, as explained above, is on other grounds already too enviable.

Forestalling possible criticism in this regard, the writer finally acknowledges the precarious nature of his position: 'I am not qualified to speak for [the Jews of Iraq]. The opinions expressed above are my own personal opinions. The Community is unfortunately too helplessly disorganized to have any co-ordinated opinion, and that is indeed why it is the more exposed.'

The position of the Jews of Iraq was, indeed, exposed, and in the end neither Daniel's analysis nor his pleas proved persuasive either to the Zionists outside or the Arab nationalists at home. As Kedourie has observed: 'With perspicacious wisdom this letter foresees the danger to its author's community posed by the style of politics which Zionism and Arabism shared in equal measure, a danger rendered all the more deadly by the indifference about public and political affairs which, as he correctly observes, was a characteristic of the Baghdad Jews.'[8]

CHAPTER 26

Mandate and Independence

When the British entered Baghdad in March 1917, the Jews were the largest single group in its population. According to the last Ottoman official yearbook of the vilayet of Baghdad, which gave the population figures for the city, the Jews there numbered 80,000, out of a total population of 202,000. The Sunnis, the Shiites and the Turks numbered 101,400; the Christians, 12,000; the Kurds, 8,000; and the Persians 800. The Civil Administration of Mesopotamia, in its annual review for the year 1920, stated that the Jewish community in the city of Baghdad 'is a very important section of the community, outnumbering the Sunnis or Shias'. Other figures which may serve as indices in this respect include a proclamation of the British military governor of the city in 1919, which fixed the number of sheep to be slaughtered daily in Baghdad east – the more populous part of the city – as 220 for Jewish butchers and 160 for Muslim butchers. A few years later in 1926, when the Baghdad Chamber of Commerce was set up, five of its fifteen-member administrative council represented Jewish merchants, four Muslim merchants, three British merchants, one each for the Persian and Christian merchants, and one represented the banks.[1]

What made the Jews the most important single element in Baghdad, however, was not only their numerical superiority *vis-à-vis* all the other religious and ethnic groups. As a community the Jews were perhaps the wealthiest and certainly the best educated. They also had the most widespread network of relations with the outside world, mainly through those of their fellow Baghdadis who had settled in India, England and the Far East, where they established themselves in commerce, the import-export trade, shipping and other branches of business. Partly through these conditions, the Jews of Baghdad in the first two decades of this century occupied a clear and acknowledged position of superiority in the Mesopotamian economy.

The Jews, then, had much to gain from the new vistas opened up to them with the coming of the British. They welcomed the change, which besides giving them a feeling of security following three years of harsh and arbitrary rule, also granted them equality of opportunity and far better facilities for trade and commerce. It was understandable, therefore, that when the British started talking about such unheard-of novelties as transferring power to 'the Arabs' these Jews began to worry. It all started with certain rumours and allegations which followed the publication of an Anglo–French Declaration promising 'to encourage and assist in the establishment of indigenous governments and administrations in Syria and Mesopotamia'. This was something the Jews could not comprehend, having lived for centuries under Ottoman rule, first as a 'protected minority' and lately as citizens formally enjoying equal rights and duties with their Muslim neighbours. Now these Muslims, or rather the Arabic-speaking Sunnis among them, were to be given the whole country to rule, most likely to lord it over the Jews, the Christians, the variety of non-Arab Muslims who had always been part of the landscape, and even their Shiite co-religionists.

Faced with these bleak possibilities, the Jews of Baghdad set to work. They petitioned the civil commissioner in Baghdad and asked that they be allowed to become British subjects. They gave three reasons for not wanting an indigenous government to rule over them. The Arabs, they said, were politically irresponsible; they had no administrative experience; and they could be fanatical and intolerant. The following year, in 1919, they submitted another petition. They reasoned:

> The proclaimed aim of the Great Allied Powers in the most tremendous world war is the complete liberation of oppressed nationalities with the object of assuring their legitimate political aspirations as well as their economical and social development. The full development of peoples whom several centuries of national lethargy plunged into a state of utter unpreparedness for self-administration is only obtainable through the material and moral co-operation of a great European Power. We are, therefore, of the opinion: that the nomination of an Amir for Mesopotamia is inadmissible; that a direct British government is indispensable for the future administration of this country.[2]

These pleas were not heeded, and Amir Faisal, the son of the Sharif Hussein ibn 'Ali, who had led the Arab Revolt against the Ottoman sultan, was brought from Mecca to govern his new domain, the Kingdom of Iraq. The Jews, however, did not give up; they decided on a last attempt. In 1921, a delegation went to see the High Commissioner, Sir Percy Cox, and again asked to be granted British citizenship. According to a contemporary British account of the meeting, the Jews 'based their claim on the fact that their country had been conquered by British troops, and that they were actually at the moment Turkish subjects under British control – and that, therefore, the British had no moral right to force them to accept a change of nationality unless they so desired it'. How the meeting ended is related in the following sentence: 'They [the Jews] were eventually appeased by the personal influence of the high commissioner, and by his assurance that ample guarantees would be afforded them by the British government against any form of local tyranny. . . .'[3]

Appeased or not, the Jews had no choice; they would have to reconcile themselves to the new situation. Kedourie, who quotes these documents, has this to say about their plight:

> The Jews of Baghdad were defeated from the start; but they did not know it and would not know it for a long time to come. The situation was completely beyond their understanding. For how could they have discerned the prodigious spectacle that then appeared, of deliquescent Liberals and *Tancred* Tories, banding together in London to utilize the might and authority of a victorious empire in order to bring about in the Middle East, consciously and willingly, such conditions as hitherto had been seen only with the decay of authority and the decline of empire? Power the Jews of Baghdad could understand, certainly, and the coarse, capricious exercise of power. The right of conquest they could cheerfully acknowledge, for all their history had taught them that there lay safety. These things and these things alone lay within their experience, and how pitifully inadequate they were going to prove! It was not by the help of this experience that they would understand the strange, exquisite perversions of the western conscience: the genial eccentricity of Mr Philby, proposing to make a thug who took his fancy the president of an Iraqi republic; or the fond foolishness of Miss Bell, thinking to stand godmother to a new Abbassid empire; or the disoriented fanaticism of Colonel Lawrence, proclaiming that he would be dishonoured if the progeny of the Sharif of Mecca were not forthwith provided with thrones. Yet it was with such people that their fate rested.[4]

Having thus failed in their efforts to stave off a danger which they felt threatened their position and their future, the Jews of Baghdad withdrew into themselves, trying to make the best of their still superior position. Though fairly sure of the dangers ahead, they had no choice but to sit and watch the spectacle of a ramshackle new administration trying to create a nation out of a motley assortment of religious, ethnic, cultural and linguistic groups. In the meantime, business was brisk, jobs in commercial and government offices were plentiful, and educational and social opportunities increasing almost day by day. On 25 October 1920 the High Commissioner set up a temporary government consisting of eight members, whose task it was to deal with the country's financial, legal, security, education, health and religious affairs. One of the eight ministers was a Jew – Sassoon Heskel, who was entrusted with the finance portfolio. Less than a year later, on 23 August 1921, Faisal was proclaimed King of Iraq. Faisal was considered a liberal and benevolent monarch, and he seems to have correctly estimated the importance of the position occupied by the Jews of his new kingdom. In 1919, he had already signed the famous Faisal–Weizmann agreement in which he declared himself sympathetic to the national aspirations of the Jews and their intention to build a national home for themselves in Palestine. When he was enthroned, the Jews of Baghdad organized a festive reception in his honour which is said to have made a great impression on him. It was held in the Great Synagogue and a large number of notables and religious leaders of all denominations were present. A Torah scroll was especially taken out of the 'temple' and the king deigned to kiss it. He also addressed his hosts, thanking them and describing the Jews as being 'the moving spirit among the inhabitants of Iraq'. Directly after ascending the throne, moreover, Faisal declared that henceforth there would be no discrimination between Muslim, Jew and Christian. 'There is only one country called Iraq', he asserted, 'and all its inhabitants are Iraqis. We all come from the same origin, our forefather being Shem. We all belong to this noble [Semitic] race. . . .'[5]

These and similar assurances were confirmed and reinforced by an article in the agreement concluded between London and Baghdad and signed on 10 October 1922, which laid down that the laws of the country guaranteed freedom of creed and conscience for all; that no one would be discriminated against because of their race, religion or language; and that every community had the right to maintain schools of its own and to educate its members in its own language. These noble sentiments were again reaffirmed in the Constitution promulgated by the constituent assembly in July 1924 and confirmed by Faisal in March the next year. Despite minor incidents and the problem of trying to realize such ideals in a country with such a long and rich experience of arbitrary rule and communal and ethnic divisions, the Jews of Iraq took full advantage of their new status and put their newly gained privileges to excellent use.

As well as securing the post of Finance Minister and a few other senior positions in the new administration, the Jews were also adequately represented in the new parliament, which had been elected in accordance with the law promulgated in 1924 and opened in July 1925. Of the thirty-three Deputies elected in the three main *Liwas*, five were Jews (two representing the Jews of Baghdad, two those of Basra, and one representing the Jews of Mosul). The remaining Deputies consisted of twenty-four Muslims (ten, five and nine respectively) and four Christians (one, one and two).

Throughout the Mandate period (1922–32) and until the death of King Faisal in 1933, the Jews were more or less left alone to work for their own economic, social and educational advancement – and to dabble in politics only superficially. Even during this peaceful period, however, voices began to be heard decrying the Jews' apparent control of the economy, their generally superior social status, and the fact that they were quite disproportionately represented in government offices. Nor did the first signs inside their ranks of open sympathy and active support of the Zionist cause go uncriticized.

About this period, which preceded the declaration of independence and the signing of the Anglo–Iraqi treaty of alliance, Longrigg has this to say concerning the position of the Jews: 'The Jews were still compact, assiduous, self-sufficient and unambitious. They had had their outstanding Finance Minister, kept their place in government offices, dominated many of the markets, owned property, and supported their own schools and hospitals; and when Iraq approached its independence, were not so foolish as to compromise their future by open protest. The art of living in Iraq, and surviving bad times, was no new one to them. . . .'[6] The fate of the Jews of Iraq, however, was to be linked willy-nilly to the vexed 'Palestine Problem'. The kind of distinction which men like Menahem Daniel and a few other heads of the community tried to introduce, namely between Judaism as a faith and Zionism as a modern European national movement, in order to keep Iraqi Jewry out of the squabble, did not and could not succeed. In the words of Longrigg again:

> Iraqi, like all Arab, feeling was strong against the Zionist movement in Palestine; ugly and violent street demonstrations, accompanied by the usual marshalled schoolboys and armed roughs, greeted Sir Alfred Mond when he visited Baghdad on business in February

1928; and in the year following demonstrations in the mosques and city, a two-minute silence in Parliament, black-edged newspapers, and telegrams to London marked Iraqi disapproval of the 'pro-Jewish' policy of Great Britain. But the day when these feelings would descend on the heads of the timid and law-abiding Baghdadi Jews, anxious only to find a secure place in the State and to dissociate themselves from Zionism, lay still some years ahead.[7]

The participation of Jews in the general economic and administrative development of Iraq from the early 1920s was as extensive as it was effective. Among the prominent names of that period are those of Sassoon Heskel, who was Minister of Finance and a member of parliament continuously for close on thirteen years (1920–32); Menahem Daniel, who represented the Jews in the twenty-member Iraqi Senate between 1925 and 1932, when he was replaced by his son Ezra Menahem Daniel; and Dawood Samra, who was appointed in 1923 as member of the High Court of Appeal, a post he held until his retirement in 1946. The most outstanding of these, however, was Sassoon Heskel, whose name used to be on a par with those of Abdul Rahman al-Naqib and Talib Pasha as the three most prominent men in Baghdad. Prior to the British occupation, Heskel Afandi was chosen as one of the Deputies of the vilayet of Baghdad in the House of Representatives in Istanbul following the Young Turks revolution of 1908. He remained in this position for nearly ten years; then in 1909 he was appointed a member of the Turkish delegation that went to London to negotiate with the British government. He was an active member of the House, where he headed the budget committee; in 1913 he became adviser to the Ministry of Commerce and Agriculture. Shortly after returning to Baghdad in 1920, he was appointed Minister of Finance, and in March 1921 he participated together with Ja'far al-'Askari in the Cairo Conference, where it was decided to establish the kindom of Iraq with Faisal as the first monarch. According to Abdul Razzaq al-Hasani, the Iraqi chronicler of this period, Heskel told Winston Churchill, then Secretary for the Colonies, that the custom thus far for the countries which used to be part of the Ottoman Empire had been for the princes who had been brought to govern them to come from the north to the south, and not the other way round. To which the British minister is said to have retorted: 'Yes, quite so; but don't forget that Mr Kornowallis is accompanying Prince Faisal – and *he* comes from the north!' Though this was obviously a derogatory remark about the level of culture of the king-designate (the reference to other parts of the empire was to some of the countries of the Balkans, e.g. Greece, to which a prince from the north had been brought to become monarch), this did not in the least affect future relations between Heskel and Faisal.[8]

As Minister of Finance in the first Iraqi administration, Heskel was responsible for setting up the ministry literally from scratch – departments, committees, officials and all. More significantly, he laid the foundations for a regular budgetary system, laid down rules of income and expenditure, saw to the promulgation of tax laws, and watched over his colleagues so that they did not exceed the figures fixed in their respective budgets. It is even said that in 1925 he threatened to resign when Faisal himself sought to force him to increase the Royal Court's budget for postal letters and telegrams. His crowning achievement, however, lay in the fact that in the negotiations conducted with the British Petroleum Company in 1925 he insisted that payment of oil revenues be calculated on the basis of gold. After much wrangling he got his way – and when Britain abolished the Gold Standard, Iraq as a result gained considerable additional revenue from its oil.[9]

CHAPTER 27

The *Farhud* and its Consequences

In 1932, shortly after Great Britain extended formal recognition of full independence to the young kingdom, Iraq was admitted as member of the League of Nations. In a 'Declaration on the Subject of Minorities' made by the Iraqi government to the League's Council, certain principles were stipulated, including an undertaking that 'full and complete protection of life and liberty will be assured to all inhabitants of Iraq, without distinction of birth, nationality, language, race or religion'. Other lofty ideals of equality were included in plenty: an electoral system ensuring 'equitable representation to racial, religious and linguistic minorities'; a stipulation that differences of race, language or religion 'will not prejudice any Iraqi national in matters relating to the enjoyment of civil and political rights . . .'; and unrestricted, free use was guaranteed 'of any language, in private intercourse, in commerce, in religion, in the press or in publications of any kind, or at public meetings'.

This document was submitted to the Council of the League of Nations on 29 February 1932. In September 1933, King Faisal I died, to be succeeded on the throne by his son Ghazi, a weak ruler and something of a nationalist enthusiast who lacked the experience, native wisdom and statesmanship of his father. Whereas Faisal succeeded in keeping the country intact amidst a motley assortment of difficulties, tribal unrest, and serious murmurings on the part of a Shiite majority unhappy with being ruled by a Sunni monarch, Ghazi encouraged the new and predominantly Sunni nationalist forces and permitted them to conduct political activities. As far as the Jews were concerned, two parallel developments seem to have helped weaken their position at this juncture: firstly, the rise of the Nazis in Germany; and secondly, the fact that Iraq had become something of a haven for Arab nationalist activists from Syria and Palestine, seeking refuge in the first Arab country to attain independence from the British. The activities of these exiles, some of whom were appointed as schoolteachers while others insinuated themselves into the higher echelons of the administration and the political parties, coincided with the activities of the German envoy, Dr F. Grobba, who disseminated Nazi propaganda and made friends and influenced people in high places – senior officials, directors-general of sensitive offices, and even ministers. On the home front, too, things reached boiling point, and during the six years of his rule Ghazi – who was to be killed in a car accident in 1939 – had to deal with numerous tribal uprisings and five military revolts.

Although no new regulations were issued, no laws passed and no discriminatory measures of any kind were formally taken against the Jews, just a little over thirty months after the Declaration had been submitted to the League of Nations, the first signs of an anti-Jewish campaign in the administration appeared. In September 1934, the newly appointed Minister of Economics and Transport ordered the dismissal of dozens of non-Muslim officials of the Ministry, though some of the Jews amongst them were reinstated following protests by the Jewish community. The following year, the Ministry of Education issued secret instructions to state secondary schools and to institutions of higher learning to admit only limited numbers of Jews. Hebrew instruction in Jewish schools was curtailed, being limited only to the reading of the Bible, without translation or interpretation. Travel by Jews to Palestine, even by those Jews who applied for visitors' visas, became far more difficult through a number of obstacles – again informal and not stipulated in any new laws or regulations.

From then on the Jews began to feel the pressure and the harassment, which was to extend to personal physical safety. This reached a peak shortly after the formation of a new government by Yasin al-Hashimi, whose cabinet had been overthrown towards the end of October 1936 as a result of the military putsch led by Bakr Sidqi, the first *coup d'état* to take place in Iraq and the Arab world in modern times. The troubles intensified after the disturbances in Palestine in 1936, and in September of that year the so-called Committee for the Defence of Palestine, headed by a member of the Chamber of Disputes, issued a manifesto accusing the Jews of Iraq of lending support to the Zionists of Palestine. Three days later, on the eve of the Jewish New Year, two Jews were shot at and murdered while leaving their club, in full view of passers-by. The following day, which had been proclaimed 'Palestine Day', witnessed protest meetings, demonstrations and fiery speeches in mosques and other public places – and on the same day two more Jews were assaulted, one of whom died while the other suffered severe injuries. A few days later, on Yom Kippur (27 September) a home-made bomb was thrown into a crowded synagogue, but it did not explode.

These grave developments led the Chief Rabbi and head of the Jewish community, Sassoon Kadoori, and a number of leading Jewish intellectuals to issue declarations in which they dissociated themselves and the community from Zionist designs in Palestine. Following an official communiqué circulated by the community to the local press, Ezra Haddad – a school principal, a scholar, translator and writer – published an article in Baghdad's leading daily *Al-Akhbar* in which he declared:

> The Arab Jew, when he makes his attitude to the Zionist question clear, feels in his innermost being that he does that of his own free will and motivated by considerations of justice, conscience and . . . well-established facts. And when he speaks of the Arab lands, he speaks of homelands which from time immemorial surrounded him with generosity and affluence – homelands which he considered and continues to consider as oases in the midst of a veritable desert of injustices and oppressions which were the Jews' lot in many of the countries which boast of culture and civilization.

A previous article by Haddad printed in *Al-Bilad* carried the title: 'We were Arabs before we became Jews' (*Nahnu 'Arab qabla an nakun Yahudan*).

Ya'qub Balboul, speaking for the younger generation of Iraqi Jews, published an article in *Al-Akhbar* two years later (21 July 1938) in which he asserted that members of that generation were among the most fervent supporters of the Pan-Arab idea, which he claimed had struck roots in the minds of these young Jews to the same extent as had happened with their Muslim and Christian compatriots. At a time in which state schools and institutions welcomed Jews and extended assistance to them alongside their Muslim and Christian brethren, he wrote, 'a Jewish youth in the Arab countries expects nothing from Zionism except colonialism and domination'.[1]

A brief period of quiet followed the formation of the government of Hikmat Suleiman, who was brought to power on 29 October 1936 by Bakr Sidqi and his associates. Attacks on Jews ceased as preoccupation with the Palestine question became less pronounced. Hikmat, unlike his predecessor Yasin al-Hashimi, was known for his liberal views and for the fact that his first concern would be internal reforms rather than foreign or Arab affairs. But this spell of peace and quiet was not to last for long. In July 1937 opposition elements staged a mass demonstration in Baghdad during which, inexplicably and without any provocation, two Jewish onlookers were attacked and killed. Less than a month later, on 8 August, Bakr Sidqi was murdered – and nine days later Jamil al-Midfa'i succeeded Hikmat Suleiman as Prime Minister. The new cabinet professed more sympathy towards the Arab cause in Palestine, and events in the Holy Land again had repercussions in Baghdad, mostly in the form of demonstrations in which the Jews were eventually involved. Individual attacks on Jews, which never really stopped even during the previous year, tended to intensify, and as early as August of 1938, shortly after the formation of the Midfa'i cabinet, a group of thirty-three Jewish dignitaries saw fit to send a telegram to the British Colonial Secretary and to the League of Nations in which they expressed opposition to Zionism and pledged loyalty to Iraq as their true homeland. At home, a number of Jewish writers, journalists and scholars again wrote in the local press reiterating their Arab sympathies and dissociating their community from the activities and plans of their Zionist co-religionists. In October 1938, the government took certain measures against the inciters – and during the premiership of Nuri as-Sa'id, who formed the following three cabinets in succession (December 1938–March 1940), and Rashid 'Ali al-Gaylani's first cabinet (March 1940–January 1941) there are records only of a few isolated incidents.[2]

With the advance of Rommel's troops and other developments in North Africa and the Levant, the British began to take more interest in Iraqi politics, and this was inevitably reflected in the relations between the court – where Crown Prince Abdul Ilah had become Regent after King Ghazi's death in April 1939 – and the leading politicians. Rashid 'Ali, who was known for his general Arab nationalist sympathies if not for downright pro-German sentiments, formed a cabinet on 31 March 1940 which lasted until the end of January 1941. He was succeeded by Taha al-Hashimi, whose cabinet was toppled exactly two months after taking power (1 February–1 April 1941). Nationalist elements in the army who supported Rashid 'Ali brought him to power again with a cabinet ostensibly advocating neutrality in the war and denied access to British troops to military bases in Iraq. The Regent and some of his faithful supporters, led by Nuri as-Sa'id, fled Baghdad on the day the *coup* was staged. On 18 April Rashid 'Ali formed a new cabinet which included elements known for their Nazi connections and anti-Jewish inclinations; and at the beginning of May Rashid 'Ali declared a state of war against Great Britain.

The month of war which followed was a time of continuous harassment for the Jews of Iraq, with hardly a day passing without some Jew or other being accused of signalling to British planes flying over or bombing some Iraqi military base in the vicinity of cities and towns. And there were thirteen known cases in which Jews were murdered in various parts of the country, ten of them in the northern village of Sandur. But the real shock was to come only after Rashid 'Ali and his colleagues were defeated and fled the country, and when British troops and the pro-Regent Iraqi forces were already virtually in the capital. What happened was that Rashid 'Ali and his followers fled on 29 May, and on the same day a group of notables and army officers formed a body they called 'The Committee for Internal Security', presumably to try to manage affairs and fill the power vacuum in the absence of a lawful government. That same day, too, British troops reached the outskirts of Baghdad; but for reasons which had to do with sparing the feelings of the Iraqis they were ordered to stay put, while the Iraqi soldiers were disbanded and allowed to enter Baghdad individually or in small groups but not in formation.

Meanwhile, Colonel Yunis al-Sab'awi, the only member of Rashid 'Ali's cabinet who remained in Baghdad, summoned Chief Rabbi Sassoon Kadoori on 30 May and asked him to notify the Jews that they were not to leave their homes for the next three days, the first two of which, Saturday 31 May and Sunday 1 June, were the two days of Shavuoth (Pentecost). Sab'awi, however, was arrested by the Committee for Internal Security but was allowed to flee to Iran. The so-called 'youth brigades', a paramilitary outfit formed and armed by Sab'awi ostensibly for purposes of civil defence but which are said to have been intended to carry out anti-Jewish pogroms, were disbanded by the Committee, who also demanded that their members turn in all the arms in their possession. A third order issued by the Committee threatened severe punishment for any disorderly conduct. This served to reassure the Jews of Baghdad, who then decided that the danger was over and that they could now quietly celebrate Pentecost and also openly welcome the imminent entry into the capital of the Regent and his pro-Allied entourage.

The Jews took additional precautions, however, and hardly left their homes on the Saturday; when they did go out they restricted their movements to going to synagogues and visiting friends and relatives in their own neighbourhoods. By Sunday, they felt sufficiently secure to go out in the streets, and many of them even ventured to cross the Tigris to the Karkh, so as to be as near as possible to the spot where a festive welcome was to be held for the Regent. Because the day happened to be a feast, these Jews were dressed in their best clothes and the impression the Muslim populace got was that the festivity was due wholly to the fact that the Jews were celebrating the country's defeat at the hands of the hated British. Trouble thus started early in the afternoon of that Sunday, when a number of Jews returning from the celebrations at the airport were accosted by some demobilized soldiers, who murdered one Jew and wounded sixteen others, in full view of members of the military police. Soon after, Jews were attacked in the city's main street and in certain poor neighbourhoods, resulting in the death of ten and the wounding of many more.

For the rest of that Sunday and much of the following day, acts of pillage and murder spread, perpetrated mainly by returning soldiers and members of the security forces who were later joined by mobs coming from slum neighbourhoods. Hordes of tribesmen, getting wind of the disorders, soon joined the rioters. Throughout these events, those who were nominally responsible for the city's security and the safety of its inhabitants – who manned the Committee for Internal Security – refused to take action against the rioters. Towards the end of Monday, when the situation threatened to get out of hand and even non-Jewish life and property were in jeopardy, the governor of the *Liwa* of Baghdad asked the Regent for permission to shoot at the attacking mob. Finally, at five that same evening a curfew was imposed and troops were ordered to shoot at the rioters. Scores of these were killed, and within one hour the streets were quiet and empty, except for members of the security forces and part of the loot the rioters decided to leave while running for their lives. Apart from a few sporadic incidents on the following two days, quiet then prevailed. It is estimated that between 170 and 180 Jews were killed and many more wounded, and even larger numbers of non-Jews, including rioters, security men and Muslims who came to the defence of their Jewish neighbours, were among the dead and injured. On 2 June the Regent named Jamil al-Midfa'i Prime Minister and a cabinet was formed, and five days later a commission of enquiry was set up to investigate these events.

The commission, manned by Sa'di Salih, Abdullah al-Qassab and Muhammed Tawfiq an-Nayib, did a hasty and highly unreliable job, and submitted its report on 8 July. Apart from telling the story of the two-day *farhud*, the report contained the commission's opinions on two interesting issues, namely the causes of the disturbances and the men who were to be held responsible for them. With regard to the former question, the commission listed six causes: Nazi propaganda disseminated by the German Legation; the Grand Mufti of Jerusalem, Amin al-Husseini, who in the name of Arabism and Islam conducted 'Nazi propaganda' and incited 'against the Jews and the British'; Palestinian and Syrian schoolteachers, who 'poisoned the minds of their students' with anti-government Nazi propaganda; Arabic broadcasts from Germany, which 'greatly helped Nazi propaganda in Iraq'; Iraqi radio broadcasts, which during the months of April and May spread reports of 'non-existent misdeeds in Palestine containing open and fierce incitement against the Jews. . . .', and the *Futuwwa* and Youth Brigades (*katayib al-shabab*) whose members 'imbibed Nazism from the Palestinians and the Syrians' and who systematically harassed the Jews during the month of May, when they were made responsible for keeping the peace in the capital. As to those whom the commission held responsible for the disturbances, these included the Director-General of the Police, the Mutasarrif (governor) of Baghdad, the police commanders of various Baghdad neighbourhoods, and the Committee for Internal Security, whose members were censured for letting Sab'awi and his associate Siddiq Shanshal leave Iraq, going so far as to hand the former the sum of 100 Iraqi dinars, his monthly salary. The Chairman of the Committee, Arshad al-'Umari, was the only one who somehow escaped the commission's damning remarks.[3]

Naturally, the commission did not so much as mention what must be reckoned the most bizarre and astonishing aspect of the whole affair, namely that the riots took place *after* the pro-Nazi regime of Rashid 'Ali was toppled and in full view, so to speak, of the British, the Regent and the loyalist army and police commanders. One British participant, the intelligence officer of the force which stood at the outskirts of Baghdad at the time, later expressed the opinion that the entry of the force into Baghdad was prevented because such an action would have been 'lowering to the dignity of our ally, the Regent, if he were seen to be supported on arrival by British bayonets'. This tallies with what the British ambassador, Sir Kinahan Cornwallis, is reported to have told the Iraqi armistice delegates: 'Many years ago I fought, together with King Faisal the lamented who was my friend for the freeing of the Arabs, and together we built up the Kingdom of Iraq. And do you think I would willingly see destroyed what I myself have helped to build?'[4]

One more point about the *farhud* of the first and second of June is worth mentioning here. Throughout the disturbances, with a few exceptions, Jewish homes in mixed neighbourhoods were defended and hundreds of Jews were saved by the willingness of their Muslim neighbours to protect them, in some cases at the cost of their own lives and limbs. According to one account, the spiritual head of the Shiite community in Baghdad, Sayyid Abu'l Hasan al-Musawi, helped save many Jewish lives by ordering his followers to refrain from taking part in the looting and the killing and by refusing to issue a *fatwa* (religious edict) calling on Muslims to declare holy war (*jihad*) against the Jews.[5]

CHAPTER 28

Youth in Revolt

Towards the end of the 1920s open Zionist activity in Iraq came to an end. The disturbances of 1929 in Palestine led to a wave of protest in Baghdad which in a way forced the government to take cognizance of the work then conducted by the Zionist Association and its leader Aharon Sassoon and bring it to an end. Popular anti-Zionist sentiment surged, with both the pro-government At-Taqaddum Party and the opposition Ash-Sha'b Party joining forces in the campaign. On 30 August 1929, a mass gathering was held at the Haidarkhana Mosque which was attended by thousands and in which Sheikh Ja'far Abu'l- Timman (a prominent Shiite leader) and Yasin al-Hashimi (a Sunni) spoke. Funds were raised, partly from Jews, and sent to Jerusalem as a token of support for the cause of the Palestinians. In the following month, representatives of Jewish communities all over the country issued statements in which Zionism was condemned and loyalty to the Kingdom of Iraq pledged. Sassoon himself, who was then headmaster of the Pardes Ha-Yaladim school in Baghdad, was asked to leave the capital within ten days. Pleading that he could not leave the school at a time when his pupils were preparing for the final examinations, and promising not to continue with his Zionist activity, Sassoon was thereupon asked by the British Adviser to the Ministry of Interior to undertake 'to put an end to all Zionist activities in Baghdad', which meant, in reality, no emigration, no collecting of donations for the Jewish National Fund, and no selling of shekels. He was also asked to undertake not to disseminate Zionist propaganda, in or outside the school.

Sassoon's protestations produced no results. Refusing to sign the undertaking, he wrote to the High Commissioner, arguing mainly that his group had a licence from the Colonial Office and that throughout the years the work done by him and his colleagues had gone smoothly without annoying anyone. This, too, was to no avail, and after the authorities 'remembered' that Pardes Ha-Yaladim had no government licence and threatened to close the school down unless he resigned as principal, Sassoon finally signed an undertaking not to 'spread Zionist ideas' in the school. It is thus possible to say that as of the end of 1929 open Zionist work in Iraq ceased and a kind of semi-clandestine activity was carried out – and this only until 1935, when 'the Teacher' emigrated to Palestine. It is to be noted here, however, that even when the Zionist Association was officially allowed to work, it conducted its activities under the name of 'the Jewish Literary Society', the name Zionist Association being used only in correspondence with Zionist bodies abroad. (In 1924, the group adopted the name 'the Zionist Federation of Mesopotamia', and in the same year Sassoon wrote to London announcing that his federation had branches or representatives in Basra, Khanaqin, 'Amara and Arbil; he also reported that the Federation had 1,000 members.)[1]

Despite official disapproval and escalating popular feeling, however, Zionist activity of some kind or other never stopped, and the 1930s witnessed the establishment of several groups and societies which, though not openly, continued the work under various disguises. The most interesting of these was a group which called itself 'Ahi'eber', which was formed under the guidance of a teacher–emissary from Palestine and did clandestine work in the fields of emigration, Hebrew instruction, meetings and lectures, and fund-raising for the JNF. Consisting almost wholly of young students from the schools of Shammash, the *Alliance* and Rahel Shahmoon (At-Ta'awun), some of its members planned a Zionist march in the streets of Baghdad in the summer of 1934, and when voted down they formed a splinter group with the name 'Shemesh', which proved more active but far less cautious, and in the end both Shemesh and Ahi'eber were discovered and dispersed by the security authorities. Other Jewish groups which engaged in Zionist activity in the 1930s were the Young Men's Hebrew Association, the Society for Distribution of Products from Eretz Yisrael, Hebrew Book Distributors, the Hebrew Youth Association, the Maccabee Sports Organization, and others.

By the early 1940s, however, what with increasing unrest in Palestine and repercussions in Iraq, the activities of most of these groups came to a standstill. The events of May and June 1941 thus found the Jews of Iraq totally unprepared, and after experiencing the *farhud* and its scenes of pillage and murder growing voices began to be heard about the need for the community to be better prepared for such eventualities. This need was deemed to increase in urgency in view of developments on the North African front, where the fall of Tobruk to the Germans was greeted with open jubilation in certain nationalist circles in

Baghdad, some of which even openly threatened the Jews with a bigger and more thorough assault than the *farhud*. At this point encouragement started coming from Zionist organizations in Palestine, and it naturally fell on rather receptive ground. For the fact was that, shortly after the *farhud*, a group of young Jews formed a clandestine self-defence group with the name 'Shabab al-Inqadh' (Salvation Youth), followed by a group calling itself 'Unity and Progress' and another with the name 'Community of Free Jews' ('Edath Hofshim'). The Salvation Youth organization, which like the other two was initiated and manned almost wholly by high school students, was the most active and determined; in a leaflet it distributed among the community it called on the youth to rise and defend their honour. The group also argued that the 100,000 Jews of Baghdad could defend themselves effectively provided they possessed the necessary weapons.

It was at this juncture that a number of emissaries from Palestine made their appearance in Baghdad and some other Jewish centres in Iraq. A more propitious moment could not have been envisaged. Not only were the Jews of Iraq, especially of the younger generation, still reeling under the shock of the *farhud* and willing to contemplate practical measures to safeguard their future or even emigrate from the country; the war, and the involvement of the Jews of Palestine in the war effort, offered a rare opportunity for these emissaries to cross the border to Iraq and back freely, either as volunteers in the British army or as its employees. Enzo Sereni, for instance, arrived in Baghdad as a representative of the large construction company Solel Boneh; he began organizing the Zionist underground in Baghdad in 1942. Two others came as truck drivers in the employ of the British (Ezra Kadoori of Kibbutz Ma'oz Hayyim and Shmaryahu Guttmann of Kibbutz Na'an). Earlier in the year, in March 1942, Shaul Avigur arrived as emissary of the Haganah; his mission was decided upon after the Zionist Organization saw the leaflets being distributed by the members of the Salvation Youth organization. Through some mutual acquaintances, Avigur met the group's leader Salim Khalifa, a lad of eighteen just out of high school. Deciding that Salvation Youth was not exactly his idea of a Zionist underground group, Avigur promised to send trained emissaries from Palestine to organize such a group. In April, first Kadoori and Guttmann and then Sereni duly arrived and immediately established contact with Khalifa and his comrades.

The three emissaries soon got to work, each taking upon himself one of the three branches of the new underground. Sereni became responsible for the Halutz movement, which took care of Zionist indoctrination and Hebrew instruction; Kadoori undertook to organize the apparatus of self-defence, known as *Ha-Shurah*, which took care of military training and defence unit formation, as well as acquisition of weapons; and Guttmann took charge of illegal immigration to Palestine (*Aliyah Bet*). Sometimes this division of labour between the three emissaries was not always observed, and some of them often involved themselves in work that was supposed to be done by another, resulting in a number of mishaps, the most serious of which was the apprehension and arrest of five 'illegals' on their way to Palestine. It so happened that the flight of these five Jews was organized by Ezra Kadoori, who was formally in charge of military training and defence organization. This mishap resulted in the suspension of the work of all three emissaries and in a good deal of recrimination, and one version of the reason as to why the suspension was decided upon was that the Jewish youth of Iraq were not 'ripe' for military training and emigration and that the movement ought, therefore, to concentrate on Hebrew instruction and Zionist education. According to Cohen, however, the real reason was the controversy and the mutual recriminations which followed the capture of the five illegal immigrants and which involved various Zionist groups in Palestine itself, rather than the quality of the youth they had undertaken to educate and train.[2]

Be that as it may, following a brief spell of uncertainty and virtual stoppage the Halutz and the Haganah arms of the Zionist movement resumed full activity early in 1943. The former, indeed, held its first convention in April of the same year; some 100 attended the clandestine gathering, which was held in the basement of the home of the Sehayiq family, in the presence of the three Palestinian emissaries. Apart from the many precautionary measures taken to protect the participants, who must have included the majority of all active members of the organization, secrecy was kept with the help of a simple device: the date chosen coincided with Passover and the gathering was disguised as a Passover celebration. In December, a second convention was held, again at the home of an active member. This appears to have been a more business-like proposition: the deliberations lasted nine hours and, for the first time, delegates from sister organizations in Basra and Mosul took part; fifty instructors and activists attended, including a fifteen-year-old girl from Basra. According to the testimony of some of the participants, it was in this convention that the basic aims and guidelines of the movement were formulated. They included:

- Spreading knowledge of Hebrew and Jewish literature
- Jewish resurgence and Jewish defence both in Palestine and in the Diaspora
- Working for the Jewish National Fund
- Immigration to Palestine under all conditions and by all the means available
- A life of labour, self-defence and active settlement in Palestine
- Liberation of the Jewish woman from the fetters of social bondage in all spheres of life
- Personal self-fulfilment

It is estimated that in 1942 membership of the movement in the three major cities of Baghdad, Basra and Mosul totalled some 300; in 1944, 550, of whom 400 were in Baghdad; in 1946, 1,000; and in 1948 the total increased to 2,000. In 1948 the movement also boasted 120 instructors and sixteen branches, half of which were in Baghdad. Many others had already found their way to Palestine after being duly trained and instructed.

It would be wrong, however, to conclude from these figures either that the Zionist movement was widespread among the Jews of Iraq as a whole or that for Jewish youth in Baghdad and the other main cities – even the most politically active and conscious among them – Zionism and Zionist activity constituted the only or even the main outlet. For one thing, the years which followed the *farhud*, and especially those up to the end of World War II, witnessed an unprecedented growth in the economy and in all branches of business. Trade flourished, prices increased by the day, with profit margins increasing accordingly, and there was much activity in the financial sphere. In all these branches of business the Jews occupied a predominant position, and the prosperity which the war years brought with them served to divert attention from recent experiences and dim considerations of possible dangers to come. And so the Jews, at least those of the older generation, virtually forgot the trauma of 1941 and became fully preoccupied with their daily pursuits.

Not so members of the young generation. These, or rather the minority amongst them that took an interest in public affairs and felt committed to some sort of involvement, were in a very valid sense 'youth in revolt'. Their revolt, however, took two broad directions. Firstly, there were those who concluded that whatever they did or refrained from doing the Jews of Iraq would have no future there and were ultimately destined to join in the work of national resurgence in

Palestine; it was these who decided to join the ranks of the Zionists and enrolled in one or other of the activities of 'the Movement'. As is plain from the last two items in the list of aims and guidelines quoted above, the driving force behind these young men and women was not solely or even mainly 'national' but also social and personal. The liberation of the Jewish woman and 'personal self-fulfilment' were, perhaps, as strong a motive for youth as was national resurgence and the settlement of Palestine by Jews. As a matter of fact, precisely by engaging in clandestine collective activities of the kind the movement was conducting – Hebrew classes, military training and illegal emigration – they were already attaining some measure of women's liberation and self-fulfilment at least for themselves, since in all of these activities young women were as prominent as young men. (The second Halutz convention referred to above was chaired jointly by a man and a woman.)

The other leading outlet which committed Jewish youth found open to them in those years was communism, which during the last years of the war and the few which followed it increased in strength very considerably and was being propagated almost in the open. The Jews who were attracted by this movement naturally threw in their lot with that of the people of Iraq as a whole and were, in fact, anti-Zionist throughout. They were a considerable force in the communist movement and attained positions of leadership in it, and when the Party's General Secretary was arrested and executed, a Jew was chosen to take the helm, and he suffered a similar fate. They also set up a new organization called the League for the Fight against Zionism ('Usbat Mukafahat al-Sahyoniyya), which was eventually disbanded and its leaders imprisoned on the absurd ground that its name meant 'the league for the fight *for* Zionism' rather than *against* it – an interpretation which was lent credibility owing to a certain casuistic grammatical ambiguity. An idea of the size and seriousness of Jewish involvement in the communist movement in Iraq can be had from a report read during a meeting of the secretariat of the Baghdad branch of the Halutz movement in March 1947 in which it was asserted that the number of the movement's members had decreased by about 100 'owing to communism'. Like their friends from the same age-groups who chose to join the Zionist movement, these young Iraqi Jews were also motivated as much by social and individual factors as by public concerns. Curiously enough, the fact that, in the end, the nationalists among these Jews emerged triumphant while their internationalist co-religionists were defeated was part of a not uncommon pattern, as witness what happened in Russia with the Bolsheviks and in Poland in the case of the Bundists.

Though it is neither easy nor completely accurate to draw dividing lines between the activities of the three main arms of the Zionist movement in Iraq in the 1940s, it would still be useful to sum up the attainments of each separately up to the establishment of the State of Israel. We have little exact information, and even fewer figures, about the extent of the work done by or the attainments made by the Halutz movement in the field of Hebrew instruction and its declared aim of spreading knowledge of Jewish culture and literature. Hebrew classes were held, to be sure, in various ramshackle forms and places; modern Hebrew names were adopted by activists as underground nicknames; attempts were made to introduce Hebrew instruction in Jewish schools under various covers and disguises; Hebrew songs were sung among members and the *Hora* was danced secretly. However, since the declared aim of these activities was ultimately emigration to Palestine, and since many of the young men and women involved did take that step, we do not now know what all these activities achieved beside raising their morale and preparing them for life in the Holy Land.

Ha-Shurah, the defence arm of the movement (also known as the Haganah), was founded and led by Ezra Kadoori, an Iraqi-born Jew who had emigrated to Palestine when he was twelve years old, had lived in Kibbutz Ma'oz Hayyim and joined the Palmach (the military arm of the Haganah). Shortly after his arrival in Baghdad in 1942, Kadoori recruited about twenty young men and women whom he started training in various ways of self-defence – the use of small weapons, knives, machine-guns, clubs, hand-grenades, and Molotov cocktails. The trainees also underwent physical training and were instructed in such skills as hand-to-hand combat and Judo. For the purposes of the movement, Baghdad was divided into zones – two at first, then three – and each was divided into sectors. Similar plans were drawn up for Basra and Kirkuk, and arms were secretly acquired either locally or by being smuggled in from Palestine or through Palestinian connections. It is estimated that in the first year of its operation the organization had accumulated between 700 and 1,000 guns, hidden mostly in underground caches in members' homes. Later, when tensions increased and a sizeable number of its membership had to depart to the newly established Jewish state, synagogues were also used for hiding weapons. However, apart from one or two occasions in which members of the Shurah were put on the alert after information was received about impending attacks on Jewish quarters, and which in the end proved false, the Shurah did not have any real chance of proving its mettle.

In the sphere of immigration the movement's activities would have been far more fruitful had it not been for the fact that those in Palestine itself who were in charge of illegal immigration fixed so low a quota on immigration from Iraq – five a month. In the years 1942–8 illegal immigration was conducted through four main devices: via Amman or via Damascus–Beirut after crossing the western border; forged passports or official passports obtained through bribes; British army facilities and Egged buses returning to Palestine; and in two dramatic escapes, an American aeroplane was used to smuggle in about 100 activists who were being sought by the security authorities. In a sense, indeed, it was in the field of illegal immigration that the Zionist movement in Iraq was most successful and showed the most impressive results in the eight years which preceded the establishment of the State of Israel. This work intensified greatly during the two years which preceded the publication of the 1950 law allowing the Jews to leave the country provided they surrendered their Iraqi citizenship.

CHAPTER 29

The Politics of Extortion

Four years of relative quiet and considerable material prosperity followed the events of May–June 1941. The change for the better was so pronounced that for the majority of the Jews of Iraq trouble seemed to have been over and life returned to its usual daily rhythm. Little did they know, however, what lay in store for them; for it took no more than five years for their ancient community to be virtually liquidated, themselves dispossessed and reduced to the status of destitute refugees.

Trouble started a few short months after the end of World War II. On 2 November 1945 a series of anti-Jewish riots were organized in Cairo by a small group of Fascist-type nationalists called Misr al-Fatat (Young Egypt). A synagogue was attacked and set on fire, a hospital and an old-people's home were destroyed, and a number of shops wrecked. The riots came in the wake of warnings issued by the group asking the Jews of Egypt to dissociate themselves from Zionism. Three days later, on 5 November, a group of Iraqi Arab nationalists called for a mass demonstration in the streets of Baghdad, and it was only owing to the ban imposed on the gathering by the Iraqi Minister of the Interior that anti-Jewish riots and incitement were prevented. However, even though the regime itself would not countenance any serious disorders – realizing full well that these would quickly be turned against it – the official attitude to the Jews began to undergo clear if incipient changes. Having already had an idea of the extent of Zionist activity in the three major cities, and realizing perhaps that this was something quite different from what they had encountered two or three decades earlier through the activities of 'the Teacher' and the Jewish Literary Society, the authorities started taking practical measures aimed at reducing the position of prominence which the Jews seemed to occupy. Another factor conducive to this policy was the fact that the League of Arab Nations had just recently been established, and the Palestine question became virtually the only cause on which the Arab world was ostensibly united. The involvement of a number of Jews in communist activities, too, made it easy for the government to persecute communists as alleged Zionists and vice versa.

The measures taken in this direction included strict censorship on all contacts by Jews with Palestine. Letters to relatives and friends were seized and filed, later to be used against their senders regardless of what was actually written in them; and in this connection it is claimed that nine sacks of such mail were handed over by the British to the Iraqi authorities, to be put to good use later on as a means for victimizing Jews. Following years in which the war effort and the various restrictions imposed as a result of the war necessitated the employment of many Jews in government departments, Jews were now no longer employed in such jobs, and in certain cases many were either dismissed or forced to resign the jobs they already held. An American report reaching Washington from Baghdad in 1945 spoke of a deliberate policy aimed at reducing the number of Jewish civil servants. Jewish merchants, especially those in the export-import business, were not issued the necessary papers, and many were impelled to go into partnership with Muslim businessmen in order to stay in business. The number of Jews admitted to state schools and institutions of higher education was reduced drastically. Hebrew instruction in Jewish schools was limited to religious study and prayers, and these were reduced to a bare minimum. Ministry of Education inspectors objected to the teaching of the Bible even when not accompanied by an Arabic translation or explanation, and all Jewish teachers who had come from Palestine were dismissed. The number of Muslim teachers in Jewish schools was increased, and an attempt was made to include geography and civics among the subjects which were to be taught only by non-Jewish teachers delegated by the Ministry, in addition to history and Arabic language and literature. The number of Jews admitted to institutions of higher learning was reduced: in the school year 1944–5 the Royal Medical College admitted seven Jewish students out of a total of sixty, while the Law College admitted nine Jews out of a new class of 300.

Several factors led to a further deterioration in the situation of the Jews. For one thing, Iraq was passing through one of its most serious economic crises since independence. For another, the recently formed Arab League was anxious to show some signs of life and there was no better or safer subject to inspire some sort of unity of purpose among its member states than that of Palestine. Thirdly, the Anglo–American Committee of Enquiry which had been set up to investigate conditions in Palestine was about to submit its findings and conclusions. Last but perhaps not least, popular opinion in Iraq itself, especially among the students, men of the liberal professions and junior army officers, was heading in two directions neither of which appeared to be conducive to moderation; and both were fiercely opposed to the pro-British policies of the government and of Crown Prince Abdul Ilah. On the one hand, there were the Arab nationalists of the Istiqlal Party, around which gathered all former supporters of Rashid 'Ali and the Axis powers during the war; the rising merchant class agitating for an adequate share in the largely Jewish-dominated import and wholesale trades; and certain army officers and men still reeling under the defeat of May 1941. On the other hand, there were the communists, now greatly strengthened by the few years of almost open activity made possible by the war and the common cause which had united Moscow and the Western Allies against Nazi Germany; the populist and social democratic forces which, though equally anti-British, did not share the Istiqlal Party's right-wing inclinations; and politically active, non-Zionist or anti-Zionist Jews who were affiliated to these latter two groups of the Left.

Faced with this state of affairs at home, the growing tensions in Palestine and the general Arab outcry to rally forces and close ranks against 'the Zionist enemy', successive post-war governments in Baghdad chose the easy way out, by trying to divert opposition to themselves by venting their anger and that of the populace on the Jews. Thinly-veiled threats were now being directed against the Jews, some of which came directly from the government. Ministers and semi-official organs spoke darkly of the seriousness of the situation of these Jews, blaming it all on the activities of their co-religionists in Palestine. Testifying in Cairo in March 1946 before the Anglo–American Committee of Enquiry Dr Muhammed Fadhil al-Jamali, then Director-General of the Iraqi Ministry of Foreign Affairs, first asserted that the Jews had been living in Iraq 'for thousands of years' as 'our brethren . . . in perfect peace and harmony, [enjoying] full political rights and all the rights that permit them to practice their religion and communal life as a community'; he then declared with regret that political Zionism had come 'to poison the atmosphere' and that Iraqi Jews felt 'embarrassed at what the Zionists stand for and at the bitter relationship that exists between us and the Zionist Jews'; and finally he issued the following ominous, but disguised, threat: 'It is a great burden on the Iraqi government to maintain that peace and harmony which we have enjoyed over a long period in our history.' It was no wonder, therefore, that when the Committee came to Baghdad the Jewish witnesses who testified publicly declared that all was well. To quote the words of one of its members: 'Their [the Jews'] lot was not hard, the handicaps to which they were subjected were not serious, there was no danger of another pogrom, and their economic status was generally similar to that of the Arabs.'

Tension increased as the Committee was completing its investigations and preparing its report. The day on which this report was to be submitted, demonstrations were planned by groups of students, and threats again were being heard of renewed anti-Jewish riots. A few weeks earlier, the leader of the Shiite Muslims – a group which generally had taken little if any interest in pan-Arab concerns – joined the campaign against the Jews by issuing a *fatwa* (religious edict) forbidding the sale of land to Jews in all Arab countries. In June of the same year, a meeting of the Arab League Council adopted a resolution in which Arab governments were urged to take measures against Zionism and to curtail Jewish activities in their respective countries. The Iraqi government was among the first to comply. In addition to the measures already mentioned, new ones were taken; for example, the government decided that as of the beginning of 1947 Jews were to be allowed to leave the country only if they gave a guarantee in the form of a cash deposit of 1,500 Iraqi dinars (£1,500) regardless of the purpose of their travel. In those days few people could mobilize such a sum of money, and the result was that even students and sick people seeking treatment abroad were prevented from leaving the country. In the same year Dr al-Jamali, now Foreign Minister, told the United Nations Committee on Palestine that 'the fate of the Jews in Muslim countries depends on developments in Palestine', while Nuri as-Sa'id about the same time bluntly and rather uncharacteristically declared that these Jews were 'hostages'. More ominous and more explicit threats are difficult to imagine. Nor did it take long for these threats to be put into practice.

Another cause of tension, which on the face of it had nothing whatever to do with the Jews or with Palestine but which, nevertheless, served to worsen the situation as far as the Jewish community was concerned, was the new treaty of alliance and co-operation which the government of Salih Jabr negotiated with the British government towards the end of 1947. This agreement, known as the Portsmouth Treaty, was concluded in order to regulate relations between London and Baghdad following the expiry of the 1922 treaty. Even as Jabr and the Iraqi delegation were negotiating the new agreement, mass demonstrations were staged in the streets of Baghdad against it, the nationalists and the Left this time finding a cause common to them both. The demonstrations gradually took on such a serious turn that the government was forced to resign following incidents in which several demonstrators were killed by the police. Jews of various political persuasions and from all walks of life – students, men of the liberal professions, communists, the Left, and Jews whose position required them to show sympathy with the populace – participated in some of these demonstrations and strikes. However, although the movement (which came to be known as *al-wathba* – 'the leap' – in Iraqi political parlance) ostensibly emerged triumphant, Jewish participation and sympathy angered the pro-British establishment, and the anti-Jewish stance was strengthened, while many of the Jewish participants were eventually brought to court later when circumstances made this possible.

These developments coincided with the aftermath of the adoption by the United Nations General Assembly on 29 November 1947 of the resolution calling for the partitioning of Palestine into separate Jewish and Arab states. Inevitably, therefore, the authorities sought to divert attention from the economic difficulties at home and the imminent renewed alliance with London to the new developments in Palestine. Even before Iraqi troops joined the war against the newly established Jewish state, agitation was rampant in Baghdad following the fighting which erupted in Palestine itself between Jews and Arabs soon after the publication of the partition resolution. A group of Iraqi 'volunteers' was sent, with official encouragement and full financial help, to join the Arab forces fighting under Qawuqji; and a campaign was launched to raise funds from the Jews themselves for what was called 'the rescue of Palestine'. Again, Chief Rabbi Sassoon Kadoori was impelled to issue a statement rejecting Zionism and expressing support for Arab rights in Palestine.

Following an interlude of a few weeks in which the Iraqi government and public became fully preoccupied with the crisis resulting from the Portsmouth Treaty, and which ended on 21 January with the resignation of Salih Jabr's government, attention was again directed to Palestine. The death of Abdul Qadir al-Husaini, the most prominent commander of the Arab fighters in Palestine, in a battle which took place near Jerusalem, led to a mass demonstration in which the main slogan was 'Death to the Jews!'. Pressure was brought to bear on the government to despatch troops to help in the fight against the Zionists; the distinction between 'Zionist' and 'Jew' grew more unclear every day; and on 27 April a Baghdad synagogue was attacked and desecrated by a group of angry demonstrators. At about this time, a group of Jewish communists decided to set up a new anti-Zionist League. The League, which was plainly a front organization of the outlawed Communist Party, staged demonstrations along with the Arab nationalist groups of the Right and did not confine its activities to anti-Zionist pursuits; it was eventually itself outlawed and many of its Jewish leaders were sentenced to long terms in prison.

The number of irregular Iraqi fighters who were 'encouraged' to infiltrate into Palestine to reinforce local resistance was never made known. Some estimates speak of a few hundred, others of as many as two battalions. The men included some army veterans and were recruited by a body calling itself the Palestine Defence League; their performance at the front was rather poor and their fighting capacity negligible. But in this they were no worse than similar units of irregulars recruited in other Arab League states and sent to Palestine with the same aim. Realizing that neither local Arab resistance nor these poor reinforcements could be a match for the forces the Jews in Palestine already had, the League decided, before the Mandate was officially ended, that Arab regular armies should intervene. In April, Abdul Ilah visited Amman and Cairo, accompanied by his Ministers of Defence, Finance and Foreign Affairs. Strikes, hunger strikes and demonstrations by students and other nationalist forces were organized in Baghdad to urge sending the army to Palestine; the Haifa pipeline was closed and no oil was pumped from Iraq's oilfields; official welcome was extended to exiles from Palestine; and the government, now headed by Muhammed al-Sadr, found itself impelled to follow the League's decision and prepare for large-scale military intervention in Palestine. Not only was there no adequate co-ordination of any kind between the various Arab armies which were to invade Palestine as soon as the Mandate ended, but the armies themselves were pitiably unprepared for the task. In the words of one observer, 'Iraqi forces under General Salih Sa'ib – forces ill prepared, ill equipped, and with clearly inadequate supplies and reserves – moved from their home stations some ten to twelve thousand strong in mechanized or lorry-borne units, and took up positions on the western fringes of the Jordan Kingdom. . . .'[1]

And so it was that on 15 May 1948, immediately after the State of Israel had been proclaimed, the Iraqi troops crossed into their allotted sector in Palestine. It was the first time the Iraqis had used their troops abroad. Martial law was imposed throughout Iraq. Military courts were established; civilian officials in almost all areas of life were subordinated to the military; censorship was made more strict; and a concentration camp was set up in the southern desert to accommodate a growing number of detainees, mostly communists and Jewish activists of the Left. The ensuing disruption of daily life and normal activities is eloquently described by the same observer:

> The emergency regime prohibited the carrying of firearms and the use of cipher codes, and by the suppression of many existing laws it involved a close restriction of civil rights. The clash between civil and military authorities increased as weeks went by with irritation, jealousy, and charges and counter-charges or indiscriminate severity or weak indulgence.... The press, swollen to an extraordinary number of daily sheets of trifling circulation but irresponsible violence, lost in a day the worst of its venom [except such as could be safely directed against the British or the Jews], and the few papers which refused compliance were suppressed....[2]

In such a state of affairs, and with enthusiasm rising with every false report from the front, the Jews were naturally the first to suffer. All kinds of anti-Jewish measures, open and disguised, were taken by a state apparatus now being run freely by the military. Sentences passed by courts martial could not be appealed against, and accordingly there was no need or obligation for the government to introduce special laws for which it could eventually be asked to offer an explanation or justification. When opposition elements expressed their dismay and misgivings about the new measures, fearing that emergency powers might be misused by the government, Prime Minister Muzahim al-Pachachi did not hesitate to assure them that the measures were to be applied only against the Jews. The one case in which the government sought a legal basis for its actions was an amendment to an article of the Criminal Code, which added 'Zionism' to the list of doctrines whose propagation was prohibited. Needless to say, it was an unnecessary and empty gesture. Not only had Zionists been subjected to punishment but the Jews as a whole had been penalized in a variety of ways even before the Palestine partition plan was adopted.

Anti-Jewish measures took many forms and were applied with gusto. On 15 May the cash deposit which a Jew had to pay before he was allowed to leave the country was increased to £3,000. Many Jewish civil servants were dismissed arbitrarily from their posts, the majority of them without notice or severance pay or pension; the more senior Jewish officials were offered retirement on pension or simply suspended from their duties. One of these was Ibrahim el-Kabir, the Controller-

General of the Ministry of Finance, who was retired on pension only a fortnight after he had been sent to London to negotiate a new financial agreement between Iraq and Britain. The wave of dismissals reached its peak in October when, following news of Israeli victories, the authorities issued a circular instructing all government departments to dismiss their Jewish employees. After this only a few Jews remained in government posts. Earlier, in July, the Minister of Defence issued an order whereby Jewish-owned banks were forbidden to have transactions with foreign banks and institutions.[3]

Another device used by the authorities was to charge Jews with such fanciful crimes as having Zionist leanings, expressing support for Israel or making derogatory remarks about the Iraqi state or army, aiding or abetting Zionist activities, and – most common of all – having or trying to establish contact with the Zionist enemy. For this latter charge, it was sufficient for a Jew to have sent a letter to a relative or friend in Palestine or got one from them – or even for his name to have been mentioned in passing, in any such letter. Considering that sacks of such letters had been kept in store somewhere for just such an eventuality, a great number of people were involved. The procedure was simple enough, and the fact that the work was left to the police and to military courts made it easy for petty officials and fanatics to victimize the Jews with a vengeance. First, the victim's house was searched for any evidence of such contacts with the Zionist enemy; then, whether or not such 'evidence' had been found, the accused was arrested and brought to court and summarily sentenced, almost invariably to a year or two in jail with the option of a fine of between £1,000 and £2,000.

Another category of charges was 'subversive activities' – and here, too, fat files had already been filled with names and addresses, as if in preparation for them to be opened at the first opportunity. These files usually included the names of participants in anti-government demonstrations staged some months previously in the course of 'the Leap' who were unlucky enough to be caught and their particulars noted down by the police before they were released. These included mere passers-by and onlookers who happened to be caught up with the demonstrators and were unable to escape in time. The same court procedure was applied to these, namely summary conviction and a verdict of guilty, and a sentence giving the victim the chance to choose between imprisonment and a heavy fine – and in a few cases imposing both. Again, in such cases the first step was to conduct a careful house search whose results made absolutely no difference to the inevitable sentence – unless it served to incriminate some other inhabitant of the same house.

The searches, of course, also provided an excellent opportunity for the police to indulge in acts of extortion and bribery. Such petty acts, however, were as nothing compared with the large-scale official campaign of what can best be termed judicial extortion, whereby millions of pounds were collected from Jews to cover the high cost of the country's military adventure in Palestine. In this connection it is interesting to note that the fines which the courts imposed on Jews were invariably payable to the Ministry of Defence.

The most blatant example of the kind of 'justice' meted out by the military courts to the Jews at that time was the trial and execution of Shafiq 'Adas, a very wealthy Syrian-born businessman based in Basra. 'Adas was charged with a rather serious crime though his guilt was never clearly established. Back in 1946, 'Adas sold surplus British military equipment to Italy, and these same items were now alleged to have been discovered in Palestine in the hands of 'the Zionist enemy'. The court, however, was never able to establish a connection between the accused and the alleged transfer of the material to Palestine. Nor did the authorities see fit to refer to the fact that 'Adas, in these transactions as well as in other business dealings, had Muslim partners of influence and standing. The proceedings were declared secret whenever this was deemed convenient for the prosecution, and in one bizarre incident the defence counsel was refused admission to the courtroom. Among several other absurdities, 'Adas was accused both of communism and Zionism. About the same time, in July, forty leading Jewish businessmen were arrested on a charge of trading with the Soviet Union, when in reality these transactions had been made a few years before and were the direct result of a Soviet–Iraqi trade agreement. In any case, Muslim businessmen who had made similar deals with Moscow were left unmolested. To be sure, all the forty were released, but not before they were made to pay various sums of up to £10,000 each.[4]

Shafiq 'Adas was hanged publicly on 27 September. The event was accompanied by a great deal of publicity and popular jubilation. Shortly afterwards, however, the Minister of Defence, Sadiq al-Bassam, resigned, some say against his will; the number of military courts was reduced to one instead of the four which had functioned since martial law was declared; and fewer Jews were brought before the court. The government, however, went right on in its harassment of the Jewish population, in some instances proving itself to be quite inventive. As, for example, in October, when the Ministry of Finance issued an order decreeing that all Iraqi Jews living abroad would forfeit their property should they not return to Iraq by a specified date. The Ministry of Health also stopped issuing licences to newly graduated Jewish doctors and refused to renew old ones. And at the beginning of the school year 1948–9, headmasters of state schools regretfully told their Jewish pupils that they were not in a position to guarantee their safety in the face of increasing hostility to the Jews among their Muslim colleagues. It has been estimated that by the end of October a total of £20,000,000 had been collected from the Jews in fines and by a rich variety of means and excuses – including the £5,000,000-worth estate left by Shafiq 'Adas to the Ministry of Defence.

By the end of the year, however, the anti-Jewish campaign appeared to have passed its peak. During the second half of the year, many of the discredited politicians – Salih Jabr, Nuri as-Sa'id, Shakir el-Wadi and other supporters of the Portsmouth Treaty – made a comeback, while some of the ultra-nationalists were gradually eased out from key positions. Muzahim al-Pachachi's cabinet remained in office, however, thanks largely to the support extended to him by the now much strengthened makers of the Portsmouth Treaty. But he failed to appease the army, which opposed his pro-Cairo leanings, and he resigned on 6 January 1949. Nuri as-Sa'id, who succeeded him, appeared to be something of a reassurance for a partial return to normalcy. In the event, however, more and rather harder trials lay in wait for the Jews of Iraq in the few years to come.

CHAPTER 30

The Exodus

In September 1948, shortly after the resignation of Sadiq al-Bassam as Minister of Defence, Ezra Menahem Daniel delivered a moving and fairly damning speech to a somewhat stunned Iraqi Senate. Daniel, who was the only Jewish member of the House and a universally respected man of seventy-four, reminded his fellow senators of the history and the age-old attachment of the Jews of Iraq to their homeland, surveyed the Jews' contribution to the build-up and the welfare of modern Iraq, and enumerated the many acts of discrimination, harassment and extortion to which his co-religionists had been subjected in recent years. In conclusion he appealed to the government for justice and asked that the Jews be treated as the Constitution of the State had stipulated, namely as equal citizens of the country. It is said, too, that Daniel warned his audience that he would not hesitate to make public the facts known to him and also to publish the text of his address abroad unless an end was put to the prevailing anti-Jewish campaign.

We do not possess the text of Daniel's speech, since the local press either did not want to print it or was prevented from doing so. It is known, however, that the speech had a favourable effect and was received with understanding. Assurances were given by the government that the rights of the Jews as fully fledged citizens would henceforth be observed and respected. A sort of lull followed, and Jews began to reopen their businesses and go about their daily pursuits as before.

For the Kingdom of Iraq, 1949 proved to be a time of difficulties at home and of disillusionment abroad. The Sa'idi government, formed early in January, was barely able to survive the year, plagued as it was by financial problems, inter-ministerial differences, and the embarrassment of the defeat which the armies of Iraq and five other Arab states suffered in Palestine. Shrewd and experienced statesman that he was, Nuri as-Sa'id realized early in the proceedings that there was a need now to save for the Arabs of Palestine as much as possible from the ruin brought on them by their leaders and by an ill-prepared and disorganized Arab League. He was now willing to accept partition as proposed in the 1947 resolution by the United Nations. He pleaded with his Arab counterparts, sending one of his close friends on a tour of Arab capitals to secure a unified Arab stand. Instead, not heeding Iraqi advice, Israel's Arab neighbours hastened to sign separate armistice agreements with the new state. By March, preparations were afoot for the withdrawal of Iraqi forces from Palestine – an operation which finally started in April and was completed in July. At the same time, the influx of Palestinian refugees into Iraq increased, and it is quite feasible that these two events were partly to blame for the renewed deterioration of the situation of the Jews.

It was also partly bad luck. Late in the summer of 1949 a young Jew was arrested on a charge of clandestine communist activities. It transpired, however, that this young man had been a member of the Halutz movement until 1946, when he decided that communism was a better way to salvation. In an effort to save his skin, he informed on his former comrades in the Zionist underground, furnishing the names and addresses of four of them. A wave of arrests followed, and what with torture and other inducements many members of the Halutz and the Haganah organizations were rounded up, their homes searched and themselves thrown into prison when found. Of the leadership, however, which numbered fourteen instructors and organizers, only one was apprehended, the other thirteen being hastily smuggled to Iran. But terror and harassment did not stop at the alleged culprits; as usual in these cases many innocent people found themselves implicated, and the community as a whole became frightened again. This time, however, the Zionist underground decided to set to work, accusing the Chief Rabbi and head of the community of cowardice and inaction in face of widespread victimization of the Jews. Influenced, or perhaps largely organized, by the underground, a group of Jewish mothers staged a demonstration against Chief Rabbi Kadoori, calling on him to act for the release of their sons. Other means of pressure were used. A day of prayer was observed on 22 October, on which all Jewish schools and stores were closed and Jewish employees did not report to their jobs; for a short period of time, Kosher butchers were boycotted; and leaflets were distributed calling on Sassoon Kadoori to resign. Seeing that the situation was getting out of hand and that he was not in a position to act without appearing to betray his opponents to the security authorities, the Chief Rabbi duly resigned and was replaced by a man acceptable to the Zionist underground – Heskel Shemtob, a member of the

Community Council. This was in November. In December, martial law was lifted throughout Iraq.

By unseating the head of the community, who was basically opposed to Zionism, and after the lifting of martial law, the Zionist underground gained a great deal of leeway. Its leaders and sympathizers found in Shemtob a fairly willing tool and practically took over the affairs of the community. They were, of course, helped greatly by the general mood among the Jews, who after two years of uncertainty and insecurity became rather receptive to the idea of emigration to Israel; in this sense, neither Kadoori nor Shemtob was able to behave in any other way than the one they chose to follow. It is possible, too, that the authorities were also willing to contemplate a course rather similar to the one advocated by the Zionists. Not only did they have several thousands of Palestinian refugees on their hands who could easily be accommodated and given employment should Jews in considerable numbers depart, but there was also the problem, which antedated the Palestine crisis and which had no doubt been a factor in popular anti-Jewish sentiment, of growing generations of Muslim professionals and businessmen clamouring for a niche in their respective fields and being under the impression that the Jews were barring the way before them.

Although illegal emigration from Iraq to Palestine never really stopped, the war there and martial law at home acted as deterrents, and the flow was slowed down considerably. The signing of armistice agreements on the one hand and the lifting of martial law on the other were thus a signal, and the Zionist underground got to work in earnest. Various escape routes to Iran, old and new, were used to capacity, mainly via Basra and Shat al-'Arab in the south and through the mountainous borders in the north. Arab and Kurdish 'guides' were mobilized and paid handsomely; border policemen and other security people were bribed and conveniently looked the other way; government officials in Baghdad were also easily bought when arrangements had to be made involving either them or their associates and friends; and young Jewish men and women had literally to wait in lines for their turn to go to the promised land. Things came to such a pass, indeed, that this mass evacuation operation could no longer be kept secret, since many families, too, chose to follow their children and started selling their household effects and property when everyone could see what their final destination was. Confronted with such determination, and seeing that neither the army nor the police were capable of stopping the flow, the government, its hands forced, decided to legalize emigration. On 2 March 1950 Salih Jabr, then Minister of the Interior, introduced to parliament a draft law permitting Jews to leave the country provided they surrender their Iraqi nationality. Elaborating, Jabr informed the Deputies that, 'ever since martial law had been abolished on 17 December 1949, illegal emigration has been increasing . . . and it is not in the public interest to force people to stay in the country if they have no desire to do so'. Faint voices opposing the draft law on the ground that it was inconsistent with Arab interests were heard in both Houses, but the law was finally adopted as an emergency measure.

Originally, the new move was contemplated as part of a deal involving an exchange of populations, with Iraq receiving Palestinian Arab refugees in roughly the same numbers as the Jews emigrating to Israel. The arrangement failed to come off, however, owing to strong opposition on the part of the Arab League – and ultimately Iraq received a total of less than 10,000 refugees.

The new law empowered the Council of Ministers 'to deprive any Iraqi Jew of Iraqi nationality who of his own free will chooses to leave Iraq for good'. It provided that any Iraqi Jew who left Iraq illegally, or attempted to leave illegally, should be deprived of Iraqi nationality. Finally, it decreed that 'any Iraqi Jew who had already left Iraq illegally shall be regarded as though he had left Iraq for ever unless he shall return within two months . . .'. Should he fail to return, his Iraqi nationality would be dropped after the expiration of that period. The law was to be, in effect, for a period of one year only.

During the first few weeks there was little response to the new law. The Zionist underground counselled patience, suggesting darkly that the law might be a trap, a devious way of enabling the authorities to round up suspected Zionists. The real reason, however, was that no preparation had been made in Israel itself for the expected influx of newcomers. When finally word was given that Jews could start registering for emigration, the number of Jews who actually did so was comparatively small. However, as more people decided to register, a kind of vicious circle was set in motion and many of those who had had no wish to leave the country 'for ever' decided to follow suit, finding it difficult to remain when their children, relatives, friends or business associates were about to leave. By the end of April some 50,000 had registered for departure.

It was in April that the first incident took place which was to hasten the mass exodus. On the eighth of that month, which happened to be the last day of Passover, a bomb was thrown into a crowded café on Abu

Nuwwas promenade. It was 9.30 p.m. and the café, usually frequented by Jews, was more crowded than usual since many of these came there partly to have their first taste of leavened bread after eight days of eating unleavened *matzoth*. Four Jews were seriously injured and, according to a report published in the *Jewish Chronicle* of London on 19 May, the police later announced that three Jews had been arrested in connection with the incident. The following days witnessed a sharp increase in the number of people applying for emigration. Other minor incidents followed, the most serious of which occurred on 14 January 1951, when a bomb exploded at the Mas'uda Shemtob Synagogue, which had been turned into a gathering-place for departing Jews. A seven-year-old boy was killed and twenty Jews were injured, two of them fatally. Between this incident and 10 March some 50,000 Jews registered for emigration, partly no doubt because the day was nearing when the validity of the law permitting them to do so was to expire.

Following this incident, too, the authorities blamed 'Jewish elements' for the act, and a series of searches were conducted. In the course of these, considerable quantities of arms and ammunition were uncovered, and documents, maps and printing machines were found, hidden in caches in two synagogues, those of Mas'uda Shemtob and of Hakham Heskel. A number of Jews were brought to trial and two of them were sentenced to death on the strength of a confession made by one of them. The two were eventually hanged on 19 January 1952. However, none of the evidence adduced, either in the case of these two or in those of others similarly tried and convicted, was conclusive and – in the words of a careful observer – 'It must remain an open question whether Zionists were responsible for some or all of the incidents which stretch over a period from April 1950 to June 1951.' The same observer, however, referring to the allegation made by the Iraqi government that it was Zionist agents who threw the bombs, commented: 'This may be so, for the Zionists were capable of using such tactics', a statement which he backed by citing the cases of the blowing-up of the crowded ship *Patria* at Haifa harbour in 1940 and the notorious 'Lavon Affair'.[1]

In March 1951, on the day of expiry of the law allowing Jews to leave, it was found that all Iraqi Jews with the exception of some five to six thousand, had registered to leave. It was then that the final blow was dealt. The government, led by Nuri as-Sa'id, went into secret session and decided to convoke parliament, again in secret session. Two laws were proposed and passed. The first decreed that the possessions of all Jews who had registered for emigration were to be 'frozen'; the second stipulated that Iraqi Jews who had not given up their Iraqi nationality and who were abroad would lose their nationality should they not return to Iraq within a specified period of time, in which eventuality their possessions would be forfeit to the Iraqi government. It was officially estimated that the total assets in cash to be seized would amount to £7,000,000. This did not include real estate and goods. Overnight nearly 80,000 Jews waiting to be airlifted to Israel were rendered penniless, having from now on to make do with whatever immigrant absorption authorities there would offer.

The massive airlift, which became known as 'Operation Ezra and Nehemiah', was carried out fairly smoothly although the number of emigrants by far exceeded all original estimates. While the immigration authorities in Israel had been planning to receive about 300 immigrants a day – and this with difficulty – the daily influx at its peak reached the enormous number of 1,400. Up to February 1951 Iraq allowed no direct flights from its territory to Israel, and the emigrants had to stop in Cyprus before continuing on their way to Israel. In February, however, the Iraqis relented, and flights were allowed from Baghdad and Basra direct to Lydda Airport. The total number of Iraqi Jews who surrendered their citizenship and were airlifted to Israel was 107,603, while some 16,000 had left the country by other means – some legally to various countries in the West, others illegally to Palestine. At the beginning of 1952, it was estimated that no more than 6,000 Jews remained in Iraq. By the mid-1980s almost no Jews were left in the country, with the exception of a few dozen men and women spending their last remaining years in a country in which they and their ancestors had lived for close on three millennia.

APPENDIX

The Organization of the Community by Davide Sala (Salman)*

Mutual responsibility for common welfare had deep roots both in the historical tradition of the Jewish people and in its social realities. Following the destruction of the Temple, Yohanan ben Zakkai taught that charitable acts now would take the place of sacrificial offering in securing for the Jews forgiveness of sins. Late in the third century AD, Rabbi Assi went a little further when he exclaimed: 'Charity is a counterpoise to all other commandments.'

There was, of course, an obvious element of self-interest in this idealistically overdrawn picture of Jewish charities, especially in rabbinic writings. The spirit of common responsibility of each individual for the whole group, and of the group for the individual, was in fact inspired and nurtured by the people's increasingly defensive battle for survival. Jewish sources are replete with stories and anecdotes whose common moral is that in giving for charity a man should always bear in mind that he himself or his children might come to depend on charitable acts. Rabbi Hiyya's wife thought that he had cursed her children when he had enjoined her to rush bread to beggars 'so that others may hasten to give it to your children'. To pacify her, the rabbi cited the school of Rabbi Ishmael which had already expressed this thought by punning on a Deuteronomic verse (15 : 10–*gelal galgal*): 'It is a wheel which is turning in the world.' One rabbi put it more succinctly when he stated: 'More than the wealthy man does for the poor, the poor man does for the wealthy.'

Characteristic of the rabbis' approach to the subject of charities was their postulate that the sensitivities of recipients be carefully

* Davide Sala (Salman) was active in the Jewish community of Baghdad and in its various organizations. As member and then secretary of the community's Education Board and of several social and charitable institutions of the community, he had inside knowledge of the community and of the way in which its affairs were run.

safeguarded and cognizance taken of their accustomed standard of life When an impoverished Babylonian Jew demanded from Raba funds for stuffed chicken and old wine, the rabbi asked him if he had no compunctions about straining the resources of the community. 'No,' the petitioner replied, 'I am eating not of their money, but of that of the Holy One blessed be He.' Another Babylonian sage, Mar Uqba, customarily sent 400 denarir to a poor man on the eve of the Day of Atonement. He doubled this amount upon learning that the recipient was used to drinking great quantities of precious old wine.

Needless to say, such a carefully constructed welfare structure could not have been entirely effective. There was dissent among the rich, so much so that on one occasion, in an irate mood, Rab condemned the entire wealthy class of Babylonia as 'doomed to hell'. However, actual hunger seems to have been greatly mitigated during the recurrent periods of famine. As one eminent Jewish historian has put it:

> Whether or not the idealistic picture presented by the Talmudic sources was in any way approximated in actual life, there was enough power in communal leadership, buttressed by public opinion and religious fears of retribution after death, as well as by the enlightened self-interest of a strongly interdependent community, to achieve the practical realization of at least a modicum of these postulates.[1]

During most of its existence, Babylonian Jewry enjoyed a measure of self-government which sometimes seemed to give it the status of a state within a state. This semi-autonomous status, which the Jews were granted by all the various rulers under whom they lived since the Assyrian exile, continued almost untouched even in the three decades preceding the liquidation of the community in the early 1950s. What follows is a short account of the structure of the Jewish community in modern Iraq and of the way the community was organized and its affairs run.

In 1950 the Jews of Iraq numbered about 150,000, of whom some 120,000 lived in Baghdad, the rest being scattered in other cities and towns, mainly Basra and Mosul. Up till 1948, when the persecution of Jews took a serious turn, Iraqi Jews controlled over eighty per cent of the country's foreign trade as well as nearly all the banking system. Leading doctors, engineers, architects and professionals were mostly Jews, and hundreds of Jews held key positions in various government offices. Some ministries had Jewish directors-general.

Apart from a small minority whose ancestors had come from southern Europe, the Jews of Iraq were descendants of Jews brought to the country as captives by the Babylonians almost 2,500 years ago, following the destruction of the first Temple at the hands of Nebuchadnezzar. They were first settled on the banks of the river Euphrates, mainly near the city of Babylon. In recent years, since their mass emigration to Israel, it has become the custom to call Babylonian Jews 'Sephardim'. This, however, is a misnomer, since 'Sephardi' is derived from 'Sepharad' (Spain), and there were very few Sephardic Jews in Iraq.

The Jews of Babylonia, upon arriving in the country with the armies of Nebuchadnezzar, did not waste much time lamenting their bitter fate, but soon set to work building up their lives virtually from scratch – just as their descendants were to do in 1951, when they arrived in Israel in their scores of thousands. Schools for religious instruction were soon established, led by rabbis well versed in the Torah – and it was these schools, or *yeshivoth*, that were to be the nucleus of their community life. From these religious centres sprang Judaism's greatest monument after the Bible – the Babylonian Talmud, which remains the main source of Jewish learning in all its various branches.

Torah study, trade and various crafts were Babylonian Jewry's main preoccupations up to the appearance of the Persians and the onset of Muslim–Arab rule, when a new class of rich merchants and financiers arose, and when many Jews began to interest themselves not only in business but in the administration of the community as well. The Jews under Islam also took part in the actual administration of the country, sometimes as financiers and sometimes as active officials of the government.

During the Ottoman regime, when conscription was introduced and the government imposed a levy on the Jewish community in exchange for exempting Jews from military service, a special committee was formed to supervise the collection of the tax from families affected, and in the course of time this committee started to interest itself in an increasing number of aspects of non-religious community life. But the turning-point in the organization of the community came early in the 1920s, when the Constitution of the newly formed government of Iraq extended official autonomy to the community and regulated its life by laws, administrative decrees and tradition. As a result, in the period 1932–50 the Jewish community of Baghdad was organized and run in the following manner:

- The 'president' of the community, *ra'is al-ta'ifa*, who could have been either a religious leader or a layman, was the overall figure who co-ordinated the various communal institutions. His appointment had to be approved by the authorities.
- The General Assembly, *al-majlis al-'umumi*, was a sort of parliament elected by the male adults of the community every four years.
- The Lay Council, *al-majlis al-jismani*, was a sort of council of ministers comprising nine members appointed by, and responsible to, the General Assembly. Chosen every two years, this council levied taxes, prepared budgets to be approved by the Assembly, and administered the secular life of the community either directly or by relegating power to certain bodies known as Committees or Societies.
- The Religious Council, *al-majlis al-ruhani*, was in charge of the religious aspects of the life of the community – supervision of the synagogues, religious instruction both in religious and non-religious schools, the formation of religious courts, and religious rites such as matrimony, circumcision, kosher meats and the like.

As mentioned above, the Lay Council appointed several specialized committees – equivalent to cabinet 'ministries' – through which different aspects of the non-religious life of the community were regulated. The most important of these committees were:

1. The Schools Committee, which ran the educational apparatus of the community in much the same way as the Ministry of Education did in a country-wide sense. The committee was in charge of some twenty-four primary and secondary schools in Baghdad alone, comprising about 12,000 pupils, excluding private schools, kindergartens and religious schools. The Schools Committee also appointed, in turn, a number of sub-committees in charge of such community affairs as health, welfare, architecture, auditing and physical education.
2. The Hospitals Committee
3. The Blind Welfare Society
4. The Poor Welfare Society
5. The Students Welfare Society
6. The Mother and Child Welfare Society
7. The Cemeteries Societies

Membership of all the Assemblies, Councils, Committees and Societies mentioned above – as well as of a certain number of minor societies not listed here – was honorary and unsalaried, with the exception of the religious ones. The cost of the overall administration was quite minimal compared to the work done.

In addition to the bodies listed above, the community benefited from the work of several unofficial 'advisory groups', which were usually called for consultation on matters of concern to the community and which called for expert advice. These included:

- 'The Political Group', whose members included the one Jewish member of the Iraqi Senate, most present and past members of the Iraqi Chamber of Deputies, and past and present directors-general of government ministries.
- 'The Lawyers Group'
- 'The Financial and Commercial Group'
- 'The Women's Group'

Besides these and other such 'groups', there were the various social clubs – Al-Zawraa, Al-Rashid, Al-Rafidain, the Laura Kadoori Club and the *Alliance* Schools Graduates' Club. Although formed mainly for social purposes, these clubs were an important source of public-opinion formation and were the initiators of many social and cultural activities and reforms.

Parallel to the official community administration ran the clandestine Zionist movement which, started in the early 1920s, reached its peak after the formation in 1942 of the so-called *Tenu'ah* (the movement) by the late Dr Enzo Sereni of Givat Brenner. There is no doubt that this movement contributed considerably to the high spirit and the unshaken morale which the Jewish community maintained despite the pressure and oppression it was subjected to in the later 1940s.

One feature of this difficult period that is worth emphasizing is the mutual loyalty and the solidarity manifested by the community. The Iraqi government early in the proceedings suspected the existence of the Zionist underground and tried hard to break it. However, although scores of thousands of Jews knew who its members were, and although many knew where and when these members held their meetings, not a single one of Baghdad's 120,000 Jews informed on the movement or on its members.

Chronology

BC	
1960	Ur of the Chaldees falls to Elamite invaders
1850	Terah, father of Abraham, leaves Ur with family
1650–1500	Age of the Patriarchs
1500–1300	Israel's sojourn in Egypt
1300	Exodus from Egypt
1225–1020	Period of the Judges
733	Assyria invades Israel (Tiglath-pileser)
721	Fall of Samaria, and second deportation of Jews to Babylonia
598	Nebuchadnezzar's first invasion
587	Nebuchadnezzar's second invasion
586	Fall of Jerusalem and mass deportation of Jews to Babylonia
539	Cyrus the Great of Persia conquers Babylon
538	First return of exiles to Palestine
458	Ezra the scribe and second return of exiles to Palestine
445–433	Nehemiah governor of Judea
331	Alexander the Great's troops enter Babylon; fall of the Persian Empire
247	Rise of Parthia
167	Outbreak of Maccabean revolt
160	Death of Judah Maccabeus
126	Beginning of Parthian rule in Babylonia
39–34	Hillel and Shammai; Herod the Great
10	Beginning of the age of the *tannaim*
AD	
6	Judea under Roman occupation
70	Burning of the second Temple; Vespasian allows Yohanan ben Zakkai to establish an academy at Yavneh (Yamina)
219–47	Abba Areka establishes an academy at Sura; Mar Samuel in Nehardea
220	End of the Tannaic Age with final redaction of the Mishnah to writing by Judah the Prince
220–500	Age of the Babylonian *amoraim*
224–42	Ardashir I founds Sassanian Empire in Persia

227	End of Parthian rule in Babylonia; Sassanians take control
254–99	Judah ben Ezekiel founds academy of Pumbeditha
261	Nehardea captured and destroyed by Odenath
375–427	Ashi of Sura begins redaction of Babylonian Talmud
474–99	Rabina II completes redaction of Babylonian Talmud
570	Birth of Muhammed, prophet of Islam
604–30	Perso–Byzantine wars
633–41	Muslim armies conquer Syria and Iraq; Bustanai, Exilarch
650	Age of the *Geonim* begins
711–15	Muslim conquest of Spain
754–75	Al-Mansur, Caliph
763	Baghdad becomes capital of the caliphate
767	The Karaite schism led by 'Anan ben David
772	Natronai bar Habibae, expelled Exilarch, emigrates to Spain
786–809	Harun al-Rashid, Caliph
842–58	Paltoi, *Gaon* of Pumbeditha
853–6	Natronai bar Hilai, *Gaon* of Sura
856–74	Amram, *Gaon* of Sura
882–942	Saadia ben Joseph
916	Death of Netira, founder of a great Jewish banking concern in Baghdad
916–40	David ben Zakkai, Exilarch
928–42	Saadia, *Gaon* of Sura; translates the Bible into Arabic, redacts first standard prayerbook
960	Moses ben Hanoch (Enoch) arrives in Cordoba
968–98	Sherira, *Gaon* of Pumbeditha
987	Sherira *Gaon* writes his famous *Epistle*
998–1038	Hai, *Gaon* of Pumbeditha, and presumed end of the *Gaonic* Age
1031–75	Al-Qayim, last Buwaihid caliph
1042	Death of Saadia; succeeded as *Gaon* of Sura by Joseph bar Satia
1135–1204	Moses ben Maimon (Maimonides)
1160–73	Benjamin of Tudela's journey
1180	Pethahiah ben Jacob of Ratisbon's journey
1258	Baghdad captured by the Mongols under Hulagu and end of Abbasid caliphate
1280	Ibn Kammuna publishes his *Tanqih al-Abhath fi'l-Milal al-Thalath*
1291	Assassination of Sa'd el-Dawla and other officials of the Ilkhanids; anti-Jewish riots in Iraq
1316	Rashid el-Dawla accused of causing Khan's death and executed
1336	End of Mongol rule in Iraq; beginning of the Jala'iri period

1401	Tamerlane, last of the Mongols, conquers Baghdad
1508	End of the reign of the White Sheep dynasty
1508–34	Safawi rule in Iraq
1534	Sulaiman al-Qanuni (the Magnificent), Ottoman sultan, enters Baghdad on last day of the year
1705	New era begins with appointment of Hasan Pasha to Baghdad *ayalat*
1733	Baghdad's Jews take part in effort to stave off Persian invaders
1743–1831	Plagues claim high toll of dead among Jews of Baghdad
1780–1802	Sulaiman the Great, Mamluk governor of Iraq
1817–31	Daud Pasha, last Mamluk governor of Iraq
1828	David Sassoon, son of Sheikh Sassoon ben Salih, emigrates with family to Bushire and then Bombay
1832	First Talmud Torah school opens in Baghdad
1839	Khatt-i Sherif introduces far-reaching reforms
1840	First Beth Midrash (*yeshivah*) established in Baghdad
1849	Approximate date of creation of the office of *Hakham Bashi*
1856	Khatt-i Humayun grants equality to empire's non-Muslims
1863	First Hebrew printing press opens in Baghdad
1864	*Alliance Israélite Universelle* opens first modern elementary school in Baghdad, 10 December
1876	Proclamation of the Constitution in Istanbul; Baghdad Jews represented in first Ottoman parliament
1890	*Alliance Israélite Universelle* opens vocational school for girls in Baghdad
1893	Laura Kadoori school for girls opens in Baghdad; *Alliance* school opens in Basra
1903–13	*Alliance Israélite Universelle* opens schools for boys and girls in Basra, Mosul, Hilla, 'Amara, Kirkuk and Khanaqin
1907	Second Talmud Torah school opens in Baghdad
1908	Beth Midrash Meir Eliahu opened in Baghdad; Albert Sassoon College recognized by authorities as secondary school. Constitution proclaimed for second time in Istanbul, granting non-Muslims full civic rights
1917	Baghdad falls to British forces
1919	Aharon Sassoon (*Ha-Moreh*) resumes Zionist activity
1920	'Jewish Literary Society', first Zionist group, formed 15 July; publishes weekly *Yeshurun* in Hebrew and Judeo-Arabic. Temporary Iraqi government set up by British; Sassoon Heskel is Minister of Finance
1921	Iraqi Jewish notables ask British High Commissioner to grant Jews British citizenship; Faisal, son of the Sharif Hussein, proclaimed King of Iraq

1925	First parliament opened; the Jews of Baghdad, Basra and Mosul get five out of the thirty-three Deputies
1932	Iraq admitted as member of the League of Nations
1934	First signs of official anti-Jewish measures and harassment
1936	Committee for the Defence of Palestine accuses the Jews of Iraq of extending support to the Zionists; three Jews assassinated in the streets; bomb thrown into crowded synagogue on Yom Kippur; Nazi propaganda intensifies
1940	Rashid 'Ali al-Gaylani's first cabinet formed
1941	Rashid 'Ali forms cabinet following military *coup*, 1 April; Regent and Nuri as-Sa'id flee the country; Iraq declares a state of war against Great Britain, 1 May; *farhud*, anti-Jewish rioting and pillage, 1–2 June; 170–80 Jews killed and many more wounded
1942	Zionist activity intensifies; three emissaries arrive from Palestine to organize the movement, train youths in use of arms, teach Hebrew, help organize illegal immigration to Palestine
1946	League of Arab States urges Arab governments to take measures against Zionist activities; various restrictions decreed curtailing Jewish freedom of movement
1948	State of Israel proclaimed, 15 May, and Iraqi troops join war against the new state; martial law imposed and military courts established; Jews are main sufferers; Shafiq 'Adas sentenced to death and hanged publicly, 27 September
1949	Withdrawal of defeated Iraqi forces and influx of Palestinian refugees lead to worsening of Jewish situation; Chief Rabbi Sassoon Kadoori resigns, replaced by Heskel Shemtob
1950	Law permitting Jews to leave Iraq provided they surrender their Iraqi nationality, 2 March
1950–51	107,603 Jews airlifted to Israel; estimated 16,000 reach Israel by other means

Select Bibliography

Adler, Marcus N., *The Itinerary of Benjamin of Tudela* (London, 1907).

al-Azzawi, Abbas, *Taarikh al-'Iraq bayn ihtilalayn* (*History of Iraq Between Two Occupations*), Vol. VII (Baghdad, 1955).

Altmann, Alexander, 'Saadya Gaon: Book of Doctrines and Beliefs', in *Three Jewish Philosophers* (New York, 1960).

Ashtor, Eliyahu, *The Jews of Moslem Spain*, 2 vols (Philadelphia, 1973 and 1979).

Ashtor, Eliyahu, *A Social and Economic History of the Near East in the Middle Ages* (London, 1976).

Bamberger, Bernard J., *The Story of Judaism* (New York, 1957).

Baron, Salo W., *A Social and Religious History of the Jews* (New York):
  Vol. I: 'To the Beginning of the Christian Era' (1952).
  Vol. II: 'Christian Era: The First Five Centuries' (1952).
  Vol. III: 'Heirs of Rome and Persia' (1957).
  Vol. IV: 'Religious Controls and Dissensions' (1957).

Basri, Mir, *A'lam al-Yahud fi'l 'Iraq al-Hadith* (*Prominent Jews in Modern Iraq*) (Jerusalem, 1983).

Ben-Yacob, Abraham, *Yehude Babel mi-sof tequfat ha-gaonim 'ad yameinu* (*The Jews of Iraq: From the End of the Gaonic Period to the Present Day*) (Jerusalem, 1965).

Cohen, Gerson D., 'The Talmudic Age', in Leo W. Schwarz, *Great Ages and Ideas of the Jewish People* (New York, 1956).

Cohen, Hayyim J., *Ha-pe'ilut ha-tzionit be-'Iraq* (*Zionist Activity in Iraq*) (Jerusalem, 1969).

Cohen, Hayyim J., *The Jews of the Middle East 1860–1972* (Jerusalem, 1973).

Epstein, Isidore, *Judaism: A Historical Presentation* (Harmondsworth, Middlesex, 1959).

Fischel, Walter J., 'Sassoon', in *Encyclopedia Judaica*, vol. 14, pp. 896–901.

Fisher, Sydney N., *The Middle East: A History* (London, 1971).

Goldin, Judah, 'The Period of the Talmud', in Louis Finkelstein, *The Jews: Their History, Culture and Religion* (New York, 1955).

Goldin, Judah, *The Living Talmud* (New York, 1957).

Ginzberg, Louis, *The Legends of the Jews*, Vol. III (New York, 1956).

Grayzel, Solomon, *A History of the Jews* (Philadelphia, 1968).

Guttmann, Julius, *Philosophies of Judaism* (New York, 1966).

Halkin, Abraham, 'The Judeo–Islamic Age', in Leo W. Schwarz, *Great Ages and Ideas of the Jewish People* (New York, 1956).

Hertz, J. H., *A Book of Jewish Thoughts* (London, 1917).

Hitti, Philip K., *History of the Arabs* (London, 1956).

Husik, Isaac, *A History of Medieval Jewish Philosophy* (New York, 1958).

Israel, Benjamin J., *The Jews of India* (New Delhi, 1982).

Kaufmann, Yehezkel, 'The Biblical Age', in Leo W. Schwarz, *Great Ages and Ideas of the Jewish People* (New York, 1956).

Kedourie, Elie, *The Chatham House Version and Other Middle Eastern Studies* (London, 1970).
Kedourie, Elie, *Arabic Political Memoirs and Other Studies* (London, 1974).
Keller, Werner, *The Bible as History* (London, 1956).
Khadduri, Majid, *Independent Iraq: A Study in Iraqi Politics from 1932 to 1958* (London, 1960).
Landshut, S., *Jewish Communities in the Muslim Countries of the Middle East* (London, 1950).
Lewis, Geoffrey, *Turkey* (New York, 1955).
Longrigg, Stephen H., *Four Centuries of Modern Iraq* (London, 1925).
Longrigg, Stephen H., *Iraq 1900 to 1950: A Political, Social and Economic History* (London, 1953).
Ma'ruf, Khaldun Naji, *Al-Aqaliyya al-Yahudiyya fil 'Iraq bayn sanat 1921 wa 1952* (*The Jewish Minority in Iraq 1921–1952*) (Baghdad, 1976).
Marcus, Jacob R., *The Jew in the Medieval World* (New York, 1960).
Margolis, Max and Marx, Alexander, *History of the Jewish People* (New York, 1958).
Montefiore, C.G. and Loewe, H., *A Rabbinic Anthology* (New York, 1963).
Perlmann, Moshe, 'The Medieval Polemics between Islam and Judaism', in S.D. Goitein, *Religion in a Religious Age* (Cambridge, Mass., 1974).
Perlmann, Moshe (editor and translator), *Tanqih al-Abhath l'il Milal al-Thalath* (*Examination of the Enquiries into the Three Faiths*), (Berkeley and Los Angeles, 1967).
Roth, Cecil, *A Bird's-Eye View of Jewish History* (Cincinnati, 1935).
Roux, Georges, *Ancient Iraq* (Harmondsworth, Middlesex, 1966).
Sassoon, David S., *A History of the Jews in Baghdad* (Letchworth, 1949).
Sassoon, David S., *Massa' Babel* (*Iraq Journey*) (Jerusalem, 1955).
Sassoon, David S., 'The History of the Jews in Basra', *Jewish Quarterly Review*, N.S., Vol. 17, pp. 407–69.
Shohet, Nir, *Sippurah shel Golah* (*The Story of an Exile*) (Jerusalem, 1981).
Speiser, E.A., 'Mesopotamia: Evolution of an Integrated Civilization', in E.A. Speiser (ed.), *The World History of the Jewish People*, Series 1, Vol. 1: 'At the Dawn of Civilization' (Jerusalem, 1964).
Woolley, Charles Leonard, *Ur of the Chaldees* (Harmondsworth, Middlesex, 1954).

Source Notes

Part One

1 Judah Goldin, 'The Period of the Talmud', in Louis Finkelstein, *The Jews: Their History, Culture and Religion*, p.115.

1: Roots

1 E.A. Speiser, 'Mesopotamia: Evolution of an Integrated Civilization', in E.A. Speiser (ed.), *The World History of the Jewish People*, Series 1, Vol. 1: 'At the Dawn of Civilization'.
2 *Ibid.*, p.265.
3 Charles Leonard Wooley, *Ur of the Chaldees*, p.27.
4 Yehezkel Kaufmann, 'The Biblical Age', in Leo W. Schwarz, *Great Ages and Ideas of the Jewish People*, pp.5–6.
5 *Ibid.*
6 Isidore Epstein, *Judaism: A Historical Presentation*, p.54.
7 Salo W. Baron, *A Social and Religious History of the Jews*, Vol. 1: 'To the Beginning of the Christian Era', pp.107–8.

2: The Lure of Exile

1 Bernard J. Bamberger, *The Story of Judaism*, p.33.
2 *Ibid.*, p.35.
3 Isidore Epstein, *Judaism: A Historical Presentation*, pp.63–4.
4 *Ibid.*

3: The Scribes and the Birth of the Synagogue

1 Solomon Grayzel, *A History of the Jews*, pp.18–19.
2 *Ibid.*, p.27.

4: The Way They Lived

1 Max Margolis and Alexander Marx, *History of the Jewish People*, pp.233–4.
2 Werner Keller, *The Bible as History*, pp.288–9.

5: Greeks, Romans, Seleucids, Sassanians

1 Solomon Grayzel, *A History of the Jews*, pp.41–2.
2 *Ibid.*, pp.193–4.

3 Georges Roux, *Ancient Iraq*, p.385.
4 Cecil Roth, *A Bird's-Eye View of Jewish History*, pp.122–3.

6: Family, Home and Education

1 Solomon Grayzel, *A History of the Jews*, pp.229–30.
2 Salo W. Baron, *A Social and Religious History of the Jews*, Vol. II: 'Christian Era: The First Five Centuries', pp.278–9.
3 *Ibid.*, p.279.
4 Grayzel, *op. cit.*, p.230.
5 Max Margolis and Alexander Marx, *History of the Jewish People*, p.236.
6 Baron, *op. cit.*
7 Hertz, J. H., *A Book of Jewish Thoughts*, p.178.
8 Gerson D. Cohen, 'The Talmudic Age', in Leo W. Schwarz, *Great Ages and Ideas of the Jewish People*, p.171.
9 *Ibid.*, pp.171–2.
10 *Ibid.*
11 Baron, *op. cit.*, pp.283–4.
12 *Ibid.*, p.284.
13 *Ibid.*, pp.287–8.

7: A Neat Division of Labour: Exilarch and *Gaon*

1 Max Margolis and Alexander Marx, *History of the Jewish People*, pp.240–41; Solomon Grayzel, *A History of the Jews*, pp.223–4.
2 Margolis and Marx, *Ibid.*, p.235.
3 Grayzel, *op. cit.*, p.225.
4 Gerson D. Cohen, 'The Talmudic Age', in Leo W. Schwarz, *Great Ages and Ideas of the Jewish People*, p.172.

8: From Mishnah to Talmud

1 C. G. Montefiore and H. Loewe, *A Rabbinic Anthology*, pp.694–6.
2 Solomon Grayzel, *A History of the Jews*, p.239.
3 Max Margolis and Alexander Marx, *History of the Jewish People*, pp.245–6.
4 Grayzel, *op. cit.*, p.241.

9: The Talmud in Action

1 Isidore Epstein, *Judaism: A Historical Presentation*, p.147.
2 *Ibid.*, p.146.
3 *Ibid.*, pp.147–8.
4 *Ibid.*, pp.150–53.
5 Salo W. Baron, *A Social and Religious History of the Jews*, Vol. II: 'Christian Era: The First Five Centuries', p.246.
6 *Ibid.*, pp.268–9.
7 *Ibid.*, p.224.
8 *Ibid.*, p.229.
9 *Ibid.*, p.229–35.
10 *Ibid.*, pp.236–41.

10: Babylonia Assumes Leadership

1 Solomon Grayzel, *A History of the Jews*, p.222.
2 Salo W. Baron, *A Social and Religious History of the Jews*, Vol. II: 'Christian Era: The First Five Centuries', p.205.
3 *Ibid.*, p.206.
4 *Ibid.*, p.209.
5 *Ibid.*, p.319.
6 Judah Goldin, *The Living Talmud*, pp.26–7.
7 *Ibid.*, pp.27–37.
8 Gerson D. Cohen, 'The Talmudic Age', in Leo W. Schwarz, *Great Ages and Ideas of the Jewish People*, p.170.
9 Baron, *op. cit.* p.320.
10 Grayzel, *op. cit.*, pp.242–3.
11 Baron, *op. cit.*, pp.320–21.

Part Two

1 Stephen H. Longrigg, *Four Centuries of Modern Iraq*, p.76.

11: A Deep Sigh of Relief

1 Salo W. Baron, *A Social and Religious History of the Jews*, Vol. III: 'Heirs of Rome and Persia', p.93.
2 Judah Goldin, 'The Period of the Talmud', in Louis Finkelstein, *The Jews: Their History, Culture and Religion*, p.184.
3 Baron, *op. cit.* pp.89–90.
4 David S. Sassoon, 'The History of the Jews in Basra', *Jewish Quarterly Review*, N.S., Vol. 17, pp.407–8.
5 *Ibid.*, p.417.

12: Islam and the Jews: Theory and Practice

1 Abraham Halkin, 'The Judeo–Islamic Age', in Leo W. Schwarz, *Great Ages and Ideas of the Jewish People*, p.217.
2 Salo W. Baron, *A Social and Religious History of the Jews*, Vol. III: 'Heirs of Rome and Persia', pp.132–4.
3 *Ibid.*, pp.148–9.
4 E. Ashtor, *A Social and Economic History of the Near East in the Middle Ages*, p.146; Baron, *op. cit.*, pp.150–53, 163, 167, 169; David S. Sassoon, *A History of the Jews in Baghdad*, pp.34–7.

13: Baghdad's Jewish Population

1 Judah Goldin, 'The Period of the Talmud', in Louis Finkelstein, *The Jews: Their History, Culture, and Religion*, p.186.
2 Max Margolis and Alexander Marx, *History of the Jewish People*, pp.255–6.
3 *Ibid.*, pp.256–7.

4 Solomon Grayzel, *A History of the Jews*, p.255.
5 David S. Sassoon, *A History of the Jews in Baghdad*, pp.7, 10, 12, 14–15.
6 *Ibid.*
7 *Ibid.*, pp.8–10.
8 This and the following quotations in this chapter are taken from Marcus N. Adler, *The Itinerary of Benjamin of Tudela*, pp.39–42.

14: Messianism and Karaism: Rabbinic Judaism Challenged

1 Max Margolis and Alexander Marx, *History of the Jewish People*, p.258.
2 Bernard J. Bamberger, *The Story of Judaism*, pp.145–6.
3 Salo W. Baron, *A Social and Religious History of the Jews*, Vol. IV: 'Religious Controls and Dissensions, pp.205–6.
4 I. Friedlander, quoted in Judah Goldin, 'The Period of the Talmud', in Louis Finkelstein, *The Jews: Their History, Culture and Religion*, pp.190–91.
5 Solomon Grayzel, *A History of the Jews*, p.267.
6 Jacob R. Marcus, *The Jew in the Medieval World*, pp.233–4.
7 *Ibid.*, pp.234–5.
8 Baron, *op. cit.*, p.211.
9 For an English rendering of Ha-Kohen's plea, see Marcus, *op. cit.*, pp.236–8.
10 See Baron, *op. cit.*, pp.275–7.
11 *Ibid.*, p.275.
12 Goldin, *op. cit.*, p.193.
13 *Ibid.*, pp.193–4.

15: Saadia's Legacy

1 The quotations from Saadia's work are from Alexander Altmann, 'Saadya Gaon: Book of Doctrines and Beliefs', in *Three Jewish Philosophers*, pp.13–14, 28–9.
2 *Ibid.*
3 See Isidore Epstein, *Judaism: A Historical Presentation*, p.190.
4 Jacob Marcus, *The Jew in the Medieval World*, pp.287–92; Max Margolis and Alexander Marx, *History of the Jewish People*, pp.264–72; Judah Goldin, 'The Period of the Talmud', in Louis Finkelstein, *The Jews: Their History, Culture and Religion*, pp.195–7.
5 Altmann, *op. cit.*, p.29.
6 *Ibid.*, p.117.
7 *Ibid.*, pp.43–4.
8 Judah Goldin, *op. cit.*, pp.198–9.
9 *Ibid.*
10 *Ibid.*
11 Julius Guttmann, *Philosophies of Judaism*, p.62.
12 *Ibid.*, p.70.
13 Epstein, *op. cit.*, pp.199–200.

16: The Last of the *Geonim*

1 David S. Sassoon, *A History of the Jews in Baghdad*, pp.46–58; Max Margolis and Alexander Marx, *History of the Jewish People*, pp.269–76.

17: The Dark Ages of Iraqi Jewry

1 Philip K. Hitti, *History of the Arabs*, pp.466–70.
2 *Ibid.*, p.485.
3 *Ibid.*, p.487.
4 Max Margolis and Alexander Marx, *History of the Jewish People*, p.276; David S. Sassoon, *A History of the Jews in Baghdad*, pp.59–80.

18: Lasting Imprint

1 Isaac Husik, *A History of Medieval Jewish Philosophy*, pp.XXIV–XXV.
2 *Ibid.*, pp.17–22.
3 Abraham Halkin, 'The Judeo–Islamic Age', in Leo W. Schwarz, *Great Ages and Ideas of the Jewish People*, p.805; Husik, *op. cit.*, p.55.
4 Halkin, *ibid.*, p.219.
5 E. Ashtor, *The Jews of Moslem Spain*, Vol. I, p.139.
6 *Ibid.*, pp.138–9.
7 *Ibid.*, p.237.
8 *Ibid.*, pp.121–2.
9 *Ibid.*, Vol. II, pp.35–6.
10 *Ibid.*, p.36
11 This and the following quotations in this chapter are taken from Solomon Grayzel, *A History of the Jews*, pp.285–7, and David S. Sassoon, *A History of the Jews in Baghdad*, pp.48–50.

19: 100 Years of Turmoil

1 David S. Sassoon, *A History of the Jews in Baghdad*, pp.91–4; Edward G. Browne, *A Literary History of Persia*, pp.31–6, quoted in Sasssoon, *ibid.*
2 Stephen H. Longrigg, *Four Centuries of Modern Iraq*, p.14.
3 *Ibid.*
4 *Ibid.*, pp.15–16.

20: Recovery and Reassertion

1 Moshe Perlmann, 'The Medieval Polemics between Islam and Judaism', in S.D. Goitein, *Religion in a Religious Age*, p.122; and *Tanqih. . .*, p.IX.
2 Perlmann, 'The Medieval Polemics between Islam and Judaism', in Goitein, *ibid.*, pp.122–3.
3 Perlmann, *Tanqih. . .*, p.X.
4 *Ibid.*
5 *Ibid.*
6 David S. Sassoon, *A History of the Jews in Baghdad*, pp.100–101.
7 Stephen H. Longrigg, *Four Centuries of Modern Iraq*, p.47.
8 Sassoon, *op. cit.*, p.101.
9 Abraham Ben-Yacob, *Yehude Babel mi-sof tequfat ha-gaonim 'ad yameinu* (*The Jews of Iraq: From the End of the Gaonic Period to the Present Day*), p.86.
10 Longrigg, *op. cit.*, p.88.

Part Three

1 Elie Kedourie, *The Chatham House Version and other Middle Eastern Studies*, p.316.

21: The Road to Equality

1 Geoffrey Lewis, *Turkey*, p.30.
2 Sydney N. Fisher, *The Middle East: A History*, pp.235–6.
3 *Ibid.*
4 Lewis, *op. cit.*, p.34.

22: Exilarch to *Nasi* to *Hakham Bashi*

1 Hayyim J. Cohen, *The Jews of the Middle East 1860–1972*, pp.11–12; Hayyim J. Cohen, *Ha-pe'ilut ha-tzionit be-'Iraq* (*Zionist Activity in Iraq*), p.12.
2 Cohen, *The Jews of the Middle East 1860–1972*, pp.16–17, 23–24; Sydney N. Fisher, *The Middle East: A History*, p.316; David S. Sassoon, *A History of the Jews in Baghdad*, pp.157–8.
3 Sassoon, *ibid.*, p.158; Cohen, *ibid.*, pp.23–4.
4 Benjamin J. Israel, *The Jews of India*, p.46.
5 *Ibid.*, p.47.
6 Walter J. Fischel, 'Sassoon', in *Encyclopedia Judaica*, Vol. 14, pp.896–901.

23: The Impact of Modern Education

1 Hayyim J. Cohen, *Ha-pe'ilut ha-tzionit be-'Iraq* (*Zionist Activity in Iraq*), p.16; Hayyim J. Cohen, *The Jews of the Middle East 1860–1972*, p.117.
2 Elie Kedourie, *The Chatham House Version and Other Middle Eastern Studies*, p.310.
3 Cohen, *The Jews of the Middle East 1860–1972*, pp.113–16.
4 David S. Sassoon, *A History of the Jews in Baghdad*, p.171; Cohen, *Ha-pe'ilut ha-tzionit be-'Iraq* (*Zionist Activity in Iraq*), pp.16–17.

24: World War I

1 Elie Kedourie, *The Chatham House Version and Other Middle Eastern Studies*, p.310.
2 *Ibid.*
3 Nir Shohet, *Sippurah shel Golah* (*The Story of an Exile*), pp.111–12.
4 Elie Kedourie, *Arabic Political Memoirs and Other Studies*, pp.263–72.

25: Rumours of a Brave New World

1 Quoted in Hayyim J. Cohen, *Ha-pe'ilut ha-tzionit be-'Iraq* (*Zionist Activity in Iraq*), p.28.
2 *Ibid.*, p.27.
3 The texts of this exchange, dated 4 May and 9 June 1914 respectively, are given in *ibid.*, pp.219–21.
4 *Ibid.*, pp.217–19.
5 *Ibid.*, pp.36–9, 229.
6 *Ibid.*, pp.42–3.
7 This and the following quotations are from *ibid.*, pp.237–40.
8 Elie Kedourie, *Arabic Political Memoirs and Other Studies*, p.267.

26: Mandate and Independence

1 Elie Kedourie, *The Chatham House Version and Other Middle Eastern Studies*, pp.255, 437.
2 *Ibid.*, pp.300–301.
3 *Ibid.*, p.301.
4 *Ibid.*
5 Quoted in Abraham Ben-Yacob, *Yehude Babel mi-sof tequfat ha-gaonim 'ad yameinu* (*The Jews of Iraq: From the End of the Gaonic Period to the Present Day*), p.234.
6 Stephen H. Longrigg, *Iraq 1900 to 1950: A Political, Social and Economic History*, pp.192–3.
7 *Ibid.*
8 Abbas al-Azzawi, *Taarikh al-'Iraq bayn ihtilalayn* (*History of Iraq Between Two Occupations*), Vol. VII, pp.201–2; Mir Basri, *A'lam al-Yahud fi'l 'Iraq al-Hadith* (*Prominent Jews in Modern Iraq*), p.31.
9 Basri, *ibid.*, pp.33–4.

27: The *Farhud* and its Consequences

1 Quoted in Khaldun Naji Ma'ruf, *Al-Aqaliyya al-Yahudiyya fil 'Iraq bayn sanat 1921 wa 1952* (*The Jewish Minority in Iraq 1921–1952*), Vol. II, pp.68–70.
2 Hayyim J. Cohen, *The Jews of the Middle East 1860–1972*, pp.27–8; Majid Khadduri, *Independent Iraq: A Study in Iraqi Politics from 1932 to 1958*, pp.69–159.
3 See Ma'ruf, *op. cit.*, pp.231–45 for the text of the commission's report.
4 Quoted in Elie Kedourie, *The Chatham House Version and Other Middle Eastern Studies*, pp.307–8.
5 Nir Shohet, *Sippurah shel Golah* (*The Story of an Exile*), p.169.

28: Youth in Revolt

1 Hayyim J. Cohen, *Ha-pe'ilut ha-tzionit be-'Iraq* (*Zionist Activity in Iraq*), pp.49–51.
2 *Ibid.*, pp.171–2.

29: The Politics of Extortion

1 Stephen H. Longrigg, *Iraq 1900 to 1950: A Political, Social and Economic History*, p.349.
2 *Ibid.*
3 S. Landshut, *Jewish Communities in the Muslim Countries of the Middle East*, pp.47–8.
4 *Ibid.*, p.50.

30: The Exodus

1 Elie Kedourie, *The Chatham House Version and Other Middle Eastern Studies*, pp.312, 449.

Appendix

1 Salo W. Baron, *A Social and Religious History of the Jews*, Vol. II, pp.273–4.

Index

Abaye, Rab, 56
Abbasid dynasty, 136–8
Abdallah, Adon, 177
Abdul Hamid, Sultan, 192
Abdul Majid, Sultan, 178–9
Abdul Rahman III, Caliph, 149
Abraham, 3–4, 5–6
Abraham ben Sherira, 104
Abu Hanifa, 112
Abu Issa, 106
academies, in Babylonia, 30, 43–4, 51–2, 55, 148–9
  importance of *responsa* (*q.v.*), 94
  in Islamic era, 97–8, 130, 132, 141
  mentioned, 11, 100
  see also Mahoza; Nehardea; Pumbeditha; Sura
Achaemenids, Achaemenians, 11, 15, 30
'Adas, Shafiq, 241, 242
Adiabene, 33, 43
Aggadah, 133
Aha, Rabbi, of Shabha, 95
Ahi'eber, 226
Ahmad ibn Buwaih, 137
Aleppo, 173
Alexander the Great, 30–1
'Ali abu Samuel *Gaon*, 140
'Ali ibn 'Isa, Vizier, 92
Aliyah Bet, 228
Alliance Israélite Universelle, 181, 195, 200
  schools run by, 181, 185–7, 190–1, 192–3, 196–7, 198, 201
'Amara, 186, 190
Amel-Marduk, 11
amoraim, 55
Amram, Rabbi, 96
'Ana, 167, 174
'Anan ben David, 'Ananites, 110–16
Anglo-American Committee of Enquiry, 234, 235–6
Antigonus of Soko, 54
apocalypses, 105
Arab nationalism, 217–18, 235
Arabia, 82, 83
Arabic, Babylonian Jews' use of, 147–8
Arbil, 190, 199
Ardashir I, 47
Argun Khan, 157
Arsacid Empire, 47
Artaban IV, 47
Ash'arites, 145
Ashi, Rab, 56
Assassins, 139
Assi, Rabbi, 249
Assur, 34
Assyria, 7, 8–10
atomic theory, 147
Avigur, Shaul, 227
'Azariah ben Yahalalel ben 'Azariah ben David, 161, 163

Babylon, 9–10, 11, 24, 30
Babylonia, *see* Iraq
badal el-'askar, 179
Baghdad
  Pumbeditha academy transferred to, 98
  Muslim capital, 98, 99, 117
  Jews of, in Islamic era, 98–103, 141, 147–8, 155–6, 161–3
  Exilarch moves to, 99–100
  intellectual life, sectarian confusion, 117–19, 123–4
  weakness of caliphs, decline of the city, 132, 136–9
  captured by Mongols, 139–40, 155
  Jews of, under Mongols, 155, 156–60
  Jews from Spain, 160
  Safawi rule, 164
  Ottoman conquest, 164
  the vilayet beyond the city, 164
  Jews of, under Ottoman rule, 164–8, 173–4, 177–82, 185–91, 193–9
  plague (1831), 172
  occupied by British, from 1917, 199, 210–16

Baghdad – *continued*
  Zionists in, 200–209 *passim*, 225–32 *passim*
  Jews the largest single group, in 1917, 210
  attacks on Jews in, 220, 221–4
  number of Jews in, before exodus, 250
al-Baghdadi, Abu 'Ali Hasan, 99, 121
'Baghdadis', 182–4
Balboul, Ya'qub, 219
Balfour Declaration, 203
Bar Kochba revolt, 33, 70
Baraita, 55
al-Basir (Joseph ben Abraham), 146–7
Basra
  Jews of, 84, 166–7, 174, 177, 250
  Islamic culture, 146, 147
  Alliance schools in, 186, 190
  occupied by British in 1914, 199
  Zionists in, 202–3, 228, 229, 231
ben Amram, Aaron, 89–93
ben Enoch, Moses, 149–50
ben Joseph, Benjamin, 177
ben Joseph Ibn-Sarjado *Gaon*, Aaron, 132
ben Meir, Aaron, 122
ben Rabbi Joseph, Rabbi Jacob, 178
Benjamin of Nehawend, 114–15
Benjamin of Tudela, 101–3, 141, 155–6, 173
Bension, Dr Ariel, 206, 208
Beth Hillel, David d', 177
Beth Midrash school, 189–90
Bible, Scriptures, 3, 4, 38, 55, 58–9, 125
  translations of, 54, 127–8
Black Sheep dynasty, 159, 160
Bombay, Iraqi Jews in, 182–4
Britain
  route to India via Basra, 177
  occupation of Iraq, Mandate, 187, 199, 210–16
  talks with Turkey (1909), 193
  independence of Iraq recognized, 217
  and Iraq in World War II, 220–3
  Portsmouth Treaty (1947), 236–7
British Petroleum Company, 216
Bustanai, 81–2
Buwaihids, 137–8
Byzantine Empire, 79

Calcutta, Iraqi Jews in, 184
calendar, regulation of, 121–2
Canaan, 4, 6
Carchemish, battle of, 8
charities, Jewish, 249–50
'Children of Scripture' (Karaites, *q.v.*), 115
China, Babylonian Jews' trade with, 26
Chingiz (Genghis) Khan, 138
Chosroes I, 34
Churchill, (Sir) Winston, 215
Committee for the Defence of Palestine, 218
communism, 230, 233–4, 235, 238
Cordoba, 149
Cornwallis, Sir Kinahan, 223
Cox, Sir Percy, 211–12
creation, fact of, 147
Ctesiphon, 34, 71
Cyrus, King, of Persia, 11, 15–16, 30

Damascus, 7, 8, 79
Dangoor, Rabbi Elisha ben Nissim, 181
Dangoor, Rabbi Ezra, 184
Daniel (Exilarch), 101, 103
Daniel, Ezra Menahem, 215, 243
Daniel, Menahem Salih, 196–7, 198, 206–9, 215
Daud Pasha, 167
David, King, 7
  House of, 49
David ben Zakkai, 120, 123, 129, 137
dhimmis, 85–9
Diyarbakr, 160
Dosa *Gaon*, 131

education, schools
  in Babylonia, 39–41
  in Baghdad, Iraq, 178, 181, 185–91, 196–7, 198, 201, 252
Egypt
  Israelites and, 3, 6, 7–9
  Islamic conquest, 79
  Jews of, 95; and Romans, 31, 32; Fostat, 97, 98–9, 120–1; and Zionism, 233
Elamites, 5
Eleazar ben Pedath, Rabbi, 11
Elias, Meir, 196, 197
Eliezer, Rabbi, 36, 83
Elijah ben Abraham, 111
eschatology, 105
excommunication, 52
Exilarch, Exilarchate, 48–51
  relations with rabbis and *Geonim*, 43, 99–100, 130
  in Islamic era, 80, 97, 101–3
  Baghdad becomes seat of, 99
  installation of, 100–101, 103
  office combined with *Gaonate*, 109
  disputed election (767), 110–11
  title replaced by *nasi*, 163
Ezekiel, 12, 13–15, 17
  Tomb of, 173

Ezra, 19–23, 53
  Tomb of, 173
Ezra family, 184

Faisal, Amir, later King, 211, 213, 214, 215–16, 217
family names, Jews' adoption of, 173
Fattal, Maurice, 202
fez, compulsory wearing of, in Ottoman Empire, 175
Fischel, Professor Walter, 90
Fostat, Cairo, 97, 98–9, 120–1
frock-coat, adoption of, in Ottoman Empire, 176

Gabbai, Heskel ben Yosef ben Nissim Menahem, 167
Gabbai, Rabbi Jacob ben Aharon, 167
Gabelle, 198
Gamliel I, Rabban, 54
Gamliel II, Rabban, 54
Gaonate, Geonim, 51, 108–9
  in Islamic era, 94, 97, 99–100, 137, 138, 140–3, 151–2
  see also *responsa*
Gaugamela, battle of, 30
Gemara, 55–6, 75
Genesis, Book of, 3
geniza (of Fostat, *q.v.*), 97
Gentiles, 64–5
Geonim, see *Gaonate*
Ghazi, King, 217, 218
Gnosticism, 107
God
  of Abraham, 5–6
  personal relationship with, 13–15
  belief in, 61
  existence proved, 147
Great Halakhoth, 95–6
Grobba, Dr F., 218
Guttfarb, Moritz, 166
Guttmann, Shmaryahu, 227

Ha-Cohen, Shalom ben Aharon ben Obadiah, 182
ha-Levy, 'Obadia ben Abraham, 180
Haddad, Ezra, 219
Hadrian, Emperor, 70
Haganah (*Shurah*), 226, 227, 228, 231–2, 244
haggadah, 58
Hai, Rab, *Gaon*, 99, 109, 130, 134–5, 148
Hai ben David *Gaon*, 113
Hakham Bashi (Chief Rabbi), 168, 179–80, 195–6
Hakim, Menashe, 202
Halutz movement, 228, 230, 231, 244
Hamon, Rabbi Moshe, 164
Hananiah (Exilarch), 110–11
Hananiah ben 'Ali ha-Levy, 141
Hanina bar Hamma, Rabbi, 11
Harran, 3, 5
Hasan Jala'ir, 159
Hasan Pasha, 166
Hasdai ibn Shaprut, 149
al-Hashimi, Taha, 220
al-Hashimi, Yasin, 218
Hasmoneans, 109
Hayya, Salman (Shlomo), 205
Hayyim, Rabbi Moshe, 178
Hebrews, origin of the name, 6
Hebron, 3–4, 6, 201
Hefes ben Yasliah, 148
Herod, King, 53
Heskel, (Sir) Sassoon ('Sassoon Afandi'), 193, 213, 215–16
Hezekiah (Exilarch), 109, 140
Hilla, 174, 177, 186, 190
Hillel Ha-Babli, 39, 53–4
al-Hiti, Ibn, 129
Hiwi al-Balkhi, 119
Hiyya, Rabbi, 11
Holy Land, *see* Palestine
Horesh, Rafael, 202
Hoshea, King, of Israel, 8
Hulagu, 139–40, 155
al-Humaydi, 118
al-Husaini, Abdul Qadir, 237
al-Husseini, Amin, 223

Iberian peninsula, *see* Spain
ibn 'Abbas, Jehudah ben Samuel, 144
ibn Aknin, Joseph ben Judah, 144
ibn al-Fawti, 161–2
ibn al-Furat, Muhassin, 90–1
ibn Kammuna, Sa'd ibn Mansur, 161–3
ibn Sa'idi, Abu Omar Ahmad ibn Muhammed, 118
Iggereth Rab Sherira Gaon, 98, 133
India, Iraqi Jews and, 26, 182–4
'Ini, Menahem, 178
Iraq (references to Iraq in this index include references to Babylonia and Mesopotamia)
  conquered by Persians under Cyrus, 11, 30
  conquered by Alexander, 30
  Seleucid rule, 31
  Parthian rule, 31
  wars with Rome and Persia, 33, 34, 48
  Sassanian rule, 34–5, 47, 76

Iraq – *continued*
Islamic conquest, 76, 79, 80
dynastic quarrels and Mongol invasion, 136–40, 155
rule of Safawis, and Ottoman conquest, 164
decay of Ottoman Empire, 171–2
few urban centres in south, 174
British occupation, 186, 199, 210–16, 217
Faisal becomes King, 211, 213
independence, admitted to League of Nations, 217
invasion of Israel, 238, 243
Iraq, Jews of, *see also* academies; Exilarch; *Gaonate*; Talmud
Iraq, Jews of, before Islamic era
Israelites' ancient links with Mesopotamia, 3–5
Jews deported from Israel and Judah to Babylonia and elsewhere, 8–10, 11–16, 251
and Greeks, Romans, 30–1, 33, 48
life and religion of, 17–19, 24–9, 31–2, 36–46, 47–52, 55–69, 70–3; agriculture, 24–5; alcoholic drinks, 25–6; autonomy, 50, 66; banking, 27–8; burial, cemeteries, 45–6; craftsmen, 25; education, 39–41; equality, 64; family purity, 67; fasting, days of, 18; feasts, holidays, 18; incest forbidden, 67; judges judiciary, 41, 66; labour, labourers, 26, 65; law enforcement, 66; learning, study, 39–41, 68–9; life, importance of, 66; marriage, family life, 37–8, 66–8; polygamy, 37, 67; poverty, the poor, 65; rest, days of, 18; the rich, 25, 40, 250; scribes (*soferim*), 17–18; sexual instincts, 67; shepherds, 26; slaves, 36; trade, commerce, 24, 26–7, 28; women, social status of, 68–9
numbers of Jews, 28–9, 35
Iraq, Jews of, in Islamic era, 80–4, 86–93, 94–103, 104–5, 107, 117–24, 130–5, 136, 138, 140–3, 144–54, 155–6
banking, 89–93
messianism, anti-rabbinism, 104–16
numbers of Jews, 101, 155–6
public office, Jews in, 89
taxation, 88–9
Iraq, Jews of, and Mongols, 140, 155, 156–60, 161–4, 172
numbers of Jews, 155, 159, 160
Iraq, Jews of, in Ottoman Empire, 164–8, 172–5, 177–84, 185–9, 193–9
banking, 177–8
education, 178, 181, 185–91, 196–7, 198, 252
family names adopted, 173
numbers of Jews, 174, 177, 195
in parliament, 181
taxation, 179, 198
trade, 197; in India, 182–4
Iraq, Jews of, and Zionism, *see under* Zionism
Iraq, Jews of, and British occupation, 187, 199, 210–16
numbers of Jews, 210
Iraq, Jews of, after independence, 218–24, 233–42
numbers of Jews, 250
exodus from Iraq, 243–8
Isaac ben Moses (ibn Sakni), 140
Isaac ben Reuben, 134–5
Isaac the Banker, 178
Isaiah Ha-Levy ben Rab Abba, Rab, 99
Islam, Muslims, 76, 79–80, 86, 99, 147
Jews and, 82–4, 85–93, 99, 101–2, 147–8
philosophy of religion, 118–19, 128, 145, 161–3
Ismail Shah ibn Hayder al-Safawi, 164
Israel, biblical kingdom of, 7–8
Israel, modern state of, *see under* Palestine
Israelites, tribes of, 6, 7, 12
istadh, 178, 185, 186, 188–9
Istiqbal Party, 235

Jabr, Salih, 236, 237, 242, 246
Jala'iris, 159
al-Jamali, Dr Muhammed Fadhil, 235, 236
janissaries, 175
Jehoiakim, King, of Judah, 8
Jehoiachin, King, of Judah, 8, 11
Jeremiah (prophet), 12–13, 14, 24
Jeremiah, Rabbi, 73
Jerusalem
capital of Israelites, then of Judah, 7
captured by Nebuchadnezzar, 8–9
Cyrus allows Jews to return to, 11, 15–16
Ezra and Nehemia in, 19–22
in Roman times, 32, 53
mentioned, 201
Jewish Agency, 206
Jewish Literary Society, 204–5, 226
Jewish National Fund, 202, 204
Jews
ancestors of, 3–6
of Iraq, etc., *see under* Egypt; Iraq; Palestine
Diaspora, 59–60, 95, 130; *see also under* Talmud, Babylonian
and Islam, *see under* Islam
unity of Israel, 153–4
jizya (poll-tax), 85, 179

Joseph bar Satia, 131
Joseph ben Abba, 104
Joseph ben Abraham (al-Basir), 146–7
Joseph ben Jacob bar Satia, 123
Joseph ben Phinehas, 89–93
Joshua, 7
Judah, Kingdom of, 7–9
Judah the Prince, Rabbi, 54, 55, 71
Judaism
  contribution of Palestine to, *see under* Palestine
  developed and maintained in Babylonia, 9, 12, 18–19, 30, 31–2, 36, 38, 43, 70–6, 151; *see also* academies; *Gaonate*; Talmud, Babylonian
  Ezra and, 20–1, 22–3, 53
  Hillel's influence on, 53–4
  Islam influenced by, 79
  marriage and family life in, 36
  priests not celibate, 36
  prohibited by Hadrian, 70
  reason and revelation in, 124–6
  reward and punishment in, 13–14
  salvation in, 14–15
  two main trends in, 109–10
  see also Mishnah; rabbis; synagogue; Talmud; Torah
Judges (Israelite chiefs),7

Kadoori, Sir Eliezer, 190
Kadoori, Ezra, 227–8, 231
Kadoori, Sassoon, 219, 237, 244
Kahana, Yom Tob, 120
Kairawan, 88, 98, 133
Kalam, 128, 145, 146–7
Karaites, Karaism, 106, 109, 111–16, 117, 121, 130, 134, 145
Karo, Rabbi Joseph, 173
Kastelman, Yehiel Fischel, 177
el-Kebir, Ibrahim, 239–40
Keren Hayesod, 204, 206
Khaibar, Jews of, 83
Khalifa, Salim, 227
Khanaqin, 190–1
Kirkuk, 186, 190, 195, 199, 231
Kish, 34
Kohen-Tzedek II, 120, 123
Kufa, 83–4
Kurdistan, Kurds, 174
Kuta, 9–10

Law, 54–5
  oral, *see* Mishnah
  written, *see* Pentateuch

League of Arab Nations, Arab League, 233, 234, 236, 238, 246
League of Nations, 217
learning, study, importance of, 39–41, 68, 153
Lorimer, J. G., 194, 195
Lorion, Isaac, 181
Lucena, 96

Maghariyya sect, 119
Mahasia, *see* Sura
Mahmud II, Sultan, 167, 175–6
Mahoza, 29, 71
  academy of, 48, 55
Maimonides, 125, 129, 141–2, 145
Mamluks, 167, 176
Mandeans, 107
Manicheism, 107, 119
Masada, 32
Mazdak, 107
'Men of the Great Synagogue', 54
Menahem, King, of Israel, 8
Mesopotamia, *see* Iraq
messianism, 104–8, 116
al-Midfa'i, Jamil, 220
Midhat Pasha, 181–2
Mishnah, Oral Law, 25, 38, 51, 54–8, 75, 109–10
Misr al-Fatat (Young Egypt), 233
mitzvot, 63, 153
Mongols, 138–40, 155–9, 163, 172
Mordechai, Rabbi Sassoon, 178
Moses, 7
Mosul
  Jews of, 174, 177, 250
  Alliance schools in, 186, 190
  beggars of, 195
  occupied by British in 1918, 199
  Zionists in, 228, 229
al-Mu'arri, Abu el-'Alaa, 124
Muhammed, 79, 86
al-Muqammas, David, 145–6
al-Muqtadir, Caliph, 89, 90, 92, 137
Murashu and Sons, 27–8
al-Musawi, Sayyid Abu'l Hasan, 224
Muslims, *see* Islam
al-Mustakfi, Caliph, 137
al-Mustanjid, Caliph, 155–6
al-Musta'sim, Caliph, 139
al-Mu'tadhid, Caliph, 88, 89–90, 91, 136–7
Mutakallimun, 118, 145
al-Mu'tasim, Caliph, 136
al-Mutawakkil, Caliph, 136
Mu'tazilites, 145–7

INDEX

Mysteries of Rabbi Simon bar Yohai, The, 82–3
mysticism, 104, 105

Naharwandi, Nissi, 120
Nahman, son of Jacob, 48
Nappaha, Rabbi Isaac, 44
nasi (title), 159, 163, 168
al-Nasser, Caliph, 138, 156
Nathan ben Yehudai, 120
Nathan Ha-Babli, Rabbi, 100
Natronai bar Habibae, 150
Natronai bar Hilai *Gaon*, 96, 113
Nazis, 217–18, 222–3
Nebuchadnezzar, 8–9
Nehardea, 29, 35, 48, 72
  academy of, 48, 52, 55
Nehemiah, 21–3
Nehemiah ben Kohen-Tzedek, 132
Neoplatonism, 107
Neri-glissar, 11
Nestorians, 140
Netira, 88–9, 92
Nippur, 9, 27
Nisbis, 29
North Africa, Islamic conquest of, 79–80
Noshirwan, King, 80
Nuri as-Sa'id, 220, 236, 242, 243–4, 247

Odenath, Prince of Palmyra, 35, 48
Omar ibn el-Khattab, Caliph, 81–2, 83, 86–7
Operation Ezra and Nehemiah, 248
Ottoman Empire, *see under* Turks

al-Pachachi, Muzahim, 239, 242
Palestine, Holy Land, Israel
  the Promised Land, 3, 7
  invaded by Ptolemy, 31
  Romans in, 31, 32–4, 70, 71, 76
  Judaism in, Babylonia compared, 36, 38, 43
  as centre of Jewish learning, 38–9, 40, 70–1
  succeeded by Babylonia as centre of Jewish life, 70–6
  Islamic conquest, 79
  Jews of, in Islamic era, 95, 121
  calendar regulation controversy, 121–2
  relations with Iraqi Jews before Zionist movement, 200–201
  Jewish immigration to, purchase of land in, 201, 202, 206
  as national home for Jews, Faisal's view, 213
  disturbances in, 218, 225, 226–7
  illegal immigration to, 228, 232, 245–6
  Zionist activity in, 228, 231
  United Nations Committee on, partition called for, 236, 237
  Arab troops sent to, 238, 243–4
  State of Israel proclaimed, 238
  exodus from Iraq to Israel, 245–8
Palmyra, 35, 48
Paltoi, Rabbi, 96
Parthians, 31, 32–3
Pekah, King, of Israel, 8
Pentateuch, 55, 164
'People of the Book', 85
Persia
  King Cyrus permits Jewish return to Palestine, 11, 15–16
  Babylonian Jews' trade with, 26
  conquered by Alexander the Great, 30–1
  wars with Romans, 34, 48
  Sassanids rule Mesopotamia, 34–5, 47–8, 71, 80
  Islamic invasion, 79–80
  non-Jewish sects, influence of, 107–8
  rulers of Iraq briefly in seventeenth century, 164, 166
  wars with Iraq in eighteenth century, 166–7
Pethahiah, Rabbi, of Ratisbon, 141, 156, 173
Pharisaism, 53, 109
philosophy, medieval Jewish, 128, 144–7
plague, 172
Portsmouth Treaty, 236–7
Promised Land, *see under* Palestine
prophets, 12–15
Ptolemy (general of Alexander), 31
Pumbeditha, academy of, 94, 98, 151
  founded, 55
  and Spanish Jewry, 96, 148
  transferred to Baghdad, 98, 131
  heads of, 99, 104, 109, 120, 131–2
  mentioned, 95, 122, 123

Qara Yusif, 159
Qatzin, Rabbi Raphael, 180
al-Qayim, Caliph, 138
al-Qirqisani, 115, 116, 119
al-Qumisi, Daniel ibn Musa, 115–16

Rab (Abba Areka), 38–9, 40, 44, 47, 55, 69, 250
Raba, 56, 73
rabbis, 35, 36, 38, 51–2, 61, 62–3, 64–9, 73, 109
  anti-rabbinism, 109–16
  Chief Rabbi (*Hakham Bashi*), 168, 179–80, 195–6
Rabina II, 56
al-Radhi, Caliph, 137
Rashid 'Ali al-Gaylani, 220–1

Rashid el-Dawla, 158–9
Rehum, governor of Samaria, 21
responsa (*teshuboth*), 84, 88, 94–7, 98–9, 133, 134
Romans, 26, 31–4, 48, 70, 71, 76
Rosenfeld, Hermann, 181

Saadia ben Joseph, Rab, *Gaon*, 111, 114, 117–29, 130, 145–6, 146–7, 148
al-Sab'awi, Colonel Yunis, 221
Sabbath, 18, 22, 23
Sabeism, 107
saboraim, 57
Sa'd el-Dawla, 140, 155, 156–8
Sadducees, 109–10
Sadid el-Dawla, 159
al-Sa'dun, Abdul Muhsin, 206
Safawis, 164
Safed, 173, 201
Sahl ben Masliah Ha-Kohen, 113
Salah el-Din (Saladin), 138
Salmon ben Yeruhim, 129
Salonica, 195
Salvation Youth organization (Shabab al-Inqadh), 227
Samaria, 7, 8
Samaritans, 21
Samarra, 136
Samra, Dawood, 215
Samuel (colleague of Rab), 47–8
Samuel ben 'Ali *Gaon* (ibn al-Dustur), 101, 140–2
Samuel ben Hofni, 131, 148
Sar Shalom ben Phinehas, 159
Sassanians, 34–5, 47, 71, 76, 79, 80
Sassoon, Albert David, 185
Sassoon, Benjamin, 202
Sassoon ben Eliahu Nahum, Aharon ('Ha-Moreh'), 200, 202, 203–4, 205–6, 225–6
Sassoon ben Salih, Sheikh, 177–8, 182
Sassoon family, 168, 182–4
Saul, King, 7
Schur, Wolff, 166
science, al-Muqammas' view of, 146
Scriptures, *see* Bible
'Scripturists' (Karaites, *q.v.*), 115
Seleucus, Seleucids, 31
Semah, Yom-Tob, 201–2
Sephardic Version (of prayer-book), 173
Sephardim, *see* Spain, Jews of
Septuagint, 54
Sereni, Dr Enzo, 227, 253
Shahrabani, Rabbi Menashe, 184
Shahrastani, 108
Shammai, 53–4
Shapur I, 34, 47–8
Shechem, 6
Shemesh, 226
Shemtob, Heskel, 244–5
Sherira, Rab, *Gaon*, 98, 99, 132–4, 151–2
Shiism, Shiites, 107–8, 138, 164, 174, 224, 236
Shlesinger, Rabbi Akiba Joseph, 185
Shohet, Haron Daud, 194
Shurah, *see* Haganah
Sidqi, Bakr, 218, 219, 220
Simeon ben Shetah, 54
Simon I ben Gamliel, Rabban, 54
Simon II ben Gamliel II, Rabban, 54
Simon ben Laqish, Rabbi, 72
Smooha, Rabbi Sassoon ben Elijah, 180–1
Society for Distribution of Products from Eretz Yisrael, 226
Solel Boneh, 228
Soliman, Soliman ben Jacob, 182
Solomon, King, 7
Solomon ben Samuel *Gaon*, 140–1
Solomon Ha-Kohen, 116
Somekh, Rabbi Abdallah, 178, 185
Spain, Iberian peninsula
  Islamic conquest, 80
  Jews of (Sephardim), 96, 148–50, 173, 251
study, *see* learning
Suez Canal, 181–2
Sulaiman al-Qanuni (the Magnificent), 164, 171
Sulaiman the Great, 167
Suleiman, Hikmat, 219, 220
Sumer, 5
Sura, 29, 35
  academy of, 52, 94, 98, 151; founded by Rab, 55; heads of, 56, 95, 96, 109, 117; and Spanish Jewry, 96, 148; decline of, 120, 131; mentioned, 84, 123
synagogue, 18, 38, 41–3, 44–5, 96

Tabriz, 172
Takash, 138
Talmud, 55–6, 73, 135
Talmud, Babylonian, 24, 35, 56–69, 73–6, 98, 135, 251
  aspects of: alms-giving, 63; business, conduct in, 62; ethics and morality, 61–3; faith, 61; life, right to, 62; 'person', right of, 62–3; poverty, the poor, 63; property, private, 63; religious observance, 63–4; rights, human, 62–3; Torah, importance of, 64

Talmud, Babylonian – *continued*
  commentaries on, 75–6, 134
  importance of, in Diaspora, 44, 58, 75–6, 94–6, 98, 149
Talmud, Palestinian, 56, 57, 58, 73, 135, 149
Talmud, anti-Talmudism, 106–7, 116, 134
Talmud Torah schools, 189
Tamerlane (Timur the Lame), 159
tannaim, Tannaic period, 54
Tanzimat, 178
tarqumim, 54
Tawwas, Rabbi Jacob Josef, 164
Teixeira, Pedron, 165–6
Temple, 7, 11, 15–16, 19–20, 22, 23, 32
  not to be built in Babylonia, 17
Terah, 3–4, 5
teshuboth, see *responsa*
Thabit, Rabbi David, 167
Tiberias, 201
Tiglath-pileser III, King, of Assyria, 8
Torah
  importance of, 17, 64
  established by Ezra as constitution of Judah, 22–3
  available to all, in Babylonia, 42
  restored by Hillel, 53
  last taught orally by Rabina II, 56
  Saadia and, 128–9, 129
Tosephta, 55
Trajan, Emperor, 32–3
Tughril Beg, 138
Turks, Ottoman Empire, Turkey
  Turks invade Sassanian Persia, 80
  Turks infiltrate Abbasid Mesopotamia, 136
  Saljuqs capture Baghdad, 138
  Ottomans rule Iraq, 164, 166–8
  Ottoman Empire, Ottoman reforms, 168, 171–2, 175–6, 178–9
  Young Turks, Society for Union and Progress, 192, 193
  World War I, 199
Tzemah ben Shahin, 120

Uljaitu Khan (Muhammed Khadabandah Khan), 158–9
United Nations, 236, 237
Uqba, Mar, 250
Ur, 3–5
Uzun Hasan, 160

Valerian, Emperor, 48
Vespasian, Emperor, 34

Weizmann, Dr Chaim, 206
White Sheep dynasty, 160, 163–4
Wolff, Joseph, 84, 177
Woolley, Sir Leonard, 4
World War I, 199
World War II, 220–1, 228

Yavneh (Yamina), 34, 54
Ya'qub, Khoja, 177
Yehudai, Rabbi, 95
Yezdegerd III, King, 80, 81, 82
Yohanan bar Nappaha, Rabbi, 11
Yohanan ben Zakkai, Rabbi, 34, 40, 44, 54, 72, 249
Young Egypt (Misr al-Fatat), 233
Young Men's Hebrew Association, 226
Young Turks, Ottoman Society for Union and Progress, 192, 193
Yudghan of Hamadan, 106

Zadok, house of, 109
Zechariah al-Dhahiri, 165
Zedekiah, King, of Judah, 8–9
Zilkha Yeshivah, 189–90
Zionism, Zionists
  in Iraq, 200–209, 213, 214–15, 218–20, 225–32, 233–42 *passim*, 244–8, 253
  in Palestine, 228, 231
Zionist Association of Baghdad (Jewish Literary Society, Zionist Federation of Mesopotamia), 205–6
Zoroastrianism, 47, 107
zugot (pairs), 53, 54